CHASING
EQUALITY

CHASING
EQUALITY

CHASING
EQUALITY

Women's Rights
and
US Public Policy

Susan Gluck Mezey and
Megan A. Sholar

LYNNE
RIENNER
PUBLISHERS

BOULDER
LONDON

Published in the United States of America in 2023 by
Lynne Rienner Publishers, Inc.
1800 30th Street, Suite 314, Boulder, Colorado 80301
www.rienner.com

and in the United Kingdom by
Lynne Rienner Publishers, Inc.
Gray's Inn House, 127 Clerkenwell Road, London EC1 5DB
www.eurospanbookstore.com/rienner

Library of Congress Cataloging-in-Publication Data
Names: Mezey, Susan Gluck, 1944– author. | Sholar, Megan Anne, 1978–
    author.
Title: Chasing equality : women's rights and US public policy / Susan
    Gluck Mezey, Megan A. Sholar.
Description: Boulder, Colorado : Lynne Rienner Publishers, Inc., 2023. |
    Includes bibliographical references. | Summary: "Traces the struggle for
    women's equal rights and opportunities in the US-in the political,
    economic, and social spheres-across more than a century"— Provided by
    publisher.
Identifiers: LCCN 2022043155 (print) | LCCN 2022043156 (ebook) | ISBN
    9781955055871 (hardcover) | ISBN 9781955055888 (paperback) | ISBN
    9781685852863 (ebook) | ISBN 9781685852887 (ebook)
Subjects: LCSH: Women's rights—United States. | Women—United
    States—Social conditions. | Women—Legal status, laws, etc.—United
    States
Classification: LCC HQ1236.5.U6 M494 2023 (print) | LCC HQ1236.5.U6
    (ebook) | DDC 305.420973—dc23/eng/20221207
LC record available at https://lccn.loc.gov/2022043155
LC ebook record available at https://lccn.loc.gov/2022043156

British Cataloguing in Publication Data
A Cataloguing in Publication record for this book
is available from the British Library.

Printed and bound in the United States of America

The paper used in this publication meets the requirements
of the American National Standard for Permanence of
Paper for Printed Library Materials Z39.48-1992.

5 4 3 2 1

Contents

Acknowledgments

We thank Lynne Rienner for allowing us to pursue this project. Both of us have taught classes on women's rights and public policy, and our experiences in the classroom played an important role in guiding us toward the material we wished to include here. Therefore, in addition to more traditional topics in women's rights policymaking, such as Title VII and employment, the Family and Medical Leave Act, and reproductive rights, we write about the #MeToo movement, the role of Title IX on college campuses, the disparate treatment of women and men in championship basketball tournaments, and the multifaceted efforts of the US women's national soccer team to redress their pay inequity. We hope our readers will see how these issues affect their own lives and the greater society. By explaining the influence of various institutions on policy outcomes, we also hope to provide a better understanding of how readers can participate in the fight for gender equality.

Susan thanks her husband, Michael, for his assistance in advancing this project, as he always does, by supporting her research and writing. She also extends her love to her family: her son, Jason, his wife, Deirdre, and their children, Norah, Paul, and Daniel; and her daughter, Jennifer, her husband, Jonathan, and their children, Rebecca and Benjamin. She dedicates this book to them.

Megan thanks her family and friends for the encouragement and much-needed levity they provided while she buried herself in teaching and research. In particular, she thanks Claudio Katz for the years of guidance and friendship during his time at Loyola and beyond. She is most grateful to her parents, Michelle and Mike, for their unending support. She dedicates this book to them.

1

Seeking Women's Rights in US Public Policy

FOR MUCH OF US HISTORY, WOMEN WERE EXCLUDED FROM THE political arena, and society afforded them few rights. Upon marriage, men took ownership of women's bodies and property, becoming their legal representatives in the public and private spheres. Lacking a formal setting in which to express their political opinions, women were generally viewed as apolitical beings. Yet scholars now recognize that women participated in political life and shaped political outcomes since the founding of the United States—despite largely being relegated to the private sphere. As the American Revolution loomed, women organized nonconsumption movements and boycotted English goods. When the war began, some women joined their husbands on the battlefield as nurses and cooks; a few disguised themselves as men to fight with the revolutionary army. In the newly independent United States, women continued to make their voices heard, marching in parades, attending political rallies, hosting salons to discuss politics, and publishing patriotic novels, poems, and plays (Skemp 2016).

Political Activism

In the aftermath of the revolution, many women turned their attention to the burgeoning abolition movement. At the 1840 World Anti-Slavery Convention in London, Lucretia Mott and Elizabeth Cady Stanton met for the first time. In spite of their significant work in the fight against slavery, they were not allowed to participate in the meeting because they were women. Their outrage at being forced to sit in the balcony behind a partition contributed to their decision to organize their own convention to address women's inferior standing in society. At their 1848 convention in Seneca Falls, New York, the formal women's rights movement—and the first wave of feminism—began in the United States. The document that emerged from the convention, the Declaration of Sentiments, was modeled after the Declaration of Independence and proclaimed that "all men and women are created equal." The delegates denounced the discrimination and exploitation that women faced in education, employment, and the family, and they demanded increased political and economic opportunities for women, including the rights to vote and own property (Flexner and Fitzpatrick 1996).

The organizers' demands were revolutionary for the time, and there was little chance that any of them would come to fruition in the mid-nineteenth century. Among them, suffrage proved the most controversial. While Stanton was adamant in her demand that women receive the right to vote, others such as Mott and Stanton's husband, Henry, feared ridicule if the issue were introduced at the convention. Ultimately, the resolution for suffrage passed, but it was the only plank in the Declaration of Sentiments that received less than unanimous support from convention attendees. Conventional wisdom holds that suffrage divided the participants because that demand was the most radical. More recently, some scholars have posited that Mott and other advocates of abolitionist William Lloyd Garrison rejected the proposal because they refused to participate in a political system that collaborated with slavery. Moreover, most of the women at the convention were more concerned with issues such as their limited educational and employment opportunities or their inability to control property and earnings (O'Connor 1996; Tetrault 2014). But when little progress was made on these concerns in the years after the convention, a growing number of activists recognized that the right to vote was a necessary first step on the road to equality, as it would provide women with a voice in the policymaking process and, they hoped, lead to equal rights in economic and social arenas.

The work that many of the convention participants had done in the abolition movement prepared them for the prolonged struggle for women's suffrage. One study found that women were especially effective at antislavery petitioning, collecting 50 percent or more signatories than men circulating similar petitions in the same locations. To achieve such success, women had to develop cogent political arguments to convince people to sign their petitions, a talent they taught other women in the movement. Through their antislavery work, women built activist networks and learned the organizational and planning skills necessary to launch a large-scale campaign (Carpenter and Moore 2014). As a result of the end of the Civil War and the abolition of slavery, they could turn their attention more fully to the issue of suffrage. But questions regarding the construction of rights for newly freed African Americans ultimately divided the nascent women's movement.

The Thirteenth Amendment, ratified in 1865, abolished slavery in the United States. In anticipation of the citizenship rights for African Americans and women that many hoped would follow, abolitionists and feminists formed the American Equal Rights Association in 1866 to fight for universal suffrage. However, the ratification of the Fourteenth Amendment in 1868 created a rift in the equal rights movement, for although it granted citizenship to all people born or naturalized in the United States, it singled out men's right to vote. The first time the word *male* appeared in the US Constitution, the amendment signaled a major defeat for the women's movement. Suffragists were divided on how to respond. Leaders Susan B. Anthony and Stanton did not support the amendment, believing it would weaken women's claims to citizenship and derail the fight for women's suffrage. Others, such as Lucy Stone and Frederick Douglass, argued that even if women could not win their political freedom at that time, they should still support advancements for Black men—that "this hour belongs to the negro" (Re and Re 2012, 1614). The proposal of the Fifteenth Amendment, which prohibits denial of the right to vote "on account of race, color, or previous condition of servitude" but makes no mention of sex, cemented the collapse of the American Equal Rights Association and led to the formation of two independent women's suffrage organizations (Kraditor 1981; Evans 1989).

Women's Suffrage

In 1869, Anthony and Stanton formed the National Woman Suffrage Association (NWSA), which restricted membership to women and fought for women's political, economic, and social rights. The organization committed itself to passing a constitutional amendment guaranteeing women's suffrage, as well as improving divorce laws, elevating women's positions in the church, and ending discrimination in education and employment. In that same year, abolitionists Stone; her husband, Henry Blackwell; and Henry Ward Beecher created the American Woman Suffrage Association (AWSA), which focused only on the right to vote to avoid alienating more conservative pro-suffrage community members. Unlike the NWSA, the AWSA concentrated its efforts on a state-by-state campaign for suffrage. For over two decades, these groups worked separately toward the same primary goal, often competing for resources and the support of donors and state and local suffrage organizations. By 1890, the organizations agreed to put aside their differences and merge to become the National American Woman Suffrage Association (NAWSA) (Kraditor 1981; Scott and Scott 1982).

With the formation of the NAWSA, suffrage dominated the women's rights movement for the next thirty years. As the abolition movement had influenced early suffrage activity, the Progressive and temperance movements contributed to the development of the suffrage movement in the late nineteenth and early twentieth centuries. The Progressive movement was a response to the significant changes that increased industrialization, urbanization, and immigration had brought to the United States by the late 1800s. Lamenting growing political corruption and social inequality, progressives sought to reform working conditions, end child labor, and improve living conditions for all—especially marginalized groups such as immigrants, prisoners, and people with mental illnesses. Many of the white, middle-class women in the movement felt that to achieve their goals, they had to emerge from the home and become involved with schools, communities, and all levels of government. By becoming active in the public sphere, these women believed they would be able to better fulfill what they viewed as their most important roles—that of wives and mothers (Baker 1984). Suffrage became a key demand of the movement, as women in progressive organizations sought the vote as a stepping stone to reforming the nation.

One of the reformers' top demands was temperance, believing that the abolition of liquor would help eradicate the poverty, health problems, and abuse of women and children. The Women's Christian Temperance Union (WCTU), founded in 1874 with the primary goal of banning the manufacture and sale of liquor, was one of the first progressive groups to advocate women's suffrage. By the early 1900s, the WCTU had convinced many of its 200,000 members that women's votes were necessary to influence legislators to support temperance. This argument was especially convincing in the South, where many women had been unmoved by previous calls for the vote because of justice or equality, and the WCTU became a significant organizing force for women (Bordin 1981; Giele 1995).

In addition to the extensive work of the Progressive and temperance movements, the widespread reach of women's clubs in the late nineteenth and early twentieth centuries helped attract more women to the cause of suffrage. With the development of labor-saving devices for the home, many white, middle-class women had time to join local literary clubs to study and discuss literature, art, and music with other women. As these clubs grew, they took up a variety of social causes, such as public sanitation, improved schools and libraries, and labor reforms for women and children. In 1890, sixty-three women's clubs established the General Federation of Women's Clubs (GFWC), which by 1914 had grown to one million members and declared its support for suffrage, hoping that women's votes would pave the way for the clubs' desired social reforms (Wells 1953; Blair 1980).

The suffrage movement garnered support from diverse groups across the United States, ranging from abolitionists and equal rights advocates to clubwomen and religious and temperance crusaders. To keep this fragile coalition together, suffragists often engaged in discriminatory practices that undermined the equal rights language of the movement. For example, some suffragists endorsed an educational requirement that would limit the number of immigrants and Black men who could vote. Likewise, the perceived need to limit the electoral influence of these so-called undesirable constituencies became the rallying cry of some activists, arguing that if nativist white women could vote, they would outnumber those groups at the ballot box (Kraditor 1981; Flexner and Fitzpatrick 1996). In 1901, when suffrage leader and president of the NAWSA Carrie Chapman Catt met with white politicians in the South who were concerned about suffragists' historical connection with abolitionists, she reassured them that based on the number of potential white women voters compared with Black men and Black women voters, "white supremacy will be strengthened, not weakened, by woman suffrage." As scholars point out, while there were also times when Catt showed support for racial equality, women's suffrage was her sole aim. Like many white suffragists at the time, she was willing to collaborate with racists if it furthered her cause, regardless of any personal feelings she had on the matter (Rosario 2021).

Early mainstream suffrage organizations, such as the AWSA and the NWSA, as well as their successors, the NAWSA and the National Woman's Party (NWP), founded by Alice Paul and Lucy Burns in 1916, were overwhelmingly white and generally discouraged—or outright prohibited—Black women from joining or participating (Darrah 2012). Many white suffrage organizers feared that Black women's involvement would alienate white male legislators and Southern suffrage groups that opposed Black enfranchisement. For a sizable number of women in the movement, the efforts to keep Black women out of their ranks also reflected their own racist views (Wheeler 1993). Nevertheless, Black women played a significant—though often overlooked—role in the struggle for suffrage, both as individuals and as part of Black women's clubs. One activist, Mary Ann Shadd Cary, testified before the House Judiciary Committee in 1874, declaring that as taxpayers and citizens, women should have the right to vote. In 1891, Mary Church Terrell joined other suffragists in Washington, DC, at the first convention of the National Council of Women, a group spearheaded by Anthony. Five years later, when Black reformers founded the National Association of Colored Women's Clubs, Terrell became its first president and helped consolidate Black suffrage groups around the United States. She and her teenage daughter later joined Alice Paul's "silent sentinels" to protest outside the White House. In 1913, Ida B. Wells-Barnett, best known for her journalistic work on the horrors of lynching throughout the South, founded the Alpha Suffrage Club, Chicago's first African American suffrage organization. During the 1913 women's suffrage parade in Washington, DC, Wells-Barnett, Terrell, and other Black women marched with their state delegations, defying the organizers' attempts to force them to march in the back (Terborg-Penn 1978; Terborg-Penn 1998; Kraditor 1981; Jones 2020).

As Wells-Barnett's actions demonstrate, Black women had to forge their own path toward voting rights because they were generally excluded from the larger movement led by white suffragists. Such divisions had long been the norm among women's clubs. Activist groups often relegated Black women to the fringe of their movements, and organizations such as the WCTU and the Young Women's Christian Association (YWCA) had segregated branches. As a result, Black women's clubs proliferated in the late nineteenth and early twentieth centuries. From the beginning, these clubs had recognized the importance of the vote for furthering Black women's rights, incorporating the issue alongside their social and economic reform efforts (Davis 1933; Neverdon-Morton 1989). At the same time, Black women could not separate race from gender like their white counterparts could, for their oppression was rooted in both identities. Taking an intersectional approach to their demand for rights, Black suffragists often stressed the importance of using their "vote for the advantage of ourselves and our race" (Hendricks 1994).

Throughout the first wave of feminism, activists used a variety of tactics to secure women's right to vote, such as formulating (unsuccessful) arguments against the legality of male-only voting laws. Some focused on state-level campaigns, while others sought a federal amendment. They staged parades, marches, and protests, and leading suffragists traveled the country giving speeches in favor of suffrage, but progress was uneven. In 1878, the first suffrage amendment was introduced in Congress. When Wyoming joined the union in 1890, it became the first state to guarantee women's suffrage. Over the next six years, three other states followed Wyoming's example. But between 1896 and 1910, no new states adopted women's suffrage, and suffrage bills at the national level failed to pass out of committees (Kraditor 1981; Banaszak 1996).

The nation's growing anti-suffrage movement played a major role in blocking women's progress. The opponents adopted several approaches. Some based their arguments on the idea of separate spheres for men and women, claiming that family life would collapse if women became part of the public sphere. Many elite white women worried that they would lose their long-held influence in the domestic sphere and among their social networks if they had to participate in public life. These women claimed that they did not need the vote because the men in their lives already represented them to the outside world. Business interests, such as those in the textile and manufacturing industries, feared that enfranchised women would support labor reform and eradicate female and child workers as a cheap source of labor. Similarly, liquor interests worried about the role women voters might play in banning alcohol. Political machine bosses in urban areas feared that women would advocate reforms that would disrupt the patronage system and loosen their grip on power. In the South, hostility toward the prospect of Black women gaining the right to vote often led to opposition of women's suffrage more broadly (Scott and Scott 1982; McDonagh and Price 1985; Flexner and Fitzpatrick 1996; McConnaughy 2013).

Despite the opposition, grassroots support for suffrage continued to grow, and a new generation of suffragists joined and then supplanted the first generation. Washington state's enfranchisement of women in 1910 launched a decade of activism that culminated in the adoption of the Nineteenth Amendment. In 1913, Paul and others who thought NAWSA's approach too timid formed the Congressional Union for Woman Suffrage to focus exclusively on a national constitutional amendment. Borrowing tactics from more militant suffragettes in England, these women openly campaigned against Democrats who opposed suffrage. In defiance of the NAWSA, the Congressional Union asked female voters in suffrage states to vote against Democratic candidates.

The NWP had declared itself a single-issue party focused on women's suffrage, with party members picketing the White House daily, where Paul would quote and subsequently burn copies of President Woodrow Wilson's speeches. These actions eventually led to hundreds of arrests. Even in prison, the suffragists maintained their protests and engaged in hunger strikes to support their cause. At the same time, NAWSA president Catt had begun implementing her "Winning Plan" to campaign simultaneously for suffrage at the state and federal levels. With her eye on a federal constitutional amendment, she continued an aggressive state-by-state approach that would build the support needed for ratification.

Ultimately, Catt's methodical organizing and Paul's radical maneuvers made it impossible for lawmakers to continue to ignore suffrage. After passage by both chambers of Congress in 1919, the Nineteenth Amendment was sent to the states for ratification. By the summer of 1920, suffragists were just one state short of achieving their goal. Tennessee convened a special session to vote on the amendment, and it initially appeared as if the effort would fail. But after receiving a telegram from his mother urging him to support suffrage, Representative Harry Burn changed his stance and cast the deciding vote in favor of the amendment.

On August 26, 1920, the Nineteenth Amendment, declaring "the right of citizens of the United States to vote shall not be denied or abridged by the United States or by any State on account of sex," officially became part of the US Constitution. Although this signaled a great victory for women's rights, there was still significant work to do, especially for women of color, most of whom continued to be disenfranchised by Jim Crow laws and prejudicial immigration and citizenship policies (Evans 1989; Ford 1991; Flexner and Fitzpatrick 1996).

Levels of Scrutiny

Women's rights activists struggled to overcome barriers to equal treatment under the law as far back as the nineteenth century, with suffrage one of their most important goals. When legislatures proved unwilling to satisfy their demands for equal rights, many advocates turned to the courts; unfortunately, they often found the judiciary reluctant to contravene the legislature's judgments about the proper roles of women and men in society. In assessing litigants' constitutional claims of inequality, most judges accepted the government's position that the challenged laws were constitutional because women and men were not similarly situated. In the early phases of the litigation over equality of rights, the courts rejected women's challenges to restrictions on their ability to function in the public and private spheres, upholding limitations on practicing law, voting, earning a living, and being tried by a jury of their peers (Mezey 2011). Dismissing their claims of discrimination, the judiciary largely accepted the government's stance that the laws protected vulnerable and dependent women from the harms they would suffer by participating in the public sphere.

Spurred by the activities of the second wave of the feminist movement and guided by Ruth Bader Ginsburg, a litigator for the American Civil Liberties Union (ACLU) during the 1970s, women's rights advocates increasingly mounted constitutional challenges to such laws, primarily arguing they violated women's rights under the equal protection clause of the Fourteenth Amendment of the US Constitution, ratified in 1868. The clause, declaring that "no state shall . . . deny to any person within its jurisdiction the equal protection of the laws," restricts a state's ability to enact a law that differentiates among individuals or groups unless it is based on relevant differences among them. In interpreting this clause, the Supreme Court has struggled to reach a consensus on the proper approach to laws challenged as violations of the rights of women and other marginalized groups (Tussman and ten Broek 1949; Gunther 1972; Fiss 1976). Because immutable characteristics such as race and national origin bear no relationship to ability, nor are they relevant to valid legislative goals, the Court considers such laws suspect and applies a high (strict) level of scrutiny. In addition to immutability, it applies strict scrutiny to laws affecting individuals or groups who have a history of being subject to discrimination and are politically powerless. When reviewing a law based on these characteristics, the Court requires the state to show it has a compelling reason to enact it and there is no reasonable alternative to achieving its goal. Because the state has a heavy burden in justifying such laws, the Court almost always declares them unconstitutional. At the other end of the continuum are routine social and economic government policies as well as laws based on classifications with mutable characteristics (such as wealth) or related to ability (such as age). The Court applies minimal scrutiny (also known as rational basis) to such laws, evaluating them only to determine whether they are rationally related to legitimate government aims. Because these criteria are easily satisfied, the judiciary typically upholds the challenged policies (Mezey 2011).

In 1971, the Supreme Court seemingly shifted its approach to evaluating challenges to sex-based classifications when, for the first time, it appeared to depart from minimal scrutiny and declared a legal distinction between the sexes unconstitutional, striking down an Idaho law preferring men to women as estate administrators (*Reed v. Reed*). Some 1970s opinions reflected the justices' increasing awareness that sex-based differences violated constitutional equality, but the high court nonetheless found the US Navy's preferential treatment of women in granting promotions and a Florida policy extending a local property tax exemption to widows reasonable and consistent with equal protection. Moreover, even with its growing recognition of women's roles in the workplace, the Court still upheld a California disability insurance program that excluded pregnancy benefits. Agreeing that the policy was based on pregnancy, not sex, a majority found it a legitimate cost-saving measure (Barnard and Rapp 2009).

The justices' stance in women's rights cases evolved over time. Mindful of the nation's history of discrimination against women, an increasing number were reluctant to apply minimal scrutiny to sex-based classifications after 1971. In *Frontiero v. Richardson* (1973), the Court upheld the plaintiff's challenge to the sex-based air force regulation. Yet, with only four justices willing to equate sex-based laws with racial classifications, the Court declined to apply strict scrutiny. In 1976, in striking down an Oklahoma law differentiating between men and women in "near-beer" purchases, the Court indicated it would apply a stricter scrutiny—called heightened or intermediate scrutiny—when evaluating the constitutionality of laws based on sex (*Craig v. Boren* 1976). Under a heightened scrutiny analysis, the government must show that the goal of the challenged law is important, and the classification is substantially related to achieving the goal, a difficult but not impossible burden for the government. Several years later, in *Mississippi University for Women v. Hogan* (1982), a majority rejected a women-only admissions policy in a state university's nursing program, seeming to raise the level of scrutiny even higher by requiring the government to show it has an extremely persuasive justification for a challenged law. In 1996, in disallowing the male-only admissions policy of a state-subsidized military academy, the Court appeared to adopt an even warier approach to sex-based classifications (*United States v. Virginia* 1996). Known as skeptical scrutiny, some observers questioned whether the justices had virtually adopted strict scrutiny for sex-based classifications (Delchin 1997).

From 1971 until 1996, the Supreme Court reviewed sex-based classifications more rigorously, suggesting that a majority had become dubious about the constitutionality of laws treating the sexes differently, including those privileging women. Over these twenty-five years, the

Court invalidated myriad laws stemming from traditional notion women's and men's roles in society. Notably, it struck male and fem preferential treatment laws regulating the age of majority, child custody, military allowances, retirement benefits, unemployment insurance, workers' compensation, community property, alimony, and jury selection. The rulings indicated its awareness that such policies were largely based on stereotypical assumptions about the sexes, with a majority understanding that allowing a woman's spouse or child to benefit from a pension fund or Social Security account acknowledges the value of her work and helps her achieve greater equality in the marketplace. Overall, in conceding society's historical discrimination against women, the Court more readily invalidated laws explicitly disadvantaging women. Perhaps the most significant accomplishment of the women's rights movement was to persuade the high court that sex-based laws, even as they claimed to privilege women, also reflected society's paternalistic attitudes toward them in the economic and social arenas and furthered inequality between the sexes. Most justices ultimately grew to believe that striking down such laws advanced women's goals of achieving a more sex-neutral legal environment and helped contribute to a more egalitarian society by serving notice that such laws were inconsistent with the tenets of equal protection (Mezey 2011).

Physical Sex Differences

Despite the Supreme Court's rhetorical commitment to equal rights and its increasingly skeptical view of sex-based policies, most justices nevertheless continued to believe that laws based on innate physical sex differences were constitutionally valid. In such cases, the Court was asked to decide whether the laws were based on physiological sex differences or assumptions about societal roles, with those challenging the law arguing the high court should disentangle the relationship between physical sex differences and society's norms about culturally derived roles. Stating it was applying intermediate scrutiny, a majority nevertheless upheld a male-only draft registration policy and a statutory rape law punishing men over seventeen for engaging in sex with women under seventeen; in a series of opinions on adoption laws, the Court largely allowed states to treat the sexes differently on the assumption that mothers were more committed to their children than fathers were. While purporting to use heightened scrutiny in such cases, the justices often accepted the government's asserted purpose for the law and agreed that differentiating because of sex was reasonably related to its objectives (Mezey 2011).

In these cases, although several justices implied that classifications based on sex should be presumed invalid—as are racial classifications—the Court continued to uphold laws related to physiological differences between the sexes that stemmed from societal assumptions about sex roles. The cases largely arose over challenges to the Immigration and Nationality Act (INA), initially enacted in 1952, establishing that when a child is born on foreign soil to unwed parents—one a citizen and the other a noncitizen—the child's citizenship largely depends on whether the mother or the father is the citizen (Satinoff 1998; Gallardo 2018). In appraising the constitutionality of the INA, the high court invariably deferred to Congress and affirmed the legislature's plenary authority over immigration. Rejecting claims of inequality under the Fifth Amendment's due process clause (the equal protection component of the Fifth Amendment), the Court permitted Congress to differentiate between unwed mothers and fathers, validating the legislature's beliefs about women's relationship to their children. In upholding sections of the INA, a majority ruled that Congress was legitimately acknowledging the reality of biological differences between the sexes with respect to pregnancy and childbirth and was not relying on stereotypical and overbroad generalizations about culturally determined roles. The Court held that challenged provisions of the law were justified because a mother is more likely to be the sole caretaker of a child and establish a relationship with that child, in part because she is present at birth, while the father is less likely to form such a relationship as he may not be present at the birth or play a role in his child's life. Because it believed that the INA was substantially related to the government's objective of affirming a biological relationship between a citizen parent and the child, the Court held it satisfied the heightened scrutiny test.

Decisions like this underscored the Supreme Court's tenuous commitment to heightened scrutiny. The majority largely neglected to probe Congress's assumption that women are intrinsically more willing and able to assume primary responsibility for their children while men seek to avoid accepting their duty to their offspring. Finally in 2017, the Court adopted a different approach to physical differences cases. In *Sessions v. Morales-Santana* (2017), it declared a section of the INA unconstitutional. Instead of simply accepting Congress's traditional notions of women's and men's roles in the family, it explained that society's views had advanced since the law was passed, and fathers were as likely as mothers to establish relationships with their children. In declaring the challenged provision of the act invalid, the Court reaffirmed its original understanding of heightened scrutiny in sex-based classifications, requiring the government to show that the classification is substantially related to achieving an important goal, rather than allowing the government to simply assert, without evidence, that the relationship exists (Burt 2018; Rock 2018). Another opportunity to rule on a law arguably related to physical sex differences presented itself when the Court was asked to declare a provision of the Military Selective Service Act unconstitutional. The law, requiring men to register with the Selective Service System when they turn eighteen, had been upheld in 1981 as consistent with the Fifth Amendment. Even in the absence of a draft at the time, men were subject to fines and penalties for failing to register (Stiehm 1989).

A more recent challenge to the men-only military registration policy arose when two individuals and a group called the National Coalition for Men filed suit, arguing that unlike forty years ago when the Court held that the men-only registration policy was justified by women's exclusion from combat, women were now eligible for all military service positions, including combat, and there was no reason to exclude them from the draft registration requirement. When the case reached the Supreme Court, top military leaders and members of Congress spoke out in favor of revising the male-only registration policy; a congressionally chartered National Commission on Military, National, and Public Service recommended that women be included in the draft registration policy (*Federal News Network*, March 11, 2021).

In a press release, the plaintiffs' attorneys, the ACLU, emphasized that "putting an end to the men-only registration requirement would undo one of the last examples of overt sex discrimination in federal law." The current occupant of Ginsburg's position, the Director of the Women's Rights Project of the ACLU, reiterated the harm to women in continuing to allow such legal disparities to exist, saying, "like many laws that appear to benefit women, men-only registration harms women too . . . [because] it is based on outdated and sexist notions of women's and men's abilities to serve in the military, regardless of individual ability. Limiting registration to men treats women as unfit for this obligation of citizenship and reflects the outmoded belief that men aren't qualified to be caregivers in the event of a draft. Such sex stereotypes have no place in our federal law" (American Civil Liberties Union 2021e).

Donald Trump's administration urged the Court to uphold the sex-based distinction; Joe Biden's administration took no stand on the law but sought a delay in the Court's deliberations, asking it to allow Congress to resolve the issue. In the last month of the 2020–2021 term, the high court declined to accept the case (*National Coalition for Men v. Selective Service System* 2021). By the end of 2022, the controversy remained unresolved, with the men-only registration policy still in place. Reprising the spirit of Ginsburg, Sonia Sotomayor and two other justices wrote separately to express concern about the effect of the policy on women's status in the military, citing numerous gender equality rulings reflecting the Court's decades-old stance that the government may not "discriminat[e] because of sex absent an 'exceedingly persuasive justification'" (1815). Suggesting that the registration system was constitutionally problematic considering the thousands of women serving in the military in all capacities since 2015, they quoted the commission's finding that "male-only registration sends a message to women not only that they are not vital to the defense of the country but also that they are not expected to participate in defending it" (1816). In the end, even these three justices agreed that denying the petition for review was correct given that Congress "was actively weigh[ing] the issue" and citing the Court's customary deference to the legislature on military and national security matters (1816).

Equal Rights Amendment

Over the last five decades, courts have played a significant role in eliminating legal distinctions between women and men, leaving few laws standing that explicitly differentiate on the basis of sex. Yet a substantial number of women's rights advocates remain dissatisfied with the gains that have been made and seek to expand equality by concentrating their efforts on ratification of a constitutional amendment that explicitly proclaims the standard of equal treatment under the law.

After the adoption of the Nineteenth Amendment in 1920, the fragile unity holding together the first wave of feminism disappeared. Having won the right to vote, some women turned their attention to other social causes, such as child labor, education, and maternal health; others chose to retreat from the world of activism. But most of the key figures in the suffrage movement continued to focus on the battle for women's rights. On the cusp of the amendment's ratification, the NAWSA became transformed into the League of Women Voters, a nonpartisan organization promoting informed and active participation in elections and government. Believing that suffrage was just the first step to gender equality in the United States, the NWP also worked to secure a constitutional amendment that would guarantee women equal rights with men and eliminate sex-based public policies. After a long series of drafts, the NWP's leader Paul co-wrote the Equal Rights Amendment (ERA) and assisted with its initial introduction in Congress in 1923. But aside from Paul and her supporters, the immediate response to the proposed amendment generally ranged from unenthusiastic to hostile. Not only had the passage of the Nineteenth Amendment prompted an anti-feminist backlash among conservatives fearful of women's greater autonomy, but many women's rights advocates also worried that the ERA would outlaw protective labor legislation for women. For others, the ERA was unnecessary because the Fourteenth Amendment already provided women constitutional protection. Facing an uphill battle, ERA proponents set out to change public opinion and gain congressional support (Cott 1990a; Cott 1990b; Boisseau and Thomas 2018).

After its first introduction to Congress in 1923, the ERA was reintroduced in every session through 1971. By the mid-1940s, activists had convinced several women's organizations to endorse the ERA, including the National Association of Woman Lawyers, the National Federation of Business and Professional Women's Clubs, and the GFWC, which had played a significant role in the battle for suffrage. Additionally, Republicans and Democrats added the ERA to their party platforms in 1940 and 1944, respectively. At the same time, opposition continued to emerge from the right and the left. Catholic organizations such as the National Council of Catholic Women and the National Catholic Welfare Conference lobbied members of Congress to withhold support for the amendment. The National Committee to Defeat the Un-Equal Rights Amendment, led by feminists in the Women's Bureau of the Department of Labor, brought together leadership from labor, the YWCA, and the National Councils of Catholic, Jewish, and Negro women. Without a large, organized movement to champion the ERA and push back against this opposition, legislative progress was incremental through the 1950s (Steiner 1985; Berry 1986; Freeman 1996; Boisseau and Thomas 2018).

The passage of the Civil Rights Act in 1964 marked a turning point in the battle over the ERA as Title VII of the act, prohibiting employment discrimination based on sex, led to significant changes in protective labor legislation. Within a decade of the act's passage, the Department of Labor, the Equal Employment Opportunity Commission, and the federal courts began to interpret Title VII as nullifying labor legislation that applied only to women. To meet those standards, in some cases they required that protections such as minimum wages and limits on hours be extended to all workers instead of eliminating them for women. As a result, many women's rights activists who had previously opposed the ERA out of fear that women would lose protections in the workforce began to support it. Importantly, the National Organization for Women (NOW), founded in 1966, adopted the ERA as one of its top priorities; other groups such as the National Federation of Business and Professional Women's Clubs joined its lobbying efforts. Opponents remained—primarily in the form of conservatives who predicted the ERA would upend gender roles and destroy families—but the second wave of feminism was a powerful force.

By the early 1970s, women's rights activists had persuaded lawmakers and the public of the ERA's value. In 1971, the House approved the ERA by a vote of 354 to 23. After passing in the Senate 84 to 8 the next year, the amendment was sent to the states for ratification (Mansbridge 1986; Mayeri 2004). In its final version, Section 1 of the amendment read: "Equality of rights under the law shall not be denied or abridged by the United States or by any state on account of sex." The amendment required ratification by three-fourths of states (thirty-eight) within the seven-year time frame Congress had set. Pro-ERA forces had the initial momentum, and thirty states ratified it by early 1973. But two events halted their progress: the creation of the STOP (Stop Taking Our Privileges) ERA campaign and the legalization of abortion.

In 1972, Phyllis Schlafly founded the conservative interest group Eagle Forum and became the driving force in the STOP ERA movement. According to Schlafly, feminism sought to undermine traditional family values and force women out of their rightful, privileged place in the home. As she described it, the ERA would strip women—especially housewives and stay-at-home mothers—of the special protections they deserved, such as the right to be financially supported by their husbands. Schlafly claimed that if the ERA were ratified, widows would lose their Social Security benefits, women would be drafted into military combat, and women's bathrooms and other sex-segregated public facilities would be outlawed.

While Schlafly had already gained an impressive number of followers during the first year of her STOP ERA campaign, her efforts received a significant boost when the Supreme Court legalized abortion in *Roe v. Wade* (1973). In response to the ruling, an anti-feminist movement sprang up to challenge the feminists who had been fighting for reproductive rights, particularly abortion care. Sensing an opportunity to expand their coalition, anti-ERA activists made a concerted effort to connect abortion with the amendment in the minds of Americans. Opponents doubled down on their claim that the ERA would destroy families, arguing that ratifying it would lead to abortion on demand funded by the government. Likewise, they tied the issue of gay and lesbian rights to the ERA and predicted that its passage would require courts to permit same-sex marriage. The strategy succeeded, and numerous conservatives withdrew their support for the ERA (Mansbridge 1986; Berry 1986).

Schlafly was able to convince many women (and men) that the ERA was a threat to their way of life. One of her most successful maneuvers was transforming the focus of the ERA debate from women's equal treatment under the law to the erosion of gender roles and the traditional family. Though most Americans at the time supported the former, they feared the latter. Schlafly sought to stoke this fear among voters and lawmakers in states that had not yet ratified the ERA. Logistically, she tapped into the organizational base of fundamentalist religious and politically conservative groups. Using telephone trees, she quickly mobilized her followers to lobby state legislators with home-baked goods and hand-written notes. Her campaign was aided by other conservative organizations, such as Concerned Women for America (CWA), that also made blocking ERA ratification a priority. CWA's founder Beverly LaHaye was married to fundamentalist Baptist minister Tim LaHaye, who helped form the Moral Majority. When LaHaye established the CWA in 1979, its stated goal was to promote biblical values in all levels of public policy. In the eyes of the CWA, the ERA was not compatible with such values because it would undermine traditional gender roles, eliminate special protections for women, and lead to taxpayer-funded abortions (Conover and Gray 1983; Mansbridge 1986; Klatch 1987; Marshall 1991).

Feminist groups tried to match this fervent opposition by organizing economic boycotts and staging protests in states that had not ratified the ERA. Supporters' activism thus far had focused primarily on the national level, and their state-level grassroots campaigns were weak compared with the anti-ERA movement—especially in the South. Moreover, there were divisions among women who generally supported the ERA. For some, the amendment was an important but largely symbolic gesture. Others believed that the ERA would bring about substantive legal changes—with potential positive and negative results. Many hoped it would help to close the gender pay gap, but they also feared losing child support payments and being forced to sign up for the military draft. In the end, the opposition proved too powerful to overcome. By 1978, only thirty-five states had ratified the ERA. Although Congress extended the seven-year deadline it had set in 1972, no new states ratified it during those additional three years. In 1982, three states short of ratification, the ERA was finally defeated (Berry 1986; Mansbridge 1986).

Lawmakers have reintroduced the ERA in every session of Congress since its defeat. There was little movement for decades, but the 2010s witnessed a revival for its support in response to numerous overlapping factors. The #MeToo and #TimesUp movements brought increased media attention to the widespread sexual abuse and harassment women face. The 2016 documentary *Equal Means Equal* (dir. Kamala Lopez) highlighted the gender discrimination prevalent in the United States and made the case that the ERA could improve women's status by guaranteeing constitutional equality. Finally, the election of Donald Trump—with his misogynist rhetoric and numerous allegations of sexual misconduct—galvanized ERA supporters who worried that the new president would further undermine women's rights.

In 2017, Nevada became the thirty-sixth state to ratify the ERA, just two months after women's marches took place across the country in response to Trump's inauguration. Illinois followed suit in 2018, and in 2020, Virginia became the thirty-eighth state to ratify the amendment. With Virginia's ratification, the ERA reached the threshold needed to become part of the Constitution; however, it is still in limbo because the last three ratifications came long after the 1982 deadline. Opponents of the ERA see that deadline as firm, arguing that the ratification process must start over from the beginning. Proponents say that because Congress set the deadline, it has the power to change it and add the ERA to the Constitution immediately because it received the requisite number of votes. To bolster their claim, activists point to the Twenty-Seventh Amendment on congressional pay raises that was sent to the states for ratification in 1789 but did not receive the necessary votes to become part of the Constitution until 1992. Further complicating the issue is the fact that five states (Nebraska, Tennessee, Idaho, Kentucky, and South Dakota) rescinded their ratifications of the ERA between 1973 and 1979. It is unclear if such reversals are legal and, thus far, Congress has never accepted a state's attempt to undo its ratification of a constitutional amendment (Stewart 2018; Suk 2020). The courts have also not taken a stance on the validity of a state's rescission.

Anticipating Virginia's ratification vote, on December 16, 2019, Republican attorneys general from Alabama, Louisiana, and South Dakota filed suit in an Alabama federal district court against David Ferriero, archivist of the United States (in his official capacity as the person responsible for recording states' ratification votes and amendments). Claiming that the ratification deadline set by Congress is still valid, they sought to block him from recording the amendment as ratified once Virginia voted and to demand he remove the votes of Nebraska, Tennessee, Idaho, Kentucky, and South Dakota based on their legislatures' instructions to rescind their ratifications. A statement by the attorney general of Alabama declared, "if this constitutional bait-and-switch is successful, there will be dire consequences for the rule of law. The people had seven years to consider the ERA, and they rejected it." A member of the ERA Coalition condemned the lawsuit, saying, "Alabama has filed this lawsuit to thwart the democratic process and the will of the overwhelming majority of Americans to enshrine the fundamental right to sex equality in our Constitution. The Attorney General of Alabama has done a disservice to women, including the women of Alabama" (*The Hill*, December 19, 2019).

Shortly thereafter, following Virginia's vote to ratify, ERA proponents filed suit in a Massachusetts federal district court, asking the archivist to properly record Virginia's vote and the amendment's ratification and refrain from negating the ratification votes from the five states. They primarily objected to the seven-year deadline that Congress imposed, a provision that was not included in the text sent to the states; moreover, they stated, the subsequent three-year extension (until 1982) was approved by Congress in a joint resolution, unattached to the amendment. No other proposed amendment, they claimed, was subject to the same extraconstitutional restrictions. On August 6, 2020, the Massachusetts district court judge dismissed their suit, and on June 20, 2021, the First Circuit Court of Appeals affirmed the district court in *Equal Means Equal v. Ferriero* (2021).

Meanwhile, Democratic attorneys general from the last three ratifying states—Nevada, Illinois, and Virginia—filed suit in the District of Columbia federal district court, supported by briefs from women's organizations, members of the legal profession, labor unions, state public officials, corporations, and religious groups. Most groups filing briefs favored ratification, but several anti-ERA groups (such as the Independent Women's Forum, supported by the Trump administration's Department of Justice), presented briefs against extending the deadline to ratify (*Bloomberg Law*, October 13, 2020). In addition, five other states (Alabama, Louisiana, Nebraska, South Dakota, and Tennessee), three of which had attempted to revoke their ratifying votes, asked to intervene on behalf of the archivist. On March 5, 2021, without addressing the legality of the attempted rescissions, the District of Columbia federal court judge dismissed the Democratic attorneys' general suit, holding that because the states missed the original and the extended deadline for ratification, the archivist was not required to record their votes (*Virginia v. Ferriero* 2021). Two months later, the plaintiffs appealed to the District of Columbia Circuit Court of Appeals and, in February 2022, following the election of its Republican governor, Virginia asked to be dismissed as a party in the case. At the oral arguments before the circuit court on September 28, 2022, the circuit judges seemed to question their authority to order the federal government to publish the amendment as part of the Constitution (*Washington Post*, September 28, 2022; *Bloomberg Law*, September 28, 2022).

The battle for equality of rights is not over; half the states guarantee equal rights based on sex in their constitutions, and others such as Nevada and Minnesota are attempting to amend their state constitutions to include such language. Nor is the ERA a dead issue in Congress. In 2020 and 2021, the US House of Representatives voted in favor of removing the 1982 deadline for the ERA's ratification by the states; a companion bill has yet to make it out of committee in the Senate. With proponents and opponents of the ERA filing lawsuits to either approve or block ratification, it is likely that the Supreme Court will eventually interject itself into at least one of these legal challenges (Sullivan 2020; "Equal Rights Amendment" 2021).

As the conflict over ratification advances in the legislative and judicial branches, ERA advocates urge that "only a federal Equal Rights Amendment can provide the highest and broadest level of legal protection against sex discrimination" ("Equal Rights Amendment" 2021). They fear that without a robust guarantee of equality of rights enshrined in the Constitution, equal rights protections are constantly threatened, such as Wisconsin's 2009 Equal Pay Enforcement Act that was repealed when Republicans won the majority in the state legislature in 2012 (Stewart 2018). Advocates stress that the ERA can also bolster the ability of the law to address ongoing systemic harms to women, such as pay inequity, pregnancy discrimination, and sexual violence (Neuwirth 2015). They believe that a constitutional amendment barring sex discrimination might motivate law enforcement agents and prosecutors to address the hundreds of thousands of untested sexual assault kits warehoused in police departments. Because most reported assaults are committed against women, the failure to act on this evidence could perhaps be viewed as systemic sex discrimination (Filler-Corn et al. 2020). In short, ERA supporters believe the amendment could have immeasurable positive effects on the lives of women across the United States.

Opponents argue that adding the ERA to the Constitution is antithetical to representative democracy because the final ratification vote was long delayed after being submitted to the states for their approval. In their view, the amendment is, at best, redundant because women and men have achieved constitutional equality. At worst, they declare, the ERA would eradicate the protections women have in the workplace and home and would ultimately expand the inequities between the sexes. Anti-abortion groups have allied themselves with the ERA opposition, claiming abortion rights groups would rely on the amendment to prevent states from regulating abortion as acts of sex discrimination. Similarly, groups seeking to limit transgender rights have joined in opposing the amendment, arguing it would enhance the rights of the nation's transgender community.

Conclusion

Since the early twentieth century, women in the United States have made significant political, economic, and social progress, in large part as a result of women's activism. It was women's unwavering pressure on policymakers throughout the first wave of feminism that led to the passage of the Nineteenth Amendment granting (white) women the right to vote. Similarly, the proliferation of groups fighting for women's rights during the second wave of feminism contributed to substantial policy reforms in employment, education, and reproductive rights. Throughout that period, women's growing political representation in the legislative, executive, and judicial branches has been both a cause and an effect of women's increased rights. For example, women legislators are more likely than their male counterparts to introduce bills related to women's issues (Thomas 1994; Swers 2002). As women gained greater autonomy and access to resources from legislation, they became increasingly likely to run for and win elected office, thus perpetuating a cycle allowing for the introduction of more women's rights legislation. Yet there is still much work to be done. Women's advancement has been uneven, and women of color, poor women, and women in the LGBTQ+ community continue to have less access to resources and hold fewer positions of power. The courts have contributed to myriad advances in women's rights but have not fully committed themselves to this project. Federal court judges, appointed for life, often reflect the political views of the president who appointed them. The battle over women's rights, especially in contraceptive and abortion care policies, has taken center stage as these cases are increasingly brought to the courts, highlighting that, as the ongoing debate over the ERA demonstrates, gender equality in the United States is far from a settled issue.

Plan of the Book

Building from the historical analysis of women's rights activism and policymaking in this chapter, in the remainder of the book we explore how women continue to chase equality across an array of policy issues. Chapter 2 focuses on women's struggle to secure equal opportunities in education. In particular, we analyze the evolution of the role of the executive and judicial branches in implementing Title IX in the areas of athletic programs and sexual harassment and assault in schools.

In Chapter 3, we examine women in employment, highlighting the successes and failures of legislation aimed at combating discrimination in the workforce, such as Title VII and the Equal Pay Act. We pay particular attention to the gender pay gap and sexual harassment in the workplace, delving into the rise of the #MeToo movement and its effects on workplace outcomes for women. Moving beyond the traditional workplace, we discuss the efforts of professional athletes—especially the US women's national soccer team—to achieve equity. In Chapter 4, we turn our focus to work-family balance, exploring policies that address pregnancy and employment, family leave, and affordable childcare. While Congress initially played a significant role in these issues, the country still lacks a federal paid family leave policy or childcare plan, and it has largely fallen to state and local governments to fill these gaps.

Chapter 5 analyzes the development of family planning policies over the past century, focusing on women's rights advocates' struggle to remove government restrictions on their access to birth control. While there have been two major federal policies intended to expand contraceptive access, Title X and the Affordable Care Act, changes in governmental leadership have threatened these programs, and women's access to birth control remains tenuous. In Chapter 6, we look at the tumultuous history of abortion rights in the United States. Over five decades, the courts consistently upheld a woman's right to terminate her pregnancy, arising out of her constitutional right to privacy, albeit increasingly upholding government regulations to limit that right. As a result of a conservative shift in judicial appointments, the Supreme Court overturned *Roe v. Wade* (1973), the landmark case establishing abortion rights in the nation. As the national debate over abortion continues to rage, states have virtually unfettered authority to determine the extent to which women have access to abortion care.

Finally, in Chapter 7, we summarize our observations regarding the progress women have made since the passage of the Nineteenth Amendment in 1920, as well as where we might be headed in the future. Drawing on the findings of each chapter, we analyze how the different branches and levels of government have shaped women's rights and how this might help us understand the best ways to further expand those rights.

2

Securing Equal
Opportunities in Schools

WOMEN IN THE UNITED STATES HAVE LONG STRUGGLED TO ATTAIN
equality in education. Their goal was advanced when Congress passed
Title IX of the Education Amendments of 1972 (20 USC §1681), prohibiting discrimination based on sex in federally funded institutions.
But the law contained exceptions that allowed single-sex education in
certain institutions, such as military and merchant marine academies, as
well as public undergraduate schools that historically limited admissions to students of one sex. Because of the Title IX limitations, women
turned to the federal courts for relief in the early 1970s, challenging discriminatory policies in higher education as a violation of their rights
under the Fourteenth Amendment's equal protection clause.

Ironically, the first major victory in a case involving a university's
single-sex admissions policy came in a 1982 Supreme Court ruling on
the constitutionality of excluding men from Mississippi's women-only
nursing program. In *Mississippi University for Women v. Hogan* (1982),
the Court rejected the state's position that restricting the nursing
school to women students was constitutional because it compensated
them for past discrimination. Because women were not discriminated
against in the nursing field, the majority found it inappropriate for the
nursing program to deny admission to men. The single-sex admission
policy may only be justified, the Court ruled, if the advantaged group
(in this case, women) "suffer a disadvantage related to the classification" (728). Some justices believed that the policy even harmed
women by preserving the stereotypical image of nursing as a woman's
occupation. Women's rights advocates were pleased with the ruling, in

25

part because the Court appeared to have adopted a higher level of scrutiny for gender-based discrimination laws by requiring the state to provide an "exceedingly persuasive justification" for the nursing school policy.

The Supreme Court soon added another dimension to the meaning of constitutional equality in education, deciding whether excluding women from the Virginia Military Institute (VMI), the elite state-funded military academy, violated the equal protection clause. One of the last men-only military schools in the nation (West Point and the Naval Academy began accepting women in 1976), VMI argued that the presence of women would significantly impair the school's educational environment and undermine its mission of training men for the military. In *United States v. Virginia* (1996), the Court applied a new version of scrutiny, called skeptical scrutiny, and held that the state's reasons for excluding women from the elite school were largely based on stereotypical views of women's skills and capabilities and denying them admission to the state's premier military program violated their right to equal protection. The ruling established the principle that, barring special circumstances, public universities and colleges were prohibited from restricting admission because of sex. VMI reacted to the opinion in harsh terms, with the superintendent characterizing it as "a killer," while nonetheless pledging to comply "with honor . . . and in a gentlemanly manner." One student, wearing a shirt that read "Better dead than co-ed," said "it [the decision] stinks." Several alumni explored the possibility of replacing the state's funding with private funds, but they eventually abandoned the plan given the difficulties of raising tens of millions of dollars (*Washington Post*, June 27, 1996).

Despite the high court's admonitions, in 2020, following accusations of racism and sexism at the academy, VMI commissioned an investigation by an independent law firm that concluded the school needed to reform its "overall racist and sexist culture" (*Washington Post*, June 2, 2021). Basing its analysis in part on surveys and interviews, the firm found that in addition to racism, there was a broad consensus among those surveyed that "many women students reported a consistent fear of assault or harassment by their fellow male cadets" and believed "assault complaints are not or will not be taken seriously by the VMI administration or that a cadet will suffer retaliatory consequences for reporting them." The report added, "misogyny is a major problem at VMI" and many of those surveyed, including men, think the school's "gender inequity issues are worse than its racial equality issues" (*Washington Post*, June 1, 2021). The investigation confirmed that women had not yet achieved equality at VMI. The appointment of the first woman as VMI's top military commander in 2021 did little to dispel the school's appearance of fostering sexism and misogyny. The announcement of her appointment led to a flurry of postings on VMI's social media, ridiculing her and the other women at the school. Cadets suggested her appointment was the "most unpopular" ever at the school and she was only selected "as a publicity stunt" (*Washington Post*, July 12, 2021).

Title IX

Title IX provides: "no person in the United States shall, on the basis of sex, be excluded from participation in, be denied the benefits of, or be subjected to discrimination under any education program or activity receiving Federal financial assistance." The debate over the final version of the bill in the House and Senate Conference Committee centered on court-ordered busing for racial integration, with little attention paid to the sex discrimination provision. With scant legislative history of Title IX or evidence of legislative intent, the interpretation of the law was left to the courts and the executive branch, primarily the latter. The first Title IX regulations were adopted in July 1975; since then, federal agencies have issued numerous regulations and guidance documents, with courts exercising the final judgment to ensure that agency interpretations are consistent with the intent of Congress. Unlike a regulation (also called a rule), a guidance helps "clarify the meaning of existing statutes and regulations" and, in part because it allows the agency to avoid the rigorous procedural requirements of regulatory rulemaking, it has "become a principal agency policy instrument" (Yackee 2021).

Title IX policymaking became increasingly politicized, with enforcement dependent on the views of the personnel in control of the White House and executive branch. Although its vague language with ill-defined terms suggested the law might have only symbolic value, shortly after its passage, it began to play a key role in combating gender inequities in the educational system in a wide range of arenas, including sports, scholarships, employment, and sexual misconduct and violence. Of these, the two most hotly contested disputes over the meaning of Title IX revolved around athletics and sexual harassment.

Title IX and Athletic Programs

From the start, when women's rights advocates urged a broad interpretation of the law, they encountered opposition from sports officials and school administrators who rejected their complaints of discrimination. Notwithstanding their objections, Title IX eventually became an important weapon in the struggle to end the disparities between men's and women's athletic programs (Coleman, Joyner, and Lopiano 2020). During the regulatory process following the passage of Title IX, a coalition of men's athletic organizations opposed equal treatment for women's sports programs, concerned it would shift resources from men's sports. After they were unable to exempt revenue-producing sports from the antidiscrimination provisions of Title IX, the 1974 Education Amendments directed the Department of Health, Education, and Welfare—after 1979, the Department of Education (DOE)—to publish regulations on intercollegiate athletics. The regulations barred schools from fielding sex-segregated teams in the same sport with two broad exceptions: sports in which selection is based on competitive skill and sports involving bodily contact.

With primary responsibility for enforcing Title IX, the Office for Civil Rights (OCR), a division of DOE, periodically sends policy interpretations (or guidance documents) to the schools under its authority to spell out the administration's understanding of a school's Title IX obligations. These documents rest on the agency's ultimate authority to terminate federal funding to noncompliant institutions and remind them that civil rights complaints may generate negative publicity and potentially lead to investigations and litigation. Though they are not bound by them, courts "generally give deference to OCR's regulations and interpretations" (Chamberlain, Cornett, and Yohanan 2018, 234). The 1979 Policy Interpretation, the first of several OCR documents to explain a school's obligations under Title IX, specified the regulations broadly apply to interscholastic, intercollegiate, club, and intramural athletics. The interpretation is divided into three sections: the first states that when an institution provides financial assistance to student athletes, the dollars spent on men's and women's sports must be "substantially equal." The second identifies factors and procedures for evaluating equal opportunity in participation and benefits, such as equipment and supplies, locker room facilities, coaching, and support services. The third part sets out three criteria (later collectively known as the three-part test) to determine whether institutions are satisfying their obligations to provide women an equal opportunity to participate in athletic programs.

The three-part test became the most widely used (and the most hotly litigated) measure to assess compliance with the statute (Hefferan 2016). The three parts are (1) whether a school's intercollegiate sports programs provide opportunities for women and men that are "substantially proportionate to their respective enrollments"; (2) whether, if one sex is underrepresented in intercollegiate athletic activities, the school can demonstrate it has "a history and continuing practice of program expansion" that responds to the "developing interest and abilities" of that sex; and (3) if one sex has been underrepresented, and the school cannot show it has increased opportunities in the past, it can show that "the interests and abilities" of that sex are now being "fully and effectively accommodated" (US Department of Health, Education and Welfare 1979; Anderson 2012; Hefferan 2016). Almost twenty years later, on January 16, 1996, OCR clarified that an institution satisfies its obligations under Title IX by meeting any of the parts of the three-part test and that the key to evaluating its compliance with the law is "whether students of both sexes are provided nondiscriminatory opportunities to participate in athletics" (US Department of Education, Office for Civil Rights 1996). Because of the difficulty of satisfying the second and third prongs, most schools strive to show they meet the first, the "substantially proportionate" prong (Ambrosius 2012).

Coaches and men's sports advocates contend that Title IX produced an unintended consequence of eliminating or demoting men's nonrevenue sports as universities seek to adopt cost-saving measures to fund women's sports (Shook 1996; Jurewitz 2000). In 2003, George W. Bush's administration attempted to lessen the impact of the 1979 Policy Interpretation (issued during President Jimmy Carter's term) by issuing a new guidance clarifying that OCR had not intended to encourage schools to eliminate teams to achieve equity for women because such action "diminishes opportunities for students who are interested in participating in athletics instead of enhancing opportunities for students who have suffered from discrimination" (US Department of Education, Office for Civil Rights 2003). During Bush's tenure in office, OCR made it easier for schools to demonstrate they accommodated the needs of students of the underrepresented sex. In 2005, it informed schools that Title IX does not require them "to accommodate the interests and abilities of all their students or fulfill every request for the addition or elevation of particular sports" under all circumstances and that the burden is on OCR or the complaining students to prove a school fails to comply with the regulations.

To ease the burden on the institution to show it is responsive to student concerns, OCR formally approved the use of survey questionnaires to weigh student interest in participation, emphasizing if the survey does not indicate support for additional teams, the school will be presumed to be compliant with Title IX (US Department of Education, Office for Civil Rights 2005).

Under President Barack Obama, DOE notified educational institutions that survey instruments were no longer acceptable to determine compliance with Title IX and its regulations. A 2010 DOE guidance expressed concern that surveys underrepresent women's interests in sports and then absolve the school of engaging in discriminatory conduct. The administration explained that schools will no longer be presumed to be fulfilling their obligations under Title IX even if the survey shows there are no "unmet interest or abilities of the underrepresented sex." According to this guidance, OCR will not base its findings solely on the results of a survey but will rely on "multiple indicators" to gauge compliance with the Title IX regulations (US Department of Education, Office for Civil Rights 2010).

Title IX and the Federal Courts

In 1979, the courts began to play a significant role in enforcing institutional compliance with Title IX as a result of the Supreme Court's ruling in *Cannon v. University of Chicago* (1979). Under the law, educational institutions are eligible for federal dollars if they do not discriminate because of sex. As written, Title IX did not authorize individuals to sue offending institutions for violating their rights; instead, it left enforcement to the federal agency with the authority to monitor the school's compliance and the power to terminate its funding. Even though the federal government has the authority to cut off federal funds, as of 2020, it has not done so to any school for a Title IX violation (Sindt 2020). Thus, litigation has been a crucial spur to Title IX enforcement. In *Cannon*, the Supreme Court acknowledged that terminating a school's funding would prevent institutions from using federal dollars for discriminatory practices but would not protect individuals from discrimination. Therefore, to fulfill the statute's goals, it permitted Cannon's Title IX suit against the University of Chicago Medical School to proceed. It returned the case to the lower court to determine whether the school had discriminated against her on the basis of sex as she had claimed.

The Court's next Title IX ruling, *Grove City College v. Bell* (1984), arose from a challenge to the federal government's interpretation of the scope of the law. Grove City College, a small liberal arts college in western Pennsylvania, refused to sign the requisite assurance of compliance with Title IX, stating it was not a funding recipient within the meaning of the statute because it received federal dollars only indirectly through its student aid program. However, it argued, if the Court were to hold that Title IX protection is triggered by such indirect aid—grants and loans to students—the law only prohibits discrimination in the specific program involved. The high court held that the indirect aid to Grove City's students triggered Title IX coverage as there was no evidence to suggest that Congress intended to distinguish between direct and indirect aid. But it agreed with Grove City that the Title IX guarantees were limited to the program receiving the aid because it did not believe Congress sought to have the government's "regulatory authority follow federally aided students from classroom to classroom, building to building, or activity to activity" (573–574). Consequently, the Court declared the prohibition against sex discrimination only applied to Grove City's financial aid program and did not trigger institution-wide coverage.

The implications of this decision soon became apparent as schools successfully claimed that because their athletic programs did not receive federal funds, they were exempt from the prohibition on sex discrimination. Most courts agreed and dismissed the suits against the school athletic programs (Anderson 2012). In 1988, Congress passed the Civil Rights Restoration Act, establishing that all programs and activities in a federally funded institution were subject to Title IX. The law paved the way for scores of successful suits based on claims of inequities in athletic programs. Since then, plaintiffs have prevailed in most of the Title IX suits against college and university sports programs. By the thirtieth anniversary of its passage, relying on the three-part test, the courts largely upheld women's complaints of inequity in athletics, rejecting constitutional attacks on the statute, the regulations, and the 1979 Policy Interpretation (Eckes 2003).

One of the most widely cited Title IX cases, *Cohen v. Brown University* (1996), exemplifies the judiciary's approach to the substantial proportionality prong of the three-part test. A class action suit by women at Brown University complained that the school sought to cut costs by demoting women's volleyball and gymnastics teams and men's golf and water polo teams from university-funded varsity status to donor-funded varsity status. The women sought to have their teams reinstated, emphasizing that though it might seem even-handed to cut two teams for each sex, men were already enjoying an advantage in sports at Brown. The university contended that the three-part test of the 1979 Policy Interpretation was contrary to Title IX and its regulations as well as the Constitution. The First Circuit Court of Appeals disagreed, saying, "the [1979] Policy Interpretation represents the responsible agency's interpretation of the intercollegiate athletics provisions of Title IX and its implementing regulations," adding "an agency's construction of its own regulations is entitled to substantial deference" (*Cohen v. Brown University* 1996, 173).

The primary question for the circuit court to decide was the degree to which the school had accommodated the interests of the underrepresented sex—women—when there was a substantial gap between the percentage of women in the school and the percentage on varsity sports teams. The university contended that the difference was attributable not to its actions but to women's lack of interest in participating on intercollegiate athletic teams. The court disagreed, emphasizing this "ignore[s] the fact that Title IX was enacted in order to remedy discrimination that results from stereotyped notions of women's interests and abilities" (179). On the contrary, citing the 1979 Policy Interpretation, the appeals court stated "interest and ability rarely develop in a vacuum; they evolve as a function of opportunity and experience. The Policy Interpretation recognizes that women's lower rate of participation in athletics reflects women's historical lack of opportunities to participate in sports" (179). Based on the evidence, the judge concluded that "Brown's failure to accommodate fully and effectively the interests and abilities of the underrepresented gender is clearly established," thereby violating Title IX (180). The parties reached a settlement agreement that remained in force for over twenty years until 2020, when the university eliminated some varsity sports programs and raised sailing (available to both women and men) to varsity status. Under a threat of new litigation, the parties amended the agreement and the revised version was approved by the First Circuit in *Cohen v. Brown University* (2021).

Women in School Sports

Following the example of *Cohen*, courts were inclined to accept university actions that attempted to achieve equity between men's and women's athletic programs, often at the expense of men's sports teams, finding that schools were simply complying with Title IX in enhancing women's sports' opportunities. Representatives of men's athletic programs objected, but the rulings on equity in athletic programs were consistent with national public opinion. According to a *Washington Post*–University of Maryland national poll conducted in May 2022 with 1,503 people, a vast majority of Americans (85 percent of respondents) believed "colleges and universities should be required to award the same number of athletic scholarships for women as they do men"; over half (54 percent) thought that educational institutions had "not gone far enough" to provide equal opportunities for women (*Washington Post*, June 22, 2022).

There are numerous indicators that Title IX has had a significant impact on women's participation in sports in high schools and colleges. At its fortieth anniversary in 2012, "the number of high school girls participating in sports ha[d] risen tenfold . . . while six times as many women compete[d] in college sports" (National Coalition for Women and Girls in Education 2012, 2). More recent data show that the number of women engaged in high school athletics grew to more than 3.4 million in 2018–2019 (Hefferan 2016; Coleman, Joyner, and Lopiano 2020, 72). By 2020, there was a "435% increase in intercollegiate athletics" (Belkoff 2020, 46). Title IX's effect on sports was similarly evident at the 2012 Summer Olympics, with women representing more than half the members of the US Olympic teams and winning fifty-eight medals, more than half the total scored by the Team USA athletes. Their numbers had improved sharply compared to their record in the 1972 Summer Olympics in Munich, where they earned only twenty-two medals, amounting to less than a quarter of the US medal count (Hefferan 2016, 583). Although women have made progress in expanding their access to athletics, "the work of eradicating discrimination in sports is far from over" (George 2010, 3).

Nearly fifty years after the passage of Title IX, inequities between men's and women's teams in the 2021 college basketball tournament underscored that women's sports teams are not as greatly valued as men's. The 2021 National Collegiate Athletic Association (NCAA) men's and women's basketball tournaments, popularly known as "March Madness," beginning on March 18, 2021, were accompanied by reports of numerous discrepancies in men's and women's facilities, equipment, publicity, and game coverage. Highlighting the need for improvement in advancing equal rights in the sports world, the most widely publicized difference between the teams was the equipment in the fitness and weight rooms. While the men had access to a fully equipped weight room, the women shared a set of dumbbells and yoga mats. The NCAA reacted to photos illustrating the differences between the two workout facilities by explaining there was "limited space" available for the women and it was "actively working to enhance existing resources" (*On Her Turf*/NBC Sports, March 25, 2021).

A video made by a player on the University of Oregon basketball team and posted to social media revealed the differences between men's and women's facilities. It went viral, and sportswriters and fans brought other disparities to the nation's attention. The NCAA did not refer to the women's tournament games as "March Madness," nor did it publicize photos of the women's games despite putting thousands of pictures of the men's games on its website. The postgame press conferences for the men's teams were transcribed during all rounds of play; press conferences for the women's teams were transcribed only after the teams reached the Sweet 16 round. The difference in branding (identifying markers informing viewers they are watching tournament play) was evident in that no women's games were played with March Madness logos on their courts; the NCAA reserved March Madness for the men's games. Only one women's court had an identifying logo, and it was simply labeled "Women's Basketball." In addition, the women's penultimate round of play was labeled the "Women's Final Four" to mark a clear separation from the men's Final Four. One analyst pointed out the NCAA's excuse for these distinctions—that "men generate more revenue"—is circular: "the NCAA doesn't understand the simple math: photos and transcripts make it easier to get media coverage . . . media coverage generates interest . . . Interest generates viewers . . . Viewers generate revenue" (*On Her Turf*/NBC Sports, March 25, 2021).

In addition to the inequities in training, playing conditions, and publicity, the NCAA even provided different Covid-19 tests for the players: the men were given the more sensitive PCR tests and the women were given the cheaper antigen tests that were less likely to reveal the virus in its early stages. Social media reports also indicated the men were fed more lavishly from a buffet while the women received prepackaged meals (*On Her Turf*/NBC Sports, March 25, 2021; NPR, March 19, 2021; *New York Times*, March 25, 2021).

Reeling from the criticism, with apologies from the NCAA's top leadership for the disparities in training facilities and the other discrepancies in resources, the organization commissioned an outside law firm to review the status of gender equity in the collegiate basketball-playing community. When released several months later, the report raised questions about the validity of some of the organization's claims and confirmed what many already knew: the NCAA prefers men's basketball "over everything else in ways that create, normalize and perpetuate gender inequities" (*Our Fair Shot*, August 3, 2021). The NCAA Board of Governors issued a statement saying the organization "is wholly committed to an equitable experience among its championships and we know that has not always been the case." It continued, "the Division I Women's Basketball Championship is an important impetus for us to improve our championship experience so it is not repeated" (Weissman 2021; *Washington Post*, August 3, 2021). In discussing the report's findings in depth, a critic of the NCAA's record on gender equity described them as "blood-boiling." She noted that the 118-page analysis revealed great disparities in expenditures between men's and women's teams during the championship games, "fostering skepticism and distrust about the sincerity of the NCAA's commitment to gender equity, but also limiting the growth of women's basketball and perpetuating a mistaken narrative that women's basketball is destined to be a 'money loser' year after year." Adding "nothing could be further from the truth," she asks whether the NCAA's leaders' actions reflected "incompetence, malfeasance or pure swinishness" (Jenkins 2021).

In a concession to calls for reform, on September 29, 2021, the NCAA announced its Division I Women's Basketball Championship now will use "March Madness marketing and branding" from the start of the 2022 championship games. The organization also pledged to narrow the gap in spending on tournaments, including matching women's gift (swag) bags to the men's (NCAA 2021; *New York Times*, March 15, 2022).

Suggesting that basketball tournament games were not an anomaly, the 2021 Women's College Softball World Series, played each year in Oklahoma City and attracting over a million viewers, operated under different playing conditions than the Men's College Baseball World Series played in Omaha. The women's games—often played before sold-out crowds—were in a stadium with no showers and sometimes scheduled for two a day to limit housing and food costs. In contrast, the men's teams had rest days between games, received free massages, and were treated to a golf outing and a dinner. The size of the stadiums also varied: the women's with 13,000 seats and the men's at 24,000 seats. A college softball coach asserted that women basketball players are treated worse than men basketball players and women softball players are treated even worse than women basketball players. Speaking of the latter, she said, "they're the chosen ones and they're treated like afterthoughts," asking "what's lower than an afterthought? That's us" (*New York Times*, June 4, 2021).

Title IX and Sexual Misconduct in Schools

Cannon paved the way for individuals to sue federally funded educational institutions for Title IX violations, but the high court made no mention of the availability of money damages for successful plaintiffs. In a series of cases beginning in 1992, it began to address sexual harassment in K–12 schools, with the decisions broadly applying to all federally funded educational institutions.

In *Franklin v. Gwinnett County Public Schools* (1992), the Court agreed that the student who brought the suit may be entitled to money damages if the school were guilty of violating Title IX by failing to intervene when a teacher verbally and physically harassed her for over two years. The majority held that even though the law did not explicitly authorize a damage remedy, the federal courts have traditional authority to order appropriate relief for violations of federal statutes unless Congress explicitly directs otherwise (Wright 1992).

A few years later, the Supreme Court determined the standard for the school's liability in a suit filed by a student who charged a teacher with verbally harassing her and engaging in sexual intercourse with her (*Gebser v. Lago Vista Independent School District* 1998). The school principal was apparently aware of the verbal harassment but not the sexual acts. The Court hesitated to hold a school liable for an employee's misconduct of which it was purportedly unaware, ruling that it is responsible for money damages only if a school official with responsibility to correct the behavior had actual knowledge of it and deliberately failed to respond (Underwood 1999). Known as the deliberate indifference standard, a school could avoid liability if it acted reasonably; critics charged that the Court opted for this standard because it was reluctant to assign responsibility to the school for its employees' misconduct in all circumstances (Bolan 2018).

In *Davis v. Monroe* (1999), the Supreme Court considered whether a school is liable when a student harasses another student. School officials had made little effort to address a student's complaint that a classmate continually harassed her; in response to her suit, the school argued that it is not responsible for a student's misconduct directed at another student. The Court disagreed but limited the school's liability to situations in which officials knew about the harassment and failed to respond to it, whether the harasser was an employee or student. Applying the principle adopted in *Gebser*, it reiterated that a school violates Title IX when it is "deliberately indifferent to sexual harassment, of which [it has] actual knowledge, that is so severe, pervasive, and objectively offensive that it can be said to deprive the victims of access to the educational opportunities or benefits provided by the school" (*Davis v. Monroe* 1999, 650; Daw et al. 2020).

Catharine MacKinnon, a well-known scholar and authority on sexual harassment, thinks the Court set the bar too high for plaintiffs because "the standard [of deliberate indifference] is easy for schools to satisfy" (2016, 2068). Other critics agree that while *Davis* extended the reach of Title IX to encompass peer harassment, it was only a partial victory for victims because the standard adopted by the Court "encouraged schools to 'bury their heads in the sand' rather than actively prevent rights violations, lest they accrue the kind of knowledge that might trigger liability" (Tani 2017, 1861–1862; Bolan 2018). Later research has shown that courts are often reluctant to find schools responsible even when they have notice of the harassment (Daw et al. 2020).

The regulations and guidance documents on school sports programs indicate that the executive branch, primarily DOE, has had a vital role in defining the parameters of Title IX in securing equity for women in sports. Similarly, with respect to accusations of sexual misconduct, although litigation played an important role, DOE and more specifically OCR have major responsibility for enforcing Title IX. The agency is authorized to investigate student complaints of sexual misconduct to determine if the school's response meets the requirements of the law. OCR initially focused most of its efforts on securing compliance with Title IX on gender equity in athletic programs. Beginning in the late 1990s, it turned its attention to enforcing a broader prohibition against sex discrimination in K–12 schools as well as colleges and universities. Soon the agency was addressing numerous complaints of sexual harassment and sexual assault, considered "a pervasive issue at educational institutions" (Edgar 2020, 89).

Sexual violence (a term often used interchangeably with sexual assault) is prevalent in schools of higher education. A widely cited report released by the National Institute of Justice indicates that approximately 20 percent of women are victims of sexual assault during their college years, while approximately 6 percent of men were victims of sexual assault in their college years. The 2011 guidance underscored that sexual violence in schools is not limited to colleges and universities, reporting another study showing that "during the 2007–2008 school year, there were 800 reported incidents of rape and attempted rape and 3,800 reported incidents of other sexual batteries at public high schools" (US Department of Education, Office for Civil Rights 2011). Research on sexual violence consistently shows that for a variety of reasons such as fear, embarrassment, or concern about retribution, women are reluctant to report incidents of sexual misconduct to college authorities and even less likely to report them to law enforcement officials (McMullan 2019; Edgar 2020). Consequently, it is believed that most incidents of sexual misbehavior in colleges and universities are neither investigated nor punished (Vail 2019).

The executive branch's first formal attempt to respond to increasing incidents of sexual harassment, including sexual violence, in Title IX–eligible schools was in a 1997 OCR document titled "Sexual Harassment Guidance 1997: Sexual Harassment of Students by School Employees, Other Students, or Third Parties." An agency's guidance documents are not legally binding on the courts but they indicate to funding recipients the approach it would take in assessing whether the school is complying with the law. Released on March 13, 1997, the guidance clarified that sexual harassment is a form of sex discrimination within Title IX and, borrowing from language in employment discrimination cases, it broadly defined the illegal behavior as "sexually harassing conduct (which can include unwelcome sexual advances, requests for sexual favors, and other verbal, nonverbal, or physical conduct of a sexual nature) by an employee, by another student, or by a third party that is sufficiently severe, persistent, or pervasive to limit a student's ability to participate in or benefit from an education program or activity, or to create a hostile or abusive educational environment." The guidance specified that schools are expected to adopt and publicize policies and grievance procedures to allow "prompt and equitable resolution of sex discrimination complaints, including complaints of sexual harassment." Schools were also reminded of their duty to stop the misconduct, prevent its reoccurrence, and relieve its effects on the victims. Acknowledging the balance between the accused's due process rights and the victim's right to be free from discrimination, the guidance emphasized that due process should not "restrict or unnecessarily delay the protections provided by Title IX to the complainant" (US Department of Education, Office for Civil Rights 1997).

In January 2001, OCR released a subsequent guidance in light of the Supreme Court's rulings in *Gebser* and *Davis*. Similar in many respects to the 1997 version, the 2001 guidance reaffirmed sexual harassment as a type of sex discrimination prohibited under the law. It borrowed language from the 1997 guidance and characterized sexual harassment as "unwelcome conduct of a sexual nature . . . [that] can include unwelcome sexual advances, requests for sexual favors, and other verbal, nonverbal, or physical conduct of a sexual nature."

The 2001 guidance included physical contact in the definition of harassment but was unclear about the relationship between verbal harassment and rape or other forms of sexual violence (Harnik 2018). It took pains to differentiate between private litigation and OCR enforcement, stressing that the deliberate indifference standard established in *Gebser* and *Davis* was expressly limited to private suits for money damages and that OCR, in contrast, has authority to punish noncompliant institutions (US Department of Education, Office for Civil Rights 2001). Finally, the guidance reminded schools of their responsibility to establish procedures to investigate charges of harassment, calling for them to use "common sense and reasonable judgment" in weighing circumstances of the harassment to determine if it rose to the level of illegal behavior. Some of the factors it suggested should be used in making this determination were the type of harassment, the relationship between the victim and the harasser, and the effect on the student's education (Moorman and Osborne 2016; Bolan 2018, 821–822, n.104).

Title IX and the Obama Administration

The Obama administration initiated a new approach to sex-based misconduct in schools. When elected in 2008, Obama committed his administration to more effective enforcement of Title IX to combat sexual harassment in schools, especially sexual violence. To effectuate his pledge, OCR issued a Dear Colleague Letter (DCL) in April 2011, the first executive branch effort to focus on student-on-student sexual violence, expanding the requirements of postsecondary as well as K–12 schools to meet their obligations under Title IX (US Department of Education, Office for Civil Rights 2011; Tani 2017).

Like a guidance, a DCL does not have the force of law and "does not add requirements to existing law but provides information and examples to inform recipients about how the Departments evaluate whether covered entities are complying with their legal obligations" (US Department of Justice, Civil Rights Division and US Department of Education, Office for Civil Rights 2016). In addition to informing federally funded recipients of their legal obligations, the 2011 DCL served to educate the public about their rights under the law (US Department of Education, Office for Civil Rights 2011). It offered guidelines on the treatment of sexual assault complaints, leaving it to institutions to establish their own disciplinary policies and practices. Much of the language referred specifically to postsecondary institutions, but the document also applied to elementary and high schools.

The 2011 DCL marked the beginning of the federal government's efforts to draw attention to sexual violence on campus by assisting institutions in conforming to the requirements of the law. It clarified that the statute encompasses acts of physical sexual violence when the victim does not, or is unable to, give consent. In releasing it, "OCR kicked it up a notch, pressuring colleges and universities to make their processes more complainant-friendly by launching probes into non-compliant institutions and threatening to withdraw their federal funding if they refused" (Ward 2018, 1085.) It retained the definition of sexual harassment as "unwelcome conduct of a sexual nature," emphasizing that sexual violence, broadly defined as "rape, sexual assault, sexual battery, and sexual coercion," is within the definition of sex discrimination prohibited by Title IX. The document also explained that OCR would base its assessment of a school's compliance with the law on the extent to which it adhered to the procedures outlined in the DCL, including establishing educational programs to satisfy its obligation to prevent incidents of misconduct.

Citing the National Institute of Justice's figure that about 20 percent of women are victims of sexual assault and calling it "deeply troubling," the 2011 DCL reminded institutions of their duty to promptly resolve complaints of peer sexual harassment, especially of sexual violence, and that failing to do so was a breach of their duty under Title IX, possibly leading to funding termination. In some schools, the punishment could amount to a loss of hundreds of millions of federal dollars. In addition, the document indicated that schools are responsible for addressing students' sexual harassment complaints even if the behavior takes place outside the school (US Department of Education, Office for Civil Rights 2011).

The DCL strengthened existing enforcement mechanisms by requiring federally funded institutions to post notices that Title IX obliges them to do the following: adopt and publicize grievance procedures; establish education and training programs for students and staff; explain the role of Title IX coordinators; protect victims and inform them that their decision to file criminal charges has no bearing on the university's obligation to promptly investigate and assess their complaints; and take appropriate steps to punish the responsible party, ranging from probation to expulsion. The document also emphasized that institutions must treat the complainant and the accused equally, stressing that both sides must have an opportunity to present testimony and character witnesses, have access to documents, and be represented by counsel. Urging the school to avoid exacerbating the victim's trauma and fear, it warned against parties directly addressing each other during a hearing. Moreover, acknowledging that public institutions must accord accused students due process, the DCL emphasized that procedural fairness does not diminish the school's obligations to the victim (US Department of Education, Office for Civil Rights 2011; Moorman and Osborne 2016; Buzuvis 2017; Tani 2017; Mann 2018).

Perhaps the most significant effect of the DCL was its advice to schools that, in assessing the accused's responsibility, a "preponderance of the evidence" (guilt is more likely than not) standard correctly balances the interests of the victim and the accused and is consistent with the "standard of proof established for violations of the civil rights laws." In contrast, the DCL noted, the "clear and convincing evidence" (highly probable or reasonably certain) standard favors the accused (US Department of Education, Office for Civil Rights 2011). Most schools had already adopted the preponderance of the evidence standard before the DCL's advice about its appropriateness (Cantalupo 2019; Edgar 2020).

The Obama administration was committed to battling sexual violence in schools, but "investigatory practices were considered inconsistent or ineffective, and remedies and punishments were often seen as inadequate" (Moorman and Osborne 2016, 545). On April 29, 2014, responding to requests for more specific information, OCR issued another Title IX guidance, supplementing the 2011 DCL and the 2001 guidance. In a series of questions and answers, it stressed that schools must carry out their responsibilities under the law, offering suggestions for preventing acts of sexual violence and protecting victims. Moreover, it clarified that schools must conduct investigations whether or not students file criminal complaints (US Department of Education, Office for Civil Rights 2014). For the first time, OCR committed itself to investigating complaints of sexual violence related to gender identity (Edwards 2015).

The 2014 guidance represented the federal government's effort to contend with increasing cases of sexual violence in schools aimed at women. Meanwhile, OCR was playing an even more active role in targeting sexual assaults, including publicizing the names of potentially offending institutions. In May 2014, it released a list of the fifty-five schools with "open sexual violence investigations" under review. Noting that the list was not evidence of guilt, the assistant secretary for civil rights said, "we hope this increased transparency will spur community dialogue about this important issue" (*Washington Post*, May 1,

2014). By the end of 2015, OCR cited complaints against "152 colleges and universities for possible violations of federal law based on their handling of sexual violence and harassment complaints" (Moorman and Osborne 2016, 546). At the end of the Obama administration, the number rose to 304 investigations of sexual violence at 223 schools (*Washington Post*, January 18, 2017).

Notwithstanding the Obama administration's increased attention to compliance with Title IX, there was concern that sexual harassment, especially sexual violence, remained an ongoing problem. Some thought the administration's focus on preventing sexual assault was less effective because schools believed "they are unlikely to face consequences for their failure to comply with the law" (Bolan 2018, 808). On the other hand, critics argued that the Obama administration procedures favored the victim at the expense of the accused, with one of the most frequently heard complaints pointing to the use of the preponderance of the evidence standard. Most notably in an October 2014 statement, twenty-eight Harvard Law School professors criticized the procedures for dealing with sexual assault complaints that Harvard had adopted in response to the 2011 DCL. Among other concerns, they charged that adopting the preponderance of the evidence standard unfairly favored the complainant and did not afford the accused sufficient due process rights. They believed the school preferred the lower preponderance of the evidence standard of proof because it feared incurring the wrath of the federal government (namely OCR) and the possible termination of federal funding (Edwards 2015). Other groups, such as the American Association of University Professors, expressed concern that the Obama administration's position on Title IX enforcement threatened First Amendment guarantees of freedom of speech and academic freedom (NPR, September 7, 2017).

Bolstered by such views, accused students—predominantly men—sued their institutions, claiming they unfairly found them responsible for sexual misconduct. Such actions, often called reverse Title IX suits, are commonly brought by an accused male student to challenge a judgment against him. The plaintiff in such a case variously complains that he is innocent, the disciplinary procedure is flawed, the school treats an accused woman differently, or the school is biased against him (and all male students) because it is incentivized by the federal government to favor female victims. In the case of a public university, the plaintiff also asserts that the procedure deprives him of his constitutional right to due process (Ward 2018; McMullan 2019). Some point to the growing number of such suits as evidence of procedural or substantive unfairness as well as a propensity to find an accused responsible. Others maintain the enhanced enforcement resulting from the 2011 DCL led to increases in such suits (Buzuvis 2017).

The Obama administration's focus on sexual violence and harassment intersected with the growing popularity of the #MeToo movement, "conceived [by its founder, Tarana Burke] as a way to build empathy and connection among those affected by harassment and assault" (Flaherty 2020). Burke is credited with introducing the phrase #MeToo in 2006 to call attention to the systemic abuse of women, specifically, "Black and brown women and girls" (*Washington Post*, November 9, 2017). The #MeToo movement spread nationwide. On October 15, 2017, actor Alyssa Milano advanced its profile with a tweet: "If you've been sexually harassed or assaulted write 'me too' as a reply to this tweet." The response was dramatic, as "within 24 hours, her post generated thousands of replies, comments and retweets and inspired thousands of original posts on social media, with women and men from around the world sharing personal stories" (NBC News, October 15, 2018; BBC, July 9, 2020).

Recognized for publicizing the pervasiveness of sexual assault in the nation and around the world, #MeToo was described by hopeful victims' advocates as a "watershed moment [in which] no longer would we sweep accusations of sexual assault under the rug" (Churches 2020). Some advocates hoped "with time, the #MeToo movement may instigate more significant changes in higher education institution programs for preventing sexual assault and harassment" (Daw et al. 2020, 477). The movement soon created a backlash effect on college campuses as accused students, mostly men, filed suit against their institutions, claiming they were being wrongly punished for sex discrimination, many saying the process was biased because of the Obama DCL and the #MeToo movement (Anderson 2019).

A study of 50,000 US university students showed a link between their personal stories of sexual harassment and the number of #MeToo tweets. The researchers concluded "the emergence of the #MeToo trend on social media has empowered thousands of people to share their own sexual harassment experiences," and "a majority of topics embedded in those #MeToo tweets detail sexual harassment stories" (Duong et al. 2020, 1). The #MeToo movement likely inspired significant increases in complaints of misconduct to Title IX coordinators (up from 266 in fiscal year 2017 to 416 in fiscal year 2018) as reported by Harvard University's Title IX office. According to a Harvard official, in reporting their grievances, students will often say, "I'm finally feeling I can come forward because of the #metoo movement." Another Harvard official corroborated this colleague's view, stating "it is not uncommon for a party to say, 'I felt I could now come forward with this concern because of what's going on in the national media'" (*The Crimson*, December 14, 2018).

Title IX required schools to reconcile the conflict between their responsibility to protect their students (predominantly women) from sexual harassment and assault, while guaranteeing that the accused (predominantly men) receive justice. Much of the criticism of Title IX enforcement during the Obama years revolved around the degree to which the required procedure privileges victims over the accused, with the latter denied their due process rights.

Title IX and the Trump Administration

In President Donald Trump's administration, DOE officials were sharply critical of the Obama administration's approach to sexual harassment complaints, and their disapproval primarily focused on the use of the preponderance of the evidence standard. In their view, the 2011 DCL led to false accusations, improper investigative procedures, inadequate defenses, and erroneous findings of responsibility. They argued that the clear and convincing evidence standard is a more appropriate means to determine responsibility and avoid unjust punishments. The Trump administration embarked on a three-year process to rescind Obama administration guidance documents and replace them with its interpretation of Title IX, formulating new regulations to alter the direction of OCR enforcement. Primarily intent on enhancing the rights of the accused, Secretary of Education Betsy DeVos said the administration's purpose was to "substantially amend the Obama-era guidance in the name of fairness and due process" (Ward 2018, 1075).

Groups soon lined up on both sides of the debate over Title IX, one side seeking DOE's commitment to maintaining and strengthening protections for victims and the other focusing on the harm to the accused. At the time, OCR listed 309 cases at 227 schools, including elite institutions, under investigation around the country (*New York Times*, February 18, 2017). Several university officials were optimistic that Trump's overarching commitment to deregulation would lead to easing rules they found onerous, allowing schools more flexibility in the enforcement process and reducing the number of OCR investigations.

Speaking at George Mason University in Virginia on September 7, 2017, DeVos drew attention to the upcoming changes in Title IX policy, calling the 2011 guidance "a failed system" that "isn't working" and often tramples the rights of the accused ("Transcript" 2017). Her comments focused on the rights of the accused, interspersing her presentation with anecdotes of wrongly accused men, including one who attempted suicide. She portrayed the current process as chaotic, saying one university official had told her it had run "amok," characterizing it as a "kangaroo court." Echoing Trump's perennial indictment of the "Deep State," she broadly attacked OCR staff as "unelected and unaccountable political appointees" who drive universities to collect data and are indifferent to due process concerns. Laying most of the blame on the Obama administration, DeVos characterized the current system as "policy by political letter," broadly denouncing the 2011 DCL as "shameful," "wholly un-American," and "an anathema to the system of self-governance to which our Founders pledged their lives over 240 years ago."

She also criticized DOE under Obama for "enforc[ing] ambiguous and incredibly broad definitions of assault and harassment" and requiring a process in which "too many cases involve students and faculty who have faced investigation and punishment simply for speaking their minds or teaching their classes." Educational institutions cannot fulfill all the roles OCR demands, she insisted, and urged them to "assist schools in achieving justice for all students." The secretary's talk was embedded with warnings about the dangers of complying with OCR's current interpretation of Title IX. In her view, the agency not only denied due process to the accused but also imposed contradictory and unrealistic demands on universities. She called for a system that would "ensure that students are not charged by school-based tribunals based on hearsay and incomplete evidence" and "allow educators to focus on what they do best: educate." In response to a question, she announced that DOE would soon begin the lengthy process of rescinding the Obama-era directives and replacing them with one that was, in her view, more equitable.

Concerned about DOE's new direction, sexual assault survivors feared that under Trump it would negate the advances of the past administration by signaling to advocates for the accused that it would be more solicitous of their welfare. The president of the National Women's Law Center (NWLC) called the Trump administration's posture "a blunt attack on survivors of sexual assault [that] send[s] a frightening message to all students: your government does not have your back" (*Washington Post*, September 7, 2017; *The Cut*, September 7, 2017). Conversely, an attorney representing accused men praised the Trump administration, applauding it for ending the government's preoccupation with students' sexual behavior. Echoing DeVos, she said that "on campuses throughout the country, I've seen firsthand how colleges and universities are wrongfully implementing their own kangaroo courts to adjudicate accusations of sexual misconduct and destroying the lives of wrongfully accused male students" (*Washington Post*, September 7, 2017).

A few weeks later, on September 22, 2017, DOE followed through on its commitment to realign Title IX requirements by formally rescinding the Obama administration's 2011 DCL and the 2014 documents and issued its own document that, together with the 2001 guidance, provided interim guidance until the new regulations were formalized (US Department of Education 2017b). Speaking for a survivor's group, an attorney exclaimed "this is simply unlawful, to flip civil rights on its head." On the other hand, the executive director of an individual rights group praised it as a "necessary, but not sufficient step" (NPR, September 22, 2017). In a press release the same day, DOE highlighted its efforts to "help schools as they work to combat sexual misconduct." Again, criticizing the Obama administration's narrow focus on the victims, it added, "the process also must be fair and impartial, giving everyone more confidence in its outcomes." The department pledged to undertake a formal notice and comment procedure that would "create a thoughtful rule that will benefit students for years to come." Focusing on accused students, it charged that the previous system had "ignored notice and comment requirements, created a system that lacked basic elements of due process and failed to ensure fundamental fairness" (US Department of Education 2017a).

On November 29, 2018, DOE proposed an interim rule that differed from the 2011 DCL in three significant ways. First, unlike the 2011 DCL that defined sexual harassment broadly as "unwelcome conduct of a sexual nature," the interim rule adopted the Supreme Court's narrower definition of sexual harassment as "unwelcome conduct on the basis of sex that is so severe, pervasive, and objectively offensive that it denies a person access to the school's education program or activity." The second divergence from the 2011 DCL was that the preponderance of the evidence standard was no longer the preferred approach on the grounds it failed to protect the accused's rights. Under the interim rule, schools were free to use the clear and convincing evidence standard in determining the accused's responsibility, a setback for victims. Third, under the 2011 DCL, a school could be liable for failing to act if it knew or reasonably should have known about an act of harassment or assault. Under the interim rule, a school would have to have "actual knowledge" of the harassment to be held liable. Moreover, unlike the DCL that allowed students to complain to a wide-ranging group of individuals, such as teachers, coaches, or student resident advisors, schools would only be required to investigate if a formal complaint were made to a designated individual or individuals (US Department of Education 2018).

Observers feared the proposed interim rule would lessen the institution's responsibilities under Title IX and the guarantees it offered to victims of sex-based discrimination, especially sexual misconduct (Dunham 2020). It was estimated that if adopted, there would be a 39 percent drop in investigations (Vox, November 16, 2018). In discussing the interim rule, one critic asserted that DOE's "attempt to replace the civil rights-based preponderance standard with the quasi-criminal C&C [clear and convincing] evidence standard seeks to establish a beachhead in a larger war against civil rights" (Cantalupo 2019, 303). An official for an organization called End Rape on Campus charged DOE's "long-awaited rewrite of Title IX enforcement regulation is worse than we thought [and] it will return schools to a time where rape, assault and harassment were swept under the rug." On the other side, a representative of the Foundation of Individual Rights and Expression (FIRE) said the organization was pleased with the proposed regulation for "eliminat[ing] the confusion that has led institutions nationwide to adopt overly broad definitions of sexual harassment that threaten student and faculty speech" (*Los Angeles Times*, November 16, 2018).

The final rule, mostly unchanged from the interim rule and scheduled to take effect on August 14, 2020, was published in the *Federal Register* on May 19, 2020—the first step in the requisite public notice and comment period (*Federal Register* 2020, 30026). DOE received over 100,000 comments from the public; most were opposed to the rule change (American Association of University Women 2020). Unlike guidance documents, the final rule (a 2,000+ page document) would be legally binding on all federal recipients because DOE had adhered to the lengthy and complex legal requirements of the Administrative Procedure Act. Adopting the Court's language in *Davis*, the final rule narrowly defined sexual harassment as "unwelcome conduct that a reasonable person would determine is 'so severe, pervasive, and objectively offensive' that it effectively denies a person equal access to education." In addition, borrowing from several federal statutes (the 1990 Clery Act, amended in 2014, that requires colleges and universities receiving federal funds to report certain criminal acts, and the Violence Against Women Act, passed in 1994, reauthorized in 2013 and 2022, and enhanced by the Campus Sexual Violence Act in 2013, that authorizes federal spending for grants to states to increase protections of women from violence), the final rule broadly specified that acts of "sexual assault, dating violence, domestic violence, or stalking" are violations of Title IX. It limited the institution's responsibility to act to cases in which it had actual knowledge of the misconduct and responded with deliberate indifference and only required schools to investigate formal complaints filed with specified school officials. Closely mirroring the interim rule, the final rule enhanced procedural protections for the accused by permitting schools to adopt the clear and convincing evidence standard in finding responsibility—specifying a presumption of nonresponsibility for the accused—prescribing live hearings in postsecondary institutions, including cross-examination by each party, and, unlike the 2011 DCL, allowing grievances to be informally resolved through mediation (Ward 2018; Edgar 2020).

Before the final rule took effect, opposition arose from Democrats, with eighteen Democratic attorneys general from around the country and congressional Democrats seeking to block is implementation. When it had been announced, Senator Patty Murray (D-WA), a ranking member of the Senate Committee on Health, Education, Labor and Pensions, issued a statement: "the rule issued today would weaken protections for survivors of sexual harassment and assault by making it harder for students to report incidents of sexual harassment or assault, narrowing the definition of sexual assault and harassment, and making it significantly easier for schools to escape liability for not responding to incidents" (US Senate Committee on Health, Education, Labor and Pensions 2020).

Voicing the opposite view, the Republican leader of the House Committee on Education and Labor, Representative Virginia Foxx (R-NC), praised the new regulation, saying it "ensures protections for sexual assault survivors and requires thorough investigations of sexual assault incidents. It also aligns Title IX requirements with court precedents and provides fundamental protections for due process" (Committee on Education and Labor Republicans 2020). A senior official of FIRE, an organization long critical of the Obama regulations, praised the Trump administration's adoption of "new regulations [that] require schools to provide students with a fundamentally fair process before imposing these life-altering consequences." The NWLC president warned of legal action, saying, "we refuse to go back to the days when rape and harassment in schools were ignored and swept under the rug." A Tulane University official expressed concern about students' reactions: "They're going to see this incredibly legalistic way of responding to the harms that they've experienced, including being accused of horrible things, and instead of thinking of us as people who can help, we're now here to litigate. I thought I was working in civil rights and ensuring access to education, but instead I'm going to be running a court-room" (*New York Times*, May 6, 2020).

The suits challenging the final rule variously criticized it for narrowing the definition of sexual harassment, raising the standard for investigating complaints, narrowing the circumstances under which schools are mandated to investigate complaints, allowing schools to employ a clear and convincing evidence standard of proof, allowing cross-examination of the complainant, requiring schools to omit evidence unless the individual attends the hearing, limiting the officials with whom students can file complaints, restricting the circumstances under which a school is required to undertake an investigation, and requiring live hearings with direct cross-examination in postsecondary schools (American Civil Liberties Union 2020a; National Women's Law Center 2020b).

Democratic attorneys general from seventeen states and the District of Columbia, mostly the Northeastern and Western states (under the leadership of Pennsylvania Attorney General Josh Shapiro), challenged the final rule in the District of Columbia federal district court on June 4, 2020. Arguing that it was contrary to the purpose of Title IX and that DOE had violated procedures in adopting it, the plaintiffs sought an injunction or at least a stay. Announcing the suit in a press release, Shapiro declared, "instead of making it easier for students to report, and for schools to respond, to sexual harassment, Secretary DeVos has unlawfully narrowed the reach of Title IX. . . . These new regulations turn classrooms into courtrooms and will have a chilling effect on survivors throughout this country. We cannot afford to take such a step backwards in the fight for justice." The suit charged the regulations arbitrarily narrowed the meaning of Title IX, imposed unnecessary procedures, required schools to ignore complaints that did not meet its reporting requirements, and forced schools to change policies and procedures in the middle of a national health emergency (AG Shapiro 2020).

Another suit in a New York federal district court echoed these claims. In announcing the state's legal action, Attorney General Letitia James said, "the president has repeatedly shown that he doesn't think sexual harassment is a serious matter, but his callousness now threatens our youngest and most vulnerable and could increase the likelihood of sexual harassment and abuse of students in schools" (James 2020). The court dismissed the case, saying it must defer to the regulatory agency and it was within DOE's authority to determine procedures to treat both sides fairly (*New York v. United States Department of Education* 2020).

On August 12, 2020, two days before the regulation was to go into effect, the District of Columbia federal district court denied the Democratic attorneys' general motion for an injunction. The opinion acknowledged that though the plaintiffs had made "serious arguments," they had not met the required showing for an injunction (*Pennsylvania v. DeVos* 2020). DeVos declared that "with yet another failed attempt to block our historic Title IX Rule, we can now look forward to it taking effect this Friday, requiring schools to act in meaningful ways to support survivors of sexual misconduct without sacrificing important safeguards to protect free speech and provide all students with a transparent, reliable process" (*Politico*, August 12, 2020).

Title IX and the Biden Administration

With courts generally deferring to the executive branch's interpretation of the law, most critics hoped that President Joe Biden would negate the 2020 regulations and revert to the Obama-era Title IX policies. During the campaign, Biden, who had ushered in the 2011 DCL as vice president, vowed a "quick end" to the Trump administration rules if elected and a return to the prior procedure. A spokesperson for the Trump DOE warned that eliminating the DeVos rule "send[s] a clear message that due process and fairness don't matter" (NBC News, November 12, 2020).

Because the Trump administration had relied on the formal rulemaking process, Biden's DOE had to overcome significant procedural hurdles to implement any rule changes. Barring congressional action, it would have to follow the same course of action as Trump's DOE, likely taking years to accomplish. The administration had few options, knowing that any attempts to reverse or override the existing rule would lead to litigation by men's rights advocates. On March 8, 2021 (International Women's Day), Biden began to fulfill his promise toward achieving gender equality by signing Executive Order 14020 (2021) to foster a government-wide approach to promote "gender equity and equality" in education, sexual harassment, violence, economic security, leadership, and health care. Specifically addressing sexual harassment, another order, Executive Order 14021 (2021), proclaimed "it is the policy of my Administration that all students should be guaranteed an educational environment free from discrimination on the basis of sex, including discrimination in the form of sexual harassment, which encompasses sexual violence, and including discrimination on the basis of sexual orientation or gender identity."

Biden directed Education Secretary Miguel Cardona to review the existing regulations and guidance within the next hundred days, focusing on them to find any that "are or may be inconsistent" with the stated policy and decide an appropriate action—that is, determine whether to rescind or revise them. The reaction to Biden's order predictably fell along party lines. Representative Rosa DeLauro (D-CT) praised it as "the first step toward reversing the outrageous policies carried out by Secretary DeVos." But Foxx warned that "by overturning these stakeholder-vetted, court-supported rules, key protections for victims and the due process rights of the accused would be jeopardized" (*Washington Post*, March 8, 2021).

In its first step to implement Biden's Executive Order, OCR announced it would host a five-day virtual hearing, beginning on June 7, 2021, to begin reviewing the existing regulations. The announcement indicated that the administration hoped to hear "from participants on steps that can be taken to ensure that students who experience sexual harassment, including sexual violence, receive appropriate supports" as well as measures to "ensure that schools have grievance procedures that provide for the fair, prompt, and equitable resolution of reports of sexual harassment and other sex discrimination" (US Department of Education 2021). At the end of the hearings, advocates for sexual assault survivors expressed their disappointment when the administration announced it would not release a proposed rule until May 2022; seeking to assuage them, the administration indicated it would be aligned with the president's Executive Orders and reflect "the priorities of the Biden-Harris administration" (Gravely 2021). On September 13, 2021, fifty-nine members of the House of Representatives sent a letter to Cardona, urging faster action in reversing the regulation and asking DOE to begin the rulemaking process by October 2021 (Congress of the United States 2021).

Meanwhile, other members of Congress introduced legislation to amend Title IX to undo the damage caused by the 2020 rule. On September 21, 2021, Representative Debbie Dingell (D-MI) cosponsored the Title IX Take Responsibility Act to enhance protections for survivors by increasing institutional liability. Among other things, it would broaden the definition of harassment and require schools to respond to claims more readily. In a press release, Dingell stated "the Title IX Take Responsibility Act would establish notice and reasonable care standards to hold educational institutions liable for sex discrimination, further defining criteria for how schools must exercise action to prevent and correct the impacts of sexual assault" (Dingell 2021).

A hopeful sign that DOE would act quickly came when the Senate confirmed Catherine Lhamon as assistant secretary for civil rights, head of OCR, returning her to the position she held in the Obama administration. All Senate Republicans opposed her confirmation, citing her harsh criticism of the 2020 regulation that, she said, "permits students to rape and sexually harass with impunity" (*New York Times*, October 20, 2021).

On the fiftieth anniversary of Title IX's passage—June 23, 2022—DOE issued a press release asking for public comments on proposed regulations to reverse crucial aspects of Trump's 2020 regulations (US Department of Education 2022c). Responding to concerns raised during the series of meetings in June 2021, DOE's 700-page proposal clarified that Title IX's ban on discrimination based on sex applies to sexual orientation and gender identity, as well as pregnancy and related conditions, including parental status and abortion (US Department of Education 2022b). A fact sheet accompanying the announcement made it clear that the Biden administration's intent was to revive the statute's guarantees of equal rights to the pre-Trump era, pledging that "the proposed amendments will restore vital protections for students in our nation's schools which were eroded by controversial regulations implemented during the previous Administration" (US Department of Education 2022a).

Among the most important changes in the Biden administration's proposed DOE rule was that in addition to identifying sex-based criminal conduct such as assault, violence, and stalking in the ban on sex discrimination under Title IX, the regulation would broadly define sex-based harassment as "unwelcome sex-based conduct that is sufficiently severe or pervasive, that, based on the totality of the circumstances and evaluated subjectively and objectively, denies or limits a person's ability to participate in or benefit from the recipient's education program or activity." The rule would also require institutions to return to the preponderance of the evidence standard of proof in most cases when assessing an accused's responsibility for the offense. It would loosen the reporting requirements to obligate schools to investigate complaints brought to a wide range of employees at the school, including after the student leaves the institution, and broaden the institution's responsibility to respond to claims of sex-based harassment even if the behavior occurs off-campus or outside the United States as long as it is related to the institution's programs or activities. It would eliminate cross-examination of the complaining student by the accused or a representative and the requirement that schools conduct in-person hearings in all cases, allowing students to participate remotely when live hearings are held.

Not surprisingly, there were objections to the proposed rules, with critics accusing the administration of eroding due process rights. An official of FIRE characterized the proposed rules as a "significant step backwards" (Knott 2022). The head of the Association of Title IX Administrators disagreed, saying, "this was not a throwing out of all the due process protections that were incorporated into the 2020 regs. The Department of Education has left in some of the most important protections for respondents while also broadening the scope of protections that are provided to complainants" (Gravely 2021).

Over 235,000 comments were submitted to DOE during the sixty-day comment period, which ended on September 14, 2022. After examining the comments, DOE will release the final regulations (Knott 2022).

Conclusion

This chapter examined women's efforts to secure equal opportunities in the nation's schools, chiefly focusing on the promise offered by Title IX of the Education Amendments of 1972 in two areas: equity in athletic programs and sexual misconduct in schools. Title IX was premised on banning sex discrimination in education in federally funded schools, yet it continued to allow single-sex admissions in certain types of educational institutions. A series of Supreme Court rulings declared that except under narrow circumstances, such policies violated the Fourteenth Amendment.

Congress contributed to the nation's goal of equal opportunity for women by passing Title IX; once the law was enacted, its interpretation was left to the judicial and executive branches of the federal government, primarily the latter. Initially, the courts took a narrow view of Title IX, restricting it to programs receiving federal aid, such as school financial assistance programs whose students obtained federal grants and loans; the interpretation excluded most school sports activities. The 1988 Civil Rights Restoration Act provided that all programs and activities in the institution were subject to the ban on discrimination in Title IX. This broader application of the law helped bring about greater equity in school athletic programs. But while women prevailed in many of their legal challenges, the disparate treatment between women and men in tournament play by the NCAA showed that their struggle for equal treatment was not over.

Although state and local governments have primary responsibility for regulating schools, at the federal level, DOE (more precisely, OCR) plays the key role in implementing Title IX. This chapter shows that federal enforcement of civil rights guarantees such as Title IX varies over time because, as presidential administrations change, so do their interpretations of schools' legal obligations to fight the sex discrimination that Title IX targets.

Contrasting the policies of the Obama, Trump, and Biden administrations indicates they interpreted Title IX in dramatically different ways, especially in addressing sexual harassment and assault in schools. The Obama administration took a proactive approach, requiring schools to deal expeditiously with student complaints of sexual misconduct, broadly defined. The Trump administration reversed most of the Obama policies, expressing more concern with protecting the rights of the accused. Biden has taken steps to restore the Obama-era interpretations of Title IX, swinging the pendulum back to emphasizing the needs of the victims and requiring more vigorous enforcement of the statute. Viewing Title IX enforcement through the prism of executive actions demonstrates the fragility of the nation's equal rights guarantees, subject to the priorities of government entities, especially to presidential administrations and executive branch officials.

3

Combating Employment Discrimination

IN 2021, 56.1 PERCENT OF WOMEN IN THE UNITED STATES PARTICI-
pated in the labor force, meaning that over 72 million American women
were either working or looking for work. In comparison, 67.6 percent of
American men were considered labor force participants. Even though
women make up almost half (47 percent) of the total labor force in the
United States, they continue to lack equal treatment in the workplace
(US Department of Labor, Bureau of Labor Statistics n.d.).

The Evolution of
Women's Labor Force Participation

Women in the United States have been working for wages outside
their homes since the 1800s. By the turn of the twentieth century,
about one-fifth of women were in the labor force (Ortiz-Ospina,
Tzvetkova, and Roser 2018). Most were lower-class women in the
service industry or fields traditionally dominated by women, such as
nursing, teaching, domestic labor, or clerical work. At the time,
women were not typically considered for positions outside of these
so-called pink-collar fields.

Everything changed when the United States entered World War II.
Not only did the military draft force millions of men to leave the
workforce and join the armed forces, but wartime production also created a significant number of new jobs. In response, public and private
agencies called on women to support the war effort and fill the vacancies

in high-paying industrial jobs that had previously been closed to them. The campaign worked, and by the end of the war, women made up a majority of employed people for the first time in US history. Many women embraced their new roles in the economy, appreciating the autonomy their jobs offered and planning to remain in the workforce beyond the end of the war; their hopes would soon be dashed (Barnard and Rapp 2009).

While World War II raged, women who worked outside the home were dubbed patriots contributing to the success of the war effort. But when the soldiers came home and the country returned to a peacetime economy, women—in particular, middle-class white women—were generally expected to retreat to their traditional roles in the home. Immigrant women, lower-class women, and women of color had long participated in the labor force, primarily out of economic necessity. Although the end of the war did little to upend those women's employment patterns, for much of society, middle-class white women's employment had been only a temporary necessity that could—and should—be abandoned in peacetime. Private and public sector employers made concerted efforts to induce their retreat from the postwar labor force. Some companies revived policies that prohibited employing married women; more broadly, the government ended most wartime childcare subsidies and granted veterans legal preferences to employment. Taken together, these actions ensured an exodus of women from the labor market (Barnard and Rapp 2009). Despite many women's unceremonious withdrawal—voluntarily or involuntarily—from the workforce, a considerable number of women remained. In 1950, women's labor force participation rate stood at 33.9 percent (US Department of Labor, Bureau of Labor Statistics 2000).

As more women joined the labor force, the dearth of policies promoting gender equality in employment became increasingly apparent. For example, in the 1950s, it was still legal to advertise jobs that were open only to men, and employers could deny women access to higher-paying or managerial positions. Women could be paid less than men were for the same work (Conway, Ahern, and Steuernagel 2005). Commercial airlines fired female flight attendants for changes in appearance, such as gaining weight, and many companies fired women workers when they got married or became pregnant (Hillstrom 2019). Such inequalities have not completely disappeared, though they have been lessened through legislation such as Title VII of the 1964 Civil Rights Act (42 USC §2000e).

Title VII of the 1964 Civil Rights Act

The passage of the 1964 Civil Rights Act was a key moment in the battle to secure equal employment opportunities, with Title VII prohibiting discrimination on the basis of sex, race, color, national origin, and religion. When originally proposed, Title VII did not mention sex. But in the final days of debate in the House, Representative Howard Smith (D-VA), a conservative who opposed rights for Black people, introduced an amendment to include sex as a protected category in Title VII. Conventional wisdom holds that Smith proposed the amendment to make the bill's passage less likely. However, numerous scholars reject this view as an oversimplification, pointing to Smith's long-standing support for the Equal Rights Amendment (ERA) and his friendship with the leader of the National Woman's Party, a political organization that was involved in drafting the ERA in 1923 and had lobbied to include sex as a protected class in civil rights bills for decades. Whatever Smith's motives, according to Jo Freeman (1991), the inclusion of sex in Title VII was ultimately "the product of a small but dedicated group of women, in and out of Congress, who knew how to take advantage of the momentum generated by a larger social movement to promote their own goals, and a larger group of Congressmen willing to make an affirmative statement in favor of women's rights" (183; see Osterman 2009).

Women lawmakers on both sides of the aisle quickly came out in favor of the amendment, reminding their male counterparts of the discrimination that would continue to befall the women in their lives if they did not support the inclusion of sex in the bill. Ultimately, the amendment passed the House in a 168 to 133 vote. Two days later, the whole civil rights bill cleared the House by more than a two-to-one margin (290 to 130). The House's version of the bill passed in the Senate by a 73 to 27 vote, and on July 2, 1964, President Lyndon Johnson signed the Civil Rights Act into law (Whalen and Whalen 1985). In its final form, Title VII applies to employers (and labor unions) with fifteen or more employees and provides the following:

> It shall be an unlawful employment practice for an employer—
>   (1) to fail or refuse to hire or to discharge any individual, or otherwise to discriminate against any individual with respect to his compensation, terms, conditions, or privileges of employment, because of such individual's race, color, religion, sex, or national origin; or
>   (2) to limit, segregate, or classify his employees or applicants for employment in any way which would deprive or tend to deprive any

individual of employment opportunities or otherwise adversely affect his status as an employee, because of such individual's race, color, religion, sex, or national origin.

Title VII established the Equal Employment Opportunity Commission (EEOC), which was granted the authority to enforce the statute's ban on employment discrimination. When it opened its doors in 1965, the EEOC had a small and inexperienced staff, and it demonstrated little interest in enforcing the ban on sex discrimination in employment. Rachel Osterman (2009) argues that the EEOC actually played up the idea that Representative Smith had added sex as a protected class to Title VII solely to derail the entire bill so that the agency could largely ignore the provision as a stunt. Yet it soon became clear that workers had every intention of using the EEOC to address the discrimination they were facing from their employers. Though it had been estimated that 2,000 charges would be filed in the first year, almost 9,000 claims were made. More surprising was the fact that one-third of those complaints alleged sex discrimination. Title VII was adopted in a time of increased racial tension, and most congressional and media sources had focused on racial discrimination during the policy debate. Therefore, many expected that race would form the basis for the vast majority of allegations.

In reaction to the EEOC's initially slow response to claims of sex discrimination in the workplace, participants at the Third National Conference of Commissions on the Status of Women in June 1966 in Washington, DC, sought to pressure the government to carry out its legal mandate to end such discrimination. When they were told that they had no authority at the conference, a group of frustrated conference participants determined to find another way to take action. Assembled in the hotel room of Betty Friedan, author of *The Feminine Mystique* (1963), these women created a new organization that would speak on behalf of women in the fight for their rights. On June 20, 1966, twenty-eight women signed the charter of the National Organization for Women (NOW) to help ensure that the government enforced Title VII to eradicate gender discrimination in the workplace (National Organization for Women 2011).

Realizing that addressing sex discrimination would be a significant part of the EEOC's work—and that the women's movement would continue to pressure the agency to do its job—by the early 1970s, the EEOC had adopted the position that it was a violation of Title VII to classify jobs as male or female, to separate seniority lists by sex, or to refuse to hire or promote a woman because she was married or had children. The agency likewise declared that protective labor laws, such as mandating extra breaks for women employees or prohibiting women from taking jobs that involved heavy lifting, were discriminatory. A number of judicial rulings immediately following that declaration came to the same conclusion and struck down the so-called protective legislation (US Equal Employment Opportunity Commission 2000b; Han and Heldman 2018).

Before 1972, the EEOC did not have the power to litigate on its own; it had to ask the US Department of Justice (DOJ) to act on its behalf. The Equal Employment Opportunity Act of 1972 increased the EEOC's enforcement authority by allowing it to file suit against employers, employment agencies, and unions that violated its guidelines. In addition, the act expanded Title VII protections to government workers at the federal, state, and local levels, as well as in educational institutions. The EEOC's authority continued to expand over the next two decades as it became responsible for implementing antidiscrimination legislation beyond Title VII, such as the Equal Pay Act of 1963 (EPA), the Pregnancy Discrimination Act of 1978, and laws prohibiting discrimination on the basis of age and disabilities. The EEOC's principal responsibility is to investigate complaints and attempt to settle them when it finds discrimination. If the agency cannot resolve a dispute through mediation, it has the authority to file either an individual discrimination lawsuit or a "pattern or practice" suit alleging systematic discrimination. Courts often defer to agency regulations and guidance in discrimination lawsuits but are not bound by them (US Equal Employment Opportunity Commission 2000b).

Women's employment rose dramatically after the passage of Title VII, with the percentage of women employed in professional positions increasing from 13.9 percent in 1966 to 27.1 percent in 1972. In recent decades, women's involvement in the labor market has continued to grow. From 1970 to 2019, the proportion of women workers aged twenty-five to sixty-four with a college degree quadrupled; the proportion of their male counterparts in the labor force with a college degree only doubled in the same time period. Since 1970, women have become more likely to work in full-time, year-round jobs, and women with children have significantly increased their presence in the workforce. Overall, women's labor force participation climbed steadily throughout the 1970s and 1980s before slowing in the 1990s. Since then, their participation rates have generally hovered between 57 and 60 percent (US Equal Employment Opportunity Commission 2015; US Department of Labor, Bureau of Labor Statistics 2021b).

Sexual Harassment in the Workplace

Throughout US history, women workers have been mistreated. In the eighteenth and nineteenth centuries, enslaved women and domestic workers routinely faced sexual coercion and violence. As women moved into clerical and manufacturing jobs in the early twentieth century, they often experienced verbal and physical assaults from their male bosses (Han and Heldman 2018). When a significant number of women joined the workforce in the second half of the twentieth century, there was a concurrent rise in the number of women who found themselves fending off unwanted sexual advances from their managers and coworkers. Many women saw such predatory behavior as inevitable in the workplace, especially since they were rarely taken seriously when they reported it. Most of their supervisors were men who believed their female employees were overreacting. In some cases, women were simply advised to quit if such "harmless" behavior bothered them. Although women had little power to challenge the pervasive mistreatment they faced on the job, the second wave of feminism in the late 1960s propelled them to assert their rights more forcefully (Hillstrom 2019). NOW, in particular, became a staunch opponent of such harassment in the workplace.

In the mid-1970s, there was no name for the unwelcome sexual overtures and degrading comments that many women routinely faced in the workplace. But in 1975, while teaching a course on women and work at Cornell University, journalist Lin Farley addressed this deficiency. During a consciousness raising session with her female students about their early experiences in the workforce, she found that all of them had already experienced some degree of this predatory behavior. In most cases, the women had either been fired from their positions or forced to quit after rejecting their bosses' sexual advances. As Farley reflected on these revelations, she realized that women had no common vocabulary to discuss this pervasive problem. Lacking a way to label this behavior, women often suffered in isolation without recognizing that so many others were dealing with the same issue. By coining the term "sexual harassment," Farley showed women that they were not alone in their experiences. To further elucidate the point, she created a questionnaire about sexual harassment to distribute at a campus event. Of the 155 women who responded, 70 percent said they had experienced sexual harassment themselves, and 92 percent said that it was a serious problem. At the same time, over half of the women who reported their harassment said that nothing had been done about it (Swenson 2017).

The concept of sexual harassment caught on quickly. In the year after Farley's designation of the term, *Redbook* published a survey in which 80 percent of the women who responded said they had been sexually harassed on the job (Swenson 2017). In 1977, the subject of sexual harassment appeared on the cover of *Ms.* magazine for the first time. The pages of the magazine detailed numerous examples of women who left their jobs or dropped out of school after being assaulted or propositioned for sex by their male employers, supervisors, and advisors. *Ms.* also included a survey that once again showed that an overwhelming majority of women—88 percent—from varying professions said they had been harassed at work. Despite a growing recognition of the problem, there was still not widespread acceptance of the idea that sexual harassment was a serious issue that needed to be addressed directly. For example, even though the editors at *Ms.* used puppets for their cover image (a male hand reaching into a woman's blouse) instead of a photograph because of the sensitivity of the topic, that issue of the magazine was still banned from supermarkets that were uncomfortable with the cover (Bennett 2017). More important than some people's unease with the idea of sexual harassment as a public concern was the fact that there was not yet a legal definition of the term.

The first lawsuit addressing sexual harassment was filed a year before Farley named the phenomenon. In *Barnes v. Train* (1974), the District of Columbia federal district court judge dismissed Barnes's claim that the director of her federal agency had violated Title VII by reducing her duties and eventually abolishing her position after she refused his sexual advances. According to the court, his actions were not motivated by her sex but by her unwillingness to have sexual relations with him, and therefore did not constitute sex discrimination in the workplace under Title VII (Han and Heldman 2018). The ruling was not surprising, as the courts at that time were unwilling to accept sexual harassment as a legal concept. Even though Title VII prohibits sex discrimination in the workplace, most legal challenges up to that point had focused on differences between male and female workers with regard to hiring, promotions, and wages. For many legal scholars, Title VII protections did not apply to sexual harassment because no employers had official policies that condoned such actions. Sexual harassment was considered to be a personal matter unrelated to the employment context, which meant it was not covered by employment law and an employer should not be held legally liable for it. Moreover, because both women and men can be sexually harassed, judges believed it should not be considered a sex-based offense. Early court rulings in sexual harassment cases, such as *Barnes*, generally adopted this view and dismissed claims of sexual harassment as a form of sex discrimination (Swenson 2017; Hillstrom 2019).

As more women realized they were not alone in their workplace experiences of harassment, they began filing discrimination complaints with the EEOC. Feminist activists, such as legal scholar Catharine MacKinnon (1979), sought a new interpretation of sexual harassment in the workplace, arguing that it constitutes sex discrimination under Title VII because victims' status as women is a determining factor in their harassment. Moreover, because sexual harassment denies women an equal opportunity to perform their jobs, it is also a violation of civil rights (Bennett 2017; Hillstrom 2019). In the years after *Barnes*, many courts began to adopt this perspective. In 1977, the District of Columbia Circuit Court of Appeals overruled the lower court—a signal that legal opinions were changing on the newly labeled issue of sexual harassment (Han and Heldman 2018). In 1980, the EEOC formally recognized sexual harassment as a form of sex discrimination prohibited under Title VII. The guidelines specified harassment as "unwelcome" sexual conduct, and, borrowing from MacKinnon, identified "quid pro quo" and "hostile work environment" as the two types of harassment. Soon after, most government agencies and private employers adopted the EEOC's guidelines, which came to significantly influence future legislation and court rulings (MacKinnon 1979; Hillstrom 2019). The Supreme Court ruling in *Meritor Savings Bank v. Vinson* (1986), which became a defining moment for women's rights, was a direct result of the EEOC's policy shift.

Vinson, a bank employee, claimed that her married supervisor had made sexual demands of her at work and repeatedly coerced her into having sexual relations with him before he eventually fired her. She argued that his actions created a hostile work environment. Referring to the EEOC's guidelines, the Supreme Court ruled in favor of Vinson, holding for the first time that a hostile work environment is a form of sex discrimination that violates Title VII (Bennett 2017). Revisiting the issue seven years later, in *Harris v. Forklift Systems, Inc.* (1993), the high court lowered the bar for women to succeed in hostile environment sexual harassment claims, ruling that a victim does not have to prove she suffered psychological harm as a result of the harassment. It may be relevant to her claim, it held, but is not the deciding factor.

Sexual harassment made its way into the national spotlight when President George H. W. Bush nominated Clarence Thomas as an associate justice to the Supreme Court in 1991. After the announcement of

Thomas's nomination, Anita Hill alleged that he had sexually harassed her when she worked for him in the Department of Education (DOE) in its Office for Civil Rights (OCR) and later at the EEOC; Thomas denied all claims. Hill had been reluctant to come forward, fearing the reaction her allegations might provoke. Her concerns were warranted, as she faced an immediate backlash. She was largely villainized in the press, with Thomas's supporters calling her delusional and claiming that she was seeking revenge on him for spurning her advances. Moreover, the all-male Senate Judiciary Committee repeatedly sought to undermine her credibility, attacking her testimony. Committee chair Senator Joe Biden also prevented other witnesses from testifying in the hearing to present evidence of Thomas's pattern of misconduct. The controversial hearings received exhaustive media coverage, as this was the first time a high-profile public figure had been accused of sexual harassment in this fashion (Hillstrom 2019). Thomas was eventually narrowly confirmed by the Senate, but the proceedings raised national awareness of the issue of women's treatment in the workplace, and Hill's interrogation sparked outrage among many women. Largely in reaction to the hearings, a record number of women ran for office and won the following year, which became known as the "Year of the Woman."

As the EEOC defines it, harassment is "unwelcome sexual advances, or requests for sexual favors, and other verbal or physical harassment of a sexual nature . . . and can include offensive remarks about a person's sex." The remarks rise to the rank of illegal harassment when they are "so frequent or severe" that they create a hostile working environment or result in an adverse employment decision against the victim (US Equal Employment Opportunity Commission n.d.). According to a 2016 EEOC report, between 25 percent and 85 percent of women have experienced sexual harassment on the job. The variation can largely be attributed to the way in which the respondents were questioned. When asked directly if they were ever subjected to sexual harassment at work—without the term being defined—one in four women (25 percent) reported that they had. When employees were asked if they had experienced at least one specific act of harassment, such as sexual coercion or unwanted sexual attention, approximately 60 percent of women responded affirmatively. This indicates that many people do not have a clear idea of what constitutes harassment in the workplace. Even when people view unwelcome sexually based behaviors as problematic or offensive, they often do not label them as sexual harassment (Feldblum and Lipnic 2016). Regardless of the confusion surrounding terminology, there is widespread agreement that sexual harassment of women in the workplace is pervasive: a 2018

Washington Post–ABC News poll found that 72 percent of Americans say it is a "serious problem" (Guskin 2018).

Workplace harassment has significant costs for women; in addition to the implications for their mental and physical health, it often hinders their economic prospects. To avoid their harassers, women may opt out of on-the-job training and advancement programs or promotion opportunities, transfer to a different position or field, or leave the labor force entirely. Such career interruptions can make it more difficult for women to establish themselves in a well-paying career and may contribute to the persistent gender wage gap (Shaw, Hegewisch, and Hess 2018).

There are some employment situations that increase the likelihood of women facing sexual harassment, such as working in male-dominated occupations. Indeed, 49 percent of women employed in male-dominated workplaces say that sexual harassment is a problem where they work. In gender-balanced workplaces, only 34 percent of women say harassment is a problem. That number falls to 32 percent in female-dominated workplaces (Parker 2018). More broadly, working for tips or in an isolated context such as hotel or janitorial work can increase a person's chances of experiencing harassment. Lacking legal immigration status or a permanent work visa also makes it more likely that a worker will be harassed—largely because of a perceived or actual lack of recourse. Similarly, employees in smaller, informal workplaces rarely have access to official complaint mechanisms. Those in low-paying jobs may be more likely to face harassment because they are heavily dependent on their wages and do not want to risk losing their positions by lodging a complaint. Moreover, "these structural risk factors often intersect and are exacerbated by racism, discrimination, and harassment on the basis of age, disability, or national origin" (Shaw, Hegewisch, and Hess 2018, 4).

Workplace harassment occurs at alarming rates in the United States, but only a small number of individuals report it; between 6 and 13 percent of individuals who experience harassment formally file an internal or legal complaint. Three out of four people who are harassed never raise the issue with their supervisors or union representatives. Most of these workers decline to take formal action because they fear they will not be believed, nothing will be done in response, or they will face social or professional retaliation (Feldblum and Lipnic 2016). The reality is that such fears are often warranted; in fiscal year (FY) 2017, 71 percent of sexual harassment charges included an allegation of retaliation (Frye 2017). But the #MeToo movement that exploded in 2017 has begun to change these patterns.

Thomas's confirmation hearing in 1991 was the first time that sexual harassment received extensive media coverage in the United States. The hearing brought attention to the issue of sexual harassment in the workplace, but Hill's treatment throughout the process and Thomas's ultimate confirmation sent a discouraging message to women. The Senate Judiciary Committee accused her of bringing "sleaze" into the nomination process, and pundit David Brock famously described her as "a little bit nutty and a little bit slutty." When the Senate voted to confirm Thomas after hearing Hill's allegations, the message seemed clear: "Anita Hill was the example of a strong, accomplished black woman, and if she of all people could be discredited then it seemed women, particularly women of color, had no voice when it came to sexual harassment." Still, Hill's actions undoubtedly made an impression on women, for in the year after her televised testimony, sexual harassment complaints to the EEOC grew 73 percent (Bennett 2017). This effect persisted for years after the hearing; the number of sexual harassment claims filed with the EEOC increased from 6,883 in FY 1991 to 15,618 in FY 1998 (US Equal Employment Opportunity Commission 2010).

The issue of sexual misconduct soon began to fade from the public stage. Paula Jones's sexual harassment suit against President Bill Clinton in 1994 received much attention but was eventually settled, and Clinton went on to win reelection in 1996. Even cases where women prevailed frequently turned out to be Pyrrhic victories. Navy lieutenant Paula Coughlin, who was sexually assaulted by drunken officers in 1991, won her case but faced retaliation that ultimately compelled her to leave the military. Likewise, legal secretary Rena Weeks never worked again after winning her sexual harassment case in 1994 against a partner in a well-known law firm. Many women who experienced sexual assault and harassment felt they were in a no-win situation. As sociologist Michael Kimmel observed, "I think for a long time it shut women up, at least publicly" (quoted in Bennett 2017). However, sexual harassment and assault catapulted back into the headlines during Donald Trump's 2016 presidential campaign.

#MeToo Movement

Despite more than a dozen allegations of his sexual misconduct against women, voters sent Republican Donald Trump to the White House. Although some observers initially forecasted that the public's ostensible lack of concern over the mistreatment of women would deter women from coming forward with similar complaints in the future, Trump's election ultimately seemed to galvanize women. Many were outraged by the idea of powerful men using their positions to abuse women, and in the year after the election, a growing number of women spoke out against the sexual harassment or assault they faced at the hands of men in politics, entertainment, and the media (Hillstrom 2019). But that was only the beginning of what ultimately became a global movement against sexual misconduct.

While the hashtag #MeToo went viral in 2017, it had originated more than a decade earlier. In 1997, when a thirteen-year-old girl told community organizer and activist Tarana Burke that she had been sexually abused by her mother's boyfriend, Burke was at a loss for words. When she later thought about that conversation, she wished she had said "me too" to show the girl that she was not alone, as Burke had also been assaulted as a child and a young woman. The multiple abuses she experienced were part of the motivation that led her to become a social activist. Nine years after her encounter with the girl, Burke founded Just Be Inc., an organization focused on guiding and empowering young women of color to become healthy and well-rounded adults. As part of her work with Just Be Inc., Burke also devised the Me Too campaign to bring attention to the pervasive sexual assault and harassment faced by women of color. She began using the phrase "me too" on the social networking site MySpace to reach other women of color who had been sexually abused. According to Burke, the idea behind the phrase was "empowerment through empathy." Not only did she want to show the world how widespread sexual violence is, but she also wanted other survivors to know that they are not alone (Garcia 2017; Ohlheiser 2017).

The Me Too campaign that Tarana Burke started in 2006 was relatively quiescent for over a decade; that began to change on October 5, 2017, when the *New York Times* first reported on the slew of accusations against powerful Hollywood producer Harvey Weinstein. After ten days of coverage on Weinstein's habitual sexual harassment and assault of young women throughout his thirty-year career, actor Alyssa Milano posted her now revolutionary tweet: "If you've been sexually harassed or assaulted write 'me too' as a reply to this tweet." Almost immediately, the hashtag "MeToo" tore across social media, being used more than 500,000 times on Twitter and 12 million times on Facebook in the first twenty-four hours (Garcia 2017; Rutenberg, Abrams, and Ryzik 2017).

As the number of #MeToo posts grew exponentially, reverberations were felt outside of social media. Fatima Goss Graves, president and chief executive of the National Women's Law Center (NWLC), said that in the two weeks after the Weinstein story broke, the number of calls reporting harassment to their office doubled (Rutenberg, Abrams, and Ryzik 2017). Likewise, visits to the EEOC's sexual harassment webpage more than doubled in October 2017. In the year following Milano's tweet, the EEOC received approximately 7,500 harassment complaints (a 12 percent increase over the previous year) and filed forty-one harassment lawsuits (a 50 percent increase from the previous year) targeting companies such as United Airlines and Dollar General (Chiwaya 2018). In the wake of a growing number of allegations, dozens of high-profile men in entertainment, politics, and business resigned their positions. Many likened the events following Milano's tweet to "a dam breaking, the cumulative effect of harassment claims over decades" (Bennett 2017). In 2017, *Time* magazine named "the silence breakers" of the #MeToo movement its "Person of the Year" for turning a spotlight on an issue that has long plagued women. A 2018 survey found that 81 percent of women in the United States have experienced some sort of sexual harassment in their lives, ranging from catcalls and cyberharassment to stalking, flashing, groping, and sexual assault (Stop Street Harassment 2018).

Beyond simply unearthing the pervasive problem of sexual abuse in the United States, the #MeToo movement has inspired significant legal and political activism. Founded in 2018, Time's Up is a nonprofit group dedicated to ensuring safe workplaces that are free from gender-based discrimination. Time's Up collaborated with the NWLC to launch a legal defense fund to support people who have experienced discrimination or harassment in the workplace, often by providing them with attorney consultations or assistance with legal costs. Within its first year, the fund had received over $20 million in donations and helped 3,500 women and men from all fifty states (Chiwaya 2018).

Shortly after the #MeToo movement began, one of the biggest companies in the world, Microsoft, announced that it had eliminated forced arbitration agreements with employees who make sexual harassment claims. Such agreements required workers to settle cases outside of the courtroom, which conceal them from public view and may allow serial harassers to continue their behavior. Because the process takes place behind closed doors, forced arbitration can make it difficult for employees to learn that their coworkers have experienced similar harassment or discrimination in their workplace, effectively preventing them from consolidating their efforts to address such behavior. This is partially why arbitration hearings typically favor employers. Moreover, self-interest may motivate some arbitrators to side with employers more often because the employers decide which arbitrators to hire in the future. By ending mandatory arbitration, Microsoft was acknowledging the flawed nature of the process. The company's decision "shows how the flood of harassment accusations has gone beyond individual cases to an examination of policy changes for ending the misconduct" (Wingfield and Silver-Greenberg 2017). In an attempt to speed up that process, policymakers have introduced legislation to override the corporate policies and secret workplace settlements that have long prevented women from speaking out about the abuses they suffer.

The ferocity with which the #MeToo movement spread across the United States demonstrates the deep desire by a growing number of advocates to fight the harassment that so many women face. For too long, weak laws and lack of enforcement have enabled the abuse to continue, and lawmakers have been working to change that. In 2021, Senator Kirsten Gillibrand (D-NY) and Senator Lindsey Graham (R-SC) jointly sponsored a bill to prohibit forced arbitration in sexual assault and sexual harassment cases. A companion bill in the House was introduced by Cheri Bustos (D-IL) and Morgan Griffith (R-VA). Gillibrand was vocal in her support for the bills, claiming that such legislation will protect workers and provide long-term benefits to businesses, as it will become more difficult for serial predators to rise through the ranks and perpetuate a toxic workplace (Wingfield and Silver-Greenberg 2017). The policy had strong bipartisan support, and in March 2022, President Biden signed the Ending Forced Arbitration of Sexual Assault and Sexual Harassment Act of 2021 into law (GovTrack 2021b; GovTrack 2021e).

Countless workers lack the necessary protection to allow them to participate equally in the labor force. This is especially a problem in female-dominated industries such as food service, cleaning, and care work, which have taken little action to curb discrimination and harassment. While the #MeToo movement has prompted increasing numbers of women in those fields to speak out against mistreatment, it is often unclear where they should go to report it. It is typically worse for self-employed workers who have no colleagues or human resources department to consult, and who may experience such harassment from clients or customers. Although Title VII can be an effective vehicle for combating sex discrimination in employment, including sexual harassment, it has significant procedural and substantive limitations (Kantor 2018). Recent activity at the state level has attempted to address these obstacles, largely in response to the rampant abuse that the #MeToo movement has exposed. Over a dozen states enacted legislation banning nondisclosure agreements that prevent employees from making public the harassment, discrimination, or assault they experienced (National Women's Law Center 2020a). In 2019, California tripled the statute of limitations period for employees to file a harassment, discrimination, or retaliation claim with the California Department of Fair Employment and Housing. Employees now have three years to file a claim for harassment, as well as another year after filing the complaint to bring a civil lawsuit (Mizrahi and Schwab 2019). Yet for all of the positive outcomes the #MeToo movement has produced, there have also been a number of unintended consequences that undermine gender equality.

As the #MeToo movement bourgeoned, some men began avoiding one-on-one interactions with women at work out of fear of being accused of inappropriate behavior. Such avoidance hurts women in many ways. To begin, it suggests that false accusations of misconduct made by women are common and that staying away from women altogether is the only way to escape such accusations. It sends the message that the #MeToo movement is out to punish all men, even those who have done nothing wrong. This can make men less supportive of the movement while also hurting women professionally. If men refuse to interact with women in a workplace, it may limit women's opportunities to collaborate on important projects with male colleagues or clients who can bolster their careers.

According to research from LeanIn.org and SurveyMonkey, a majority of male managers (60 percent) said they are uncomfortable participating in job-related activities with women, which means that women are more likely to miss the mentoring experiences that may be crucial to workplace advancement. Recent research also reveals that women may lose out on job opportunities as a result of these fears. A 2019 study found that 21 percent of men and 12 percent of women are now more reluctant to hire women for jobs that require them to interact closely with men, such as during business travel. Approximately 20 percent of men and 6 percent of women report that in this #MeToo era, they are less likely to hire attractive women. In an ironic twist, it appears that the backlash to #MeToo may result in fewer women being hired (Elesser 2019).

In addition to the negative effects on hiring and career development practices, this backlash may be responsible for greater hostility toward women in the workplace. A *Harvard Business Review* study compared women's experiences with workplace harassment directly before and after the #MeToo movement. From 2016 to 2018, the proportion of women reporting sexual coercion decreased from 25 percent to 16 percent;

unwanted sexual attention dropped from 66 percent to 25 percent. At the same time, reports of gender harassment increased from 76 percent of women to 92 percent. These results suggest that while blatant sexual harassment may be declining, perhaps in part as a result of the #MeToo movement, it may also be fueling increased diffused hostility toward women (Johnson, Keplinger, and Kirk 2019). A 2018 *Washington Post*–ABC poll found a similar backlash to the #MeToo movement. Almost one-third of adults (35 percent of men and 29 percent of women) in the United States said that the attention given to workplace sexual harassment has "gone too far." Republicans were the most likely to report these negative attitudes (49 percent) compared with 29 percent of independents and 23 percent of Democrats (Guskin 2018).

Still, there is reason for optimism. The #MeToo movement has exposed decades of abuse and coordinated the subsequent outpouring of support. The revelations from the movement have also boosted some women's confidence. Specifically, unwanted sexual attention had a less negative effect on women's self-esteem and self-doubt in 2018 than it did in 2016. Researchers believe that "the knowledge that so many women experience sexual harassment has tempered its deleterious effects on self-doubt and self-esteem" (Johnson, Keplinger, and Kirk 2019). Moreover, while many women have experienced some degree of backlash to the #MeToo movement at work, Scout Exchange, a recruitment marketplace provider based in Boston, found that in the first year of the movement, there was a 41 percent increase in the number of women hired for executive roles with salaries above $100,000 a year (Kalyanaraman 2018).

Women in the Military

In spite of women's significant contributions to national defense since the founding of the nation, they have often been considered only "auxiliary support." Today more than 200,000 women serve on active duty, constituting over 15 percent of the armed forces, but their full integration into the military remains elusive (Oppermann 2019). During the American Revolution (1775–1783) and the American Civil War (1861–1865), women primarily served in military camps as nurses, cooks, and laundresses, often playing a vital role in the troops' success. As many as 6,000 women provided nursing services for Union soldiers during the Civil War, and many were also more directly involved in the conflict, acting as spies or disguised as men to perform as soldiers. Over the course of the nineteenth century, the military rarely recognized these women for their service; through the early twentieth century, the only women who were allowed to join the military were nurses. It was not until the United States entered World War I in 1917 that the military permitted women who were not nurses to enlist. By World War II, more than 400,000 women served at home and abroad in noncombat roles, such as nurses, mechanics, drivers, and pilots (Oppermann 2019).

The Women's Army Corps (WAC), first created as the Women's Auxiliary Army Corps in May 1942, did not confer full military status on women. Initially, they were paid less than men and were denied life insurance, death benefits, and veterans' benefits. In July 1943, the WAC officially became a part of the army, which meant that women in the corps received similar pay and benefits as men. More than 150,000 women served in the WAC during World War II, working as weather observers and forecasters, postal clerks, radio operators and repairers, parachute riggers, aerial photograph analysts, control tower operators, and other noncombat positions (Bellafaire 2005).

In 1948, the Women's Armed Services Integration Act granted women permanent status in the military, formally recognizing the contributions they had been making since the eighteenth century. Still, the country hesitated to accept women as a core part of the military, as demonstrated by the act's provision limiting the number of women who could serve to 2 percent of the total forces in each branch. More broadly, in the aftermath of World War II, there was a return to traditional gender roles that encouraged women to embrace motherhood and domesticity. Such gender norms were at odds with the need to recruit women to serve in the Korean War, which helps explain why the armed forces had filled only 60 percent of the projected need for nurses by the start of the conflict in 1950. Still, over 50,000 women served in noncombat and combat roles in the Korean War; over 7,000 women served in the Vietnam War. In both wars, women primarily filled clerical and administrative positions to free men for combat duty (Oppermann 2019).

In 1967, the law limiting the percentage of women in the armed forces was repealed, opening the door for women's presence in the military to grow. By 1976, women were also admitted to the US military service academies, where they could train for leadership positions. But perhaps the biggest policy change came in 2016, when women finally received authorization to serve in all positions in the military—including combat roles such as the ones they had been unofficially filling in Iraq and Afghanistan for years. For hundreds of years, women have served the United States—both unofficially and officially—by performing whatever jobs the military assigned them. Yet for all their progress, women are still not fully integrated into the military (Oppermann 2019).

As a gendered institution, "gender is present in the processes, practices, images and ideologies, and distributions of power" in the US military. Gendered institutions are "historically developed by men, currently dominated by men, and symbolically interpreted from the standpoint of men in leading positions, both in the present and historically" (Acker 1992, 567). These embedded values help explain why women were excluded from combat for so long. In the 1970s, after the United States developed an all-volunteer military force, this exclusion was justified by the idea that the military was a "rational actor" that was only concerned with protecting the nation in the most efficient way. To military officials, incorporating women into combat roles would undermine that efficiency. By the 1980s, officials argued that women were "leaky bodies" that would threaten the operations of the military because of their hormones, menstruation, and pregnancies. In the 1990s, fears of sexual assault if women served with men in combat formed the basis for women's continued exclusion. After the terrorist attacks of September 11, 2001, as the United States deployed increasing numbers of troops overseas, concerns arose about how women would adjust to combat zones and the different treatment their bodies would require after returning from deployment. Even as women increasingly fought on the front lines in an unofficial capacity in Afghanistan and Iraq, the military continued to justify the ban on women in combat until it was finally ended in 2016 (Szitanyi 2020, 177).

The response to the decision to end the combat ban largely reinforced the idea of the military as a gendered institution, as demonstrated in a 2014 survey of the US Special Operations Command, which oversees the various special operations component commands of the branches of the armed forces, such as the Army Rangers and the Navy SEALs. Administered to personnel in Special Operations–controlled positions that were closed to women, the survey was designed to gauge reactions to the proposed integration of women into special operations forces (SOF). Overall, 85 percent of respondents opposed allowing women into their specialties; 71 percent opposed women in their units. Their main concerns were that standards would fall, unit cohesion would erode, and leaders would be less available to resolve conflict among members. As these results reveal, there is "strong, deep-seated, and intensely felt opposition to opening SOF specialties that have been closed to women" (Szayna et al. 2016, 78).

These exclusionary attitudes toward women can also be seen in the military's recruitment practices. In examining recruitment materials posted by the military on social media, Stephanie Szitanyi (2020) found that men were significantly more likely than women to be included in the posts, reinforcing the idea that the military is a male domain. When women were included in the posts, they were often depicted in stereotypical roles or settings; they were more likely to be shown performing medical duties or taking part in ceremonies than fighting on the front lines of a mission—even after the ban on women in combat was lifted. The military's approach to publicly honor service members also sustains the idea that it is a male domain. There are few public memorials that pay tribute to women's military service; instead, they mostly portray the idealized profile of a masculine warrior. As Szitanyi (2020) observes, "despite recent policy changes to eliminate women's exclusion from combat and to permit openly gay, lesbian, bisexual, and trans personnel to serve, the military persists as an organization that embraces notions of male superiority and preserves an institutional gender order that privileges men—heterosexual men, in particular" (191).

The idea that women are still largely considered outsiders in the armed forces is especially evident when examining the rampant sexual abuse they suffer while serving. To many men in the military, the women they serve with are challenging long-standing gender norms and undermining the cohesion of the forces. Perhaps nowhere was this more apparent than the now infamous Thirty-Fifth Annual Tailhook Association Symposium in September 1991. The Tailhook Association is a fraternal organization for active duty, reserve, and retired US military personnel involved in sea-based aviation. Each year since the group's founding in 1956, members gather for a convention that involves presentations, awards, and socializing. In 1991, around 4,000 military personnel and 1,000 defense contractors met at the Las Vegas Hilton in Nevada for the annual Tailhook convention, which quickly turned into a wild, drunken affair that took over the third floor of the hotel and caused over $20,000 in property damage. More destructive was the widespread sexual harassment and assault that victimized at least eighty-three women and seven men (Hillstrom 2019).

When the events at the convention became known, the secretary of the navy ordered the Naval Investigative Service to launch an investigation. The report published in April 1992 concluded that while some low-ranking enlisted personnel had misbehaved, no high-ranking officials bore responsibility for the events. There was dissent among some in the navy, such as Assistant Secretary of the Navy for Manpower and Reserve Affairs Barbara Pope, who felt that the investigation had been intentionally superficial to shield senior officers from criticism and avoid negative publicity. Likewise, the women who had been assaulted at the convention were frustrated by the contents of the report and the military's lack of concern about their allegations. When helicopter pilot and admiral's aide Coughlin reported that she was attacked at the convention, her complaints were dismissed and she was disparaged for drinking and wearing a short skirt, as well as for attempting to destroy a Tailhook tradition and damage the careers of other service members. Realizing she would receive no support from her supervisors, Coughlin aired her story to the news media in June 1992. Her allegations immediately gained national attention, especially since the Tailhook convention had taken place less than a week before the start of the Thomas confirmation hearings, an event that had propelled sexual harassment into the headlines. The inspector general of the Department of Defense (DoD) quickly launched a second investigation into the events of the Tailhook convention. The 2,000-page report that came out in September 1992 lambasted the first report's findings and provided a thorough examination of the events that happened, including dozens of statements from witnesses and survivors who confirmed Coughlin's account. As a result, fourteen admirals and nearly 300 aviators were subject to disciplinary action that either damaged or ended their careers (Hillstrom 2019).

Many point to the Tailhook scandal as indicative of a much larger problem in the military—namely, the treatment of women. Some Tailhook members later reported that animosity toward women seemed palpable at the 1991 convention, perhaps because earlier in the year, the largest deployment of military women in US history was sent to the Middle East. Women were still banned from combat roles at that time, but the 40,000 women who served in the Persian Gulf War had significantly more opportunities available to them than they had in the past. Many male service members did not hide their opposition to such changes to the armed forces, especially when they were confronted with the possibility of increased competition for preferred assignments. At the Tailhook convention, some male attendees even wore shirts that said "Women Are Property" or "He-Man Woman-Haters Club" as symbols of their aversion to women in the military (Hillstrom 2019). The events surrounding Tailhook also demonstrated the pervasive problem of sexual harassment and sexual assault in the armed forces, as well as the obstacles many women face from their chain of command when they report such abuse.

In FY 2020, there were 7,816 reports of sexual assault in the US military, less than a 1 percent decrease from FY 2019 (US Department of Defense 2020). With most incidents of sexual misconduct in DoD going unreported, the actual number of assaults is probably much higher. In 2018, there were 6,053 reported sexual assaults; based on survey data, it is estimated that the actual number for 2018 was more than 20,000 (Acosta, Chinman, and Shearer 2021). There were estimates that one in sixteen women (6.2 percent) and one in 143 men (0.7 percent) may experience sexual assault in the military (US Department of Defense, Sexual Assault Prevention and Response Office 2019). The rates are higher in the service academies: one in six women and one in twenty-nine men are projected to experience sexual assault. Estimates for sexual harassment in the military are one in four women and one in sixteen men. In 2019, more than 1,600 formal and informal complaints of sexual harassment were investigated by the military, but it is likely that the actual number of people experiencing harassment was closer to 119,000 (Acosta, Chinman, and Shearer 2021).

There are many reasons that sexual abuse is largely unpunished in the military. Victims may be ashamed or embarrassed, and they may want to try to forget that the incident occurred. There is also a sense of learned hopelessness in the military regarding sexual misconduct, as most victims know that perpetrators are rarely punished. In FY 2020, only 0.8 percent of reported sexual assaults ended in a sex-offense conviction under the Uniform Code of Military Justice. Paradoxically, victims often face punishment for reporting sexual harassment and assault. A 2018 DoD survey of active-duty service members found that 38 percent of women who reported their assaults experienced professional retaliation afterward. Such actions may damage a service member's career or cost them a promotion. Many women who report sexual abuse have been labeled with a mental illness diagnosis and given a less-than-honorable discharge; from 2009 to 2015, more than 20 percent of service members who left the military after reporting an assault received such a discharge (Human Rights Watch 2016; Acosta, Chinman, and Shearer 2021; Moyer 2021).

There has been growing attention paid to this massive problem in the military, in part because of the influence of the #MeToo movement. In January 2018, about thirty-five demonstrators gathered outside the Pentagon to protest the DoD's insufficient response to sexual assault and harassment in the military. Borrowing from the #MeToo movement, the protesters identified themselves with the hashtag "MeTooMilitary." Pentagon spokesperson Army Colonel Rob Manning supported the protest, saying, "no one should have to tolerate harassment as part of their military service. . . . Events like this morning's underscore the importance of the department's continued effort to eliminate sexual harassment and assault from the military" (Shinkman 2018). It remains to be seen if such verbal endorsements will turn into substantive changes in the military.

Beginning in 2013, Gillibrand, together with Senator Chuck Grassley (R-IA), has introduced a bill to reform the military justice system in every session of Congress. The legislation would move the decision to prosecute major military crimes, including sexual assault, from the chain of command to trained, independent military prosecutors (GovTrack 2021d). Opponents of the bill claim that removing commanders from the process would undermine the system that allows leadership to maintain order and discipline in the ranks. Advocates of the bill believe that such a shift would result in a greater number of assailants facing charges when reports are filed against them. In addition, the process could result in fewer delays under the proposed system; currently, it often takes months for a claim to make its way through the chain of command before a final decision about charges is made. Since the bill was reintroduced in April 2021, it has attracted more bipartisan support than ever before. Previous opponents, such as Senator Joni Ernst (R-IA) and the chair of the Joint Chiefs of Staff General Mark Milley, now endorse it. The primary reason for this shift seems to be the steady—or at times, increasing—rates of abuse in the armed forces (Moyer 2021). A growing number of decisionmakers in the military and political realms have realized that the existing reporting and prosecutorial processes are insufficient for addressing this pervasive problem.

The executive branch has also taken a more proactive approach. In January 2021, Trump signed the Deborah Sampson Act, named for the woman who pretended to be a man so she could fight in the American Revolution. The purpose of the law is to improve health care access and benefits for female veterans. Provisions in the legislation require Veterans Affairs (VA) health centers to make it easier for women to report sexual harassment or assault, establish specialized teams to process claims related to military sexual trauma, and require VA employees to report abuse. In June 2021, Secretary of Defense Lloyd Austin surprised many by publicly endorsing removing the prosecution of sexual assaults from the military chain of command (Moyer 2021).

Ultimately, procedural changes can only do so much to address the epidemic of abuse faced by women in the armed forces, as the issue is engrained in military culture. In this way, the military can be viewed as simultaneously reflecting and shaping broader society. As Szitanyi (2020) observes, "military masculinities—and the masculine warrior in particular—re-inscribe the white, heterosexual, male soldier as the embodiment of the patriot, the proper citizen, the natural leader, and the nation's honor. By comparison, women, gay, lesbian, bisexual, and gender nonconforming individuals are second class—and their continued marginalization within the military ensures that they remain as such" (194). Just as the #MeToo movement has begun to reveal the entrenched sexism that fuels the discrimination, harassment, and assault that women face in the civilian workplace, there is a growing effort to shine a light on the abuse of women in the military. Only by acknowledging the extent of this problem can it be rooted out, yet the growing impetus for military reform has met with significant resistance. Similar to the backlash to the #MeToo movement that developed in the workplace, an increasingly hostile response has been forming against the idea that female service members are mistreated and widespread changes are needed in the armed forces (Moyer 2021). Until those attitudes shift at all levels in the military, women will never be fully integrated.

The Gender Wage Gap

Women have always worked, but historically that work was primarily unpaid labor in the home. As soon as women entered the labor market, the gender wage gap materialized. During the preindustrial era, female employees earned wages 20 to 50 percent less than the wages of men performing the same work. By the early twentieth century, wage disparities reflecting the lower social value placed on work performed by women had become institutionalized in many companies. For example, the Westinghouse Corporation established a formal policy to ensure that the wages for the lowest-paying male job did not fall below the wages for the highest-paying female job. The 1913 contract for the International Ladies' Garment Workers' Union included a similar clause prohibiting the highest paid female worker from earning more than the lowest paid male worker (Bridge 1997). Such policies help to explain why, in 1929, male clerical workers earned a median income of $35.57 a week; for female clerical workers, the median wage was $22.40 a week (Barnard and Rapp 2009). The 1940 census, which included the first detailed wage data based on gender, shows that women were paid less than men working the same jobs, even when controlling for hours and weeks worked (Bridge 1997).

Companies justified this unequal treatment with society's view that even when women were employed, they were still principally regarded as wives and mothers. Employers claimed that men needed higher salaries because they were the family breadwinners, whereas women were merely "working for 'pin money'—a small amount of money for nonessential items like clothing or jewelry" (Han and Heldman 2018, 212; Bridge 1997). Even as the number of female-headed households grew—as well as the number of families that needed two incomes to survive—this mentality has persisted. Indeed, it is part of the reason the gender wage gap still exists today.

The wage gap compares the average earnings of full-time women workers to the average earnings of full-time men workers over the course of a year. In the United States in 2020, the median annual pay for a woman working full-time in a year-round job was $50,982; for a man working in a full-time, year-round job, the median annual pay was $61,417. This difference of $10,435 means that women earn only 83 cents for every dollar paid to men. However, this gap varies widely among women workers. Compared with the wages of white non-Hispanic men, white non-Hispanic women earn 79 cents to the dollar; Black women earn 64 cents, Native American women earn 60 cents, and Latinas earn only 57 cents. Among Asian American, Native Hawaiian, and Pacific Islander (AANHPI) women, the wage gap ranges from 75 cents for the women overall to 52 cents for Burmese women compared with white non-Hispanic men (Tucker 2021; National Partnership for Women and Families 2022a; National Partnership for Women and Families 2022b).

This earnings gap persists even though women in the United States are generally better educated than men. Since 2003, the percentage of employed women with a college degree has exceeded the percentage of men in the labor force with a college degree. In 2019, 45 percent of women and 37.9 percent of men in the workforce were college graduates (US Department of Labor, Bureau of Labor Statistics 2021d). That year also marked the first time that women aged twenty-five and older made up a majority (50.2 percent) of the total college-educated workforce (Fry 2019). Ironically, the gender gap in wages actually grows as women become more educated. Among workers with less than a high school diploma, women earned a weekly average of $494; men's weekly average was $644. For those with a bachelor's degree or higher, women earned an average of $1,195 a week, compared with men's weekly average of $1,573 (US Department of Labor, Bureau of Labor Statistics 2021d).

Comparing the average weekly earnings of workers based on race and ethnicity in 2019 shows that the gender gap persists in all groups. The earnings gap per week was largest among Asian workers, with Asian women earning 77 percent of what Asian men earn ($1,025 to $1,336). The next largest weekly gap was among white workers; white women earned 81 percent of what white men earned ($840 to $1,036). Among Hispanic and Latinx workers, the pay gap was 86 percent ($642 for women to $747 for men). The smallest gap was among African American workers, with women earning 91 percent of what men earned ($704 to $769) (US Department of Labor, Bureau of Labor Statistics 2021d). The narrower gender wage gap among African Americans and Hispanics and Latinx workers is likely the result of lower wages for both men and women in these groups compared with the wages of Asians and whites. In other words, because African Americans and Hispanics and Latinx workers generally earn less overall than Asians and whites, the wage gap between women and men in those groups is typically smaller as well.

The effects of the gender wage gap are significant for both society and individuals. On average, women employed in full-time, year-round jobs in the United States lose a combined total of almost $1 trillion a year because of the gap, which means they have less money to support themselves and their families. Because women have less to spend, save, and invest, the economy as a whole suffers as well. If the annual gender wage gap were eliminated, a working woman in the United States would have enough money, on average, for an additional thirteen months of groceries, twelve months of childcare, or nine months of rent per year (National Partnership for Women and Families 2022a; Tucker 2022). The earnings gap goes further than wages. It is even greater when considering workers' full compensation packages, which may include employer-sponsored health insurance, retirement benefits, and paid family and sick leave; women are less likely than men to have access to such benefits (US Council of Economic Advisers 2015).

There are multiple overlapping explanations for the persistence of the gender pay gap, some of which have changed over time. For example, Francine Blau and Lawrence Kahn (2017) found that differing levels of education and work experience between women and men explained approximately 27 percent of the gender gap in 1981; by 2010, those factors explained only around 8 percent of the gap. This is not completely surprising, as women have largely surpassed men in education. More revelatory is that during that same time period, the influence of gender segregation by occupation and industry increased dramatically, from about 27 percent to 49 percent. This occupational segregation is now the single largest cause of the gender pay gap. Male-dominated occupations generally pay more than female-dominated occupations.

Of the thirty highest-paying jobs, including chief executive and pharmacist, twenty-six are male-dominated. Of the thirty lowest-paying jobs, including cashier and childcare worker, twenty-three are female-dominated (Liner 2016). Wages in "pink-collar" jobs are often depressed in part because of the oversupply of workers compared with the demand for them (Bednarek 1998). Because women are significantly more likely than men to enter these jobs, they tend to have lower wages. In 2019, over 90 percent of secretaries and administrative assistants, dental hygienists, and preschool and kindergarten teachers were women, as were almost 90 percent of paralegals, occupational therapists, and registered nurses (US Department of Labor, Bureau of Labor Statistics 2021d).

Among full-time workers, women are much more likely than men to earn poverty-level wages. In 2019, more than 3 million full-time working women were in occupations with median weekly earnings for women less than $499, which is lower than 100 percent of the federal poverty threshold for a family of four. Only 170,000 full-time working men were in a similar occupational situation. If using the Supplemental Nutrition Assistance Program's higher poverty threshold of $644 per week for a family of four, those numbers increase to 13.8 million full-time working women and 6.6 full-time working men (Institute for Women's Policy Research 2020). As these numbers demonstrate, occupations dominated by women generally pay significantly lower wages. Some evidence even suggests that the act of women entering an occupational field in great numbers can lead average wages in that field to decline. For example, as the field of recreation, including working in parks or leading camps, went from being predominantly male in 1950 to predominantly female in 2000, median hourly wages dropped 57 percent when controlling for inflation. A similar pattern was found in the occupation of ticket agent, where wages dropped 43 percent (Levanon, England, and Allison 2009).

Not only do male-dominated jobs generally pay more than female-dominated jobs, but there is also typically a gender pay gap in each of these occupations. The wage gap persists throughout the civilian industries that employ the most full-time employees. Women working in the health care and social assistance fields make only 69 percent of men's earnings; in manufacturing the gap is 73 percent; and in retail trade the gap is 70 percent. In jobs where women make up the majority of workers, such as educational services, the gender wage gap still stands at 83 percent (National Partnership for Women and Families 2022a). Female elementary and middle school teachers—a field dominated by women—earn an average of $1,042 a week compared with $1,161 for men. In the male-dominated field of software development and application, men earn an average of $1,920 a week compared with $1,718 a week for women (Institute for Women's Policy Research 2020). Similarly, women physicians earn 71 percent of what men physicians earn and for lawyers, the gender wage gap is 82 percent (Miller 2014). This means that factors beyond occupational segregation influence the gender gap.

In the United States, motherhood helps explain why women earn lower salaries than men; mothers with full-time, year-round jobs receive 75 cents for every dollar paid to fathers (National Partnership for Women and Families 2022a). Part of this is related to the structure of the workplace in the country. Generally, companies pay employees more when they spend longer hours at the office on a regular basis and are available when needed. A lawyer working eighty hours a week at a large corporate law firm typically makes more than twice as much as a lawyer who works forty hours a week as in-house counsel for a small business (Goldin 2014). This structure disadvantages women because they bear the brunt of (unpaid) domestic work, such as cooking, cleaning, and caring for children or elderly parents, which leaves them less time to spend at the office. Relative to their male colleagues, women are more likely to desire a flexible work schedule and less likely to be available to come to the office on a moment's notice to cover a work emergency. These differences often influence a worker's chance of promotion and long-term earning potential, leaving women at a clear disadvantage (Polachek 2014; Schieder and Gould 2016).

The gender pay gap is generally most visible in jobs at opposite ends of the corporate ladder. At one end, the so-called sticky floor effect refers to women's increased likelihood to remain in the lower ranks of the job scale, even as men advance to managerial positions and earn higher wages. At the other end, the so-called glass ceiling prevents women from further advanceme
certain level. This invisible barrier keeps '
to the highest paid, most prestigious jc
level, education and skills are only part
motion; relationships of trust with clien
trust is developed over time and can be st
to-face interactions with clients. This oft
flexible with respect to their working hou
cult for women because of their great
(Goldin 2014).

Part of the "motherhood penalty" comes from its connection with human capital acquisition (Polachek 2014). The experience that individuals gain over their working lives, which encompasses education and on-the-job training, greatly influences their earnings. Workers who expect to remain a part of the labor market for a long, uninterrupted career are more likely to invest in such training resources. On the other hand, employees who expect to drop out of the workforce for any extended period of time, such as when they have children, tend to gravitate toward jobs that require less training. Solomon Polachek (2014) finds that these life cycle and human capital differences help explain why the pay gap tends to be smaller between single women and single men compared with the pay gap between married women and married men. Among people with a master's of business administration degree, women and men start their careers with nearly identical earnings. A decade after degree completion, a significant gender pay gap has developed, driven primarily by more career interruptions and shorter work hours that are tied to motherhood (Bertrand, Goldin, and Katz 2010). More broadly, Michelle Budig (2014) finds that women who return to the workforce after having children face a wage penalty of 4 percent per child, while men actually experience a 6 percent increase in wages after becoming fathers.

One of the primary sources of the gender gap is the lack of available programs in the public or private sector to help workers balance their employment with their family lives. Government-sponsored childcare is usually available only to low-income individuals, and parents often struggle to find affordable high-quality private care. The United States remains the only industrialized country in the world that does not provide paid family leave at the national level. Although a growing number of states and private companies have extended paid family leave, millions of workers are still forced to take unpaid leave—if it is available to them—or exit the workforce after the arrival of a child. Because women are typically viewed as the primary caregivers of children, they are significantly more likely to take time from work for caregiving responsibilities (Sholar 2016a). For different-sex couples, this decision often makes financial sense, as women generally have lower salaries. At the same time, that arrangement perpetuates the idea that women should be the primary caregivers, thereby reinforcing the earnings differential between women and men because the career interruptions that result from caregiving inhibit women's career potential and (Schieder and Gould 2016).

are many factors that contribute to the continuing gender when controlling for the elements that can be directly measured, such as occupational segregation, education and experience levels, and unionization rates, Blau and Kahn (2017) found that 38 percent of the pay gap remains unaccounted for. This led them to conclude that gender discrimination and unconscious bias play a significant role in keeping women's wages relatively low. Moreover, it is important to remember that the professional and familial choices that women make—choices that explain a sizable portion of the gap—do not occur in a vacuum. A study of science faculty from research-intensive universities revealed considerable bias against women applying for a laboratory manager position. In the application materials for the job, researchers randomly assigned the applicant either a female or male name. Other than the name, the applications were identical. Nevertheless, the faculty participants—regardless of their own gender—rated the male applicant as substantially more "competent and hireable," awarded him a higher starting salary, and offered greater career mentoring than to the woman with identical credentials (Moss-Racusin et al. 2012). Such bias can make it more difficult for women to receive the jobs and training necessary to help close the wage gap.

When women are hired, they are often offered lower salaries than their male counterparts. It was long suggested that this disparity stemmed from women being less assertive than men in salary negotiations. However, even when women negotiate, they still receive lower offers than men, in part because implicit gender bias causes evaluators to view women who ask for higher salaries as socially incompetent for breaking societal gender norms about how nice or how demanding women should be (Bowles, Babcock, and Lai 2007). Once in the workplace, many women experience bias against them because of their gender, especially if they work in a male-dominated environment. Thirty-seven percent of women whose workplace is mostly male report that their competence has been questioned because of their gender; 35 percent of these women say they have earned less than a man doing the same work. For women in female-dominated workplaces, those numbers are smaller but still significant: 20 percent report being treated as if they were not competent because of their gender, and 22 percent say they have earned less than a man in the same job. Overall, 34 percent of women in male-dominated workplaces say that their gender has made it more difficult for them to succeed at work; 13 percent of women in a female-dominated workplace make the same claim (Parker 2018).

Women's occupational choices—from employment field to the division of caregiving and workplace responsibilities—play a role in the gender wage gap. But these decisions are not free from gender bias;

they are shaped by years of parental, educational, societal, and work-place norms and expectations. When children are young, their parents are often more likely to expect or encourage their sons, rather than their daughters, to enter science, technology, engineering, or mathematics (STEM) fields, regardless of their children's performance in math. It is therefore not surprising that by the time young women arrive at college, they are significantly less likely than their male counterparts to be interested in STEM (Schieder and Gould 2016). Young women who enter STEM careers are significantly more likely than men to leave the field because of the industry culture. A 2008 study found that 52 percent of highly qualified women working in science, technology, and engineering quit their jobs because of excessive work pressures, such as expectations to work more than 100 hours a week while remaining available at all other times, and hostile work environments. Almost two-thirds (63 percent) of the women in those fields reported experiencing some form of sexual harassment (Hewlett et al. 2008).

The current gender pay gap is largely the result of occupational segregation, workplace harassment, gendered divisions of labor in the home and family, and the lack of policies to support caregiving—all of which stem from gender expectations and discrimination. In addition, the wage gap is "a result of implicit gender bias that causes both men and women to place a lower value on women's labor" (Han and Heldman 2018, 219). A problem with such entrenched roots is difficult to solve, and progress has been slow.

As women joined the labor market in increasing numbers in the nineteenth century, there emerged a demand for pay equity. The first organized attempt to enact equal pay legislation came after an 1869 letter to the editor in the *New York Times* revealed that the 500 women working in the Treasury Department earned only half the wages of their male colleagues. In response, the House of Representatives adopted a bill prohibiting paying women less than men for the same work in government jobs. By the time the legislation cleared the Senate, the law only applied to newly hired government employees. It ultimately brought little substantive change because it was rarely enforced, but the legislative process surrounding it prompted a larger conversation about the merits of equal pay (Han and Heldman 2018).

Over the next century, legislators slowly began to respond to mounting pressure to address the gender pay gap. In 1911, New York enacted the first binding law that mandated equal wages for female and male teachers. During World War I and World War II, the National War Labor Board decided that women and men should be paid equally for performing the same work. Unions generally supported these wartime policies because they wanted to ensure that the men returning from the war would not have to accept lower wages when they supplanted women in the workforce. In other words, during the wars, equal pay was designed to preclude a drop in wages for jobs normally held by men, rather than to make sure that women were paid equitably for their work (Han and Heldman 2018). Many saw women's employment during World War II as a temporary necessity that should largely disappear in the postwar economy, but a significant number of women chose to remain in the labor market after the war. For many of them, the idea of equal pay stayed with them, and they became part of the growing effort to secure equal pay legislation.

Not targeted to women, the Fair Labor Standards Act (FLSA) of 1938 had a lasting impact on wages for many women because it set a minimum wage for jobs in which more women were employed (Conway, Ahern, and Steuernagel 2005). In 1944, Representative Winifred Stanley (R-NY) introduced the first federal bill guaranteeing equal pay. The bill did not clear the House, but a few years later, both the Democrats and the Republicans included equal pay provisions in their party platforms (Han and Heldman 2018). Throughout the 1950s, other attempts were made to enact equal pay legislation, but none succeeded. Things changed in 1961, when Esther Peterson was appointed head of the Women's Bureau in the Department of Labor (DOL) by President John F. Kennedy.

As part of her work with the Women's Bureau, Peterson hosted hearings with working women across the country to understand the discrimination they faced and the changes they hoped to see. She suggested that Kennedy form a President's Commission on the Status of Women to advise him on these issues. Peterson prioritized the passage of pay equity legislation and was the driving force behind the Equal Pay Act (EPA). Under pressure from the White House, Congress passed the EPA and Kennedy signed it into law in 1963. The act made it illegal to pay women less than men for work performed under similar conditions that requires the same level of skill, effort, and responsibility. Wage gaps based on merit-based criteria, such as seniority or productivity, are still permitted under the law (Harrison 1988). Originally, the EPA applied only to workers covered by the FLSA; a 1972 amendment extended coverage to employees of small firms, as well as executive, administrative, and professional workers, including those in educational institutions. As a result of this amendment, female teachers could no longer be paid less than male teachers with similar training and experience (Conway, Ahern, and Steuernagel 2005). In 1974, equal pay protections were expanded again to cover federal, state, and municipal workers (Mezey 2011).

The EPA gave rise to the slogan "equal pay for equal work" (Kimball 1984). But the focus on "equal work" means that the law applies only to women and men employed in the same establishment who perform substantially equal work. Because the US workforce consists of many sex-segregated occupations, such as the so-called pink-collar jobs, the EPA has been roundly criticized for its limited ability to actually close the gender pay gap in those sectors. Moreover, professional and executive women often have difficulty proving that their jobs require the same skill and effort as those held by men. For these women, "the EPA is increasingly becoming an empty promise, unworkable and ineffective to remedy wage discrimination" (Eisenberg 2010, 22).

To overcome the EPA's equal work requirement, women's rights advocates in the 1970s and 1980s began filing Title VII actions with the hope of demonstrating discrimination in compensation. Rather than demanding equal pay for equal work, they began to call for equal pay for jobs of comparable worth. The premise of comparable worth theory is that jobs can and should be evaluated based on their worth to their employer; jobs with equal value should receive equal pay, absent any merit-based differences such as seniority. In this way, jobs predominantly performed by women, such as nurse and secretary, can be fairly evaluated alongside jobs that are predominantly performed by men, such as truck driver and physical plant worker. Proponents of comparable worth stress that sex segregation in the labor market is one of the main reasons for the persistent gender wage gap. Since women have long been channeled into low-paying jobs that are undervalued because they are female-dominated, comparable worth policies are necessary to close the gender pay gap (Blumrosen 1979; Paul 1989).

Because they "fear[ed] that they would be inundated with comparable worth suits that would require them to impose sweeping economic changes in the public and private sectors, the judiciary refused to apply comparable worth theory to Title VII wage discrimination claims, negating efforts to close the wage gap through litigation" (Mezey 2011, 109). Having made little progress on the idea of comparable worth in the courts, women's rights advocates turned their attention to legislative action at the state and local levels. By 1986, thirty-eight state legislatures had considered comparable worth, ranging from initiating a study on the issue to implementing comparable worth public policies (Chi 1986). Within four years, twenty states had implemented policies to raise the wages of civil service workers in female-dominated jobs. As a result, all twenty states successfully narrowed the gender wage gap without increasing unemployment (Hartmann and Aaronson 1994).

In the 1990s, the issue of pay inequity returned to the federal level, with little success. The Fair Pay Act of 1994, aimed at redressing pay disparities in sex-segregated occupations, would have amended the EPA to ensure that employees were paid fairly for jobs that required equivalent skill, effort, responsibility, and working conditions (Cohen 1995). The Paycheck Fairness Act (PFA), proposed in every session of Congress since 1997, seeks to close loopholes in the EPA by requiring employers to share salary data with the EEOC, thereby putting the onus on employers to justify any observed wage gaps. It requires employers to prove that pay disparities exist for legitimate, job-related reasons; prohibits employers from requiring applicants to disclose their salary history during the interview and hiring process; and assists businesses of all sizes to implement equal pay practices. Importantly, the act also prohibits employers from retaliating against workers who discuss their wages with other employees or raise concerns about gender-based wage discrimination (National Partnership for Women and Families 2021b). Such discussions can lead to greater wage transparency, which can be a powerful tool against pay inequity. Indeed, the gender pay gap in the federal government, where employees' salaries are posted online, is 7 percent (US Government Accountability Office 2020). As of 2022, the PFA remains stalled in Congress.

Equal pay advocates eventually won a significant legislative victory in 2009, but it came about in response to a crushing defeat in the courts. In 1998, Lilly Ledbetter sued Goodyear Tire & Rubber Company for sex discrimination under Title VII and the EPA. Ledbetter had been a supervisor at a Goodyear tire plant from 1979 until she retired in 1998. Although her pay was roughly equal to that of her male colleagues when she began her employment, by 1997, she was making less than all fifteen of the other area managers in Tire Assembly—all of whom were male. The lowest paid male area manager received $4,486 a month, and the highest paid received $5,236 a month; Ledbetter was paid $3,723 a month. She did not know about the wage discrepancy until she received an anonymous letter in 1998 detailing it. After this discovery, she filed a complaint with the EEOC, charging that Goodyear had discriminated against her on the basis of sex (Green 2008).

At Goodyear, salaried employees' raises are based on their performance reviews. Ledbetter alleged that her poor evaluations in the past were the result of retaliatory sex discrimination because she had rebuffed her supervisor's sexual advances for years. In the 1980s, her supervisor recommended low pay increases after she rejected him. When he became Ledbetter's performance auditor in the 1990s, he filed false audit reports when she turned him down again. According to Ledbetter, those acts of discrimination meant that her pay did not increase over time as much as it would have if she had been evaluated fairly. The Alabama federal district court judge ruled in her favor on the Title VII claim, awarded her back pay and damages, and dismissed the EPA claim. The Eleventh Circuit Court of Appeals reversed the lower court, accepting Goodyear's argument that Title VII required a plaintiff to file an EEOC complaint within 180 days of the company's first act of discrimination against her—even if she were unaware of it (*Ledbetter v. Goodyear Tire and Rubber Company* 2005). In 2007, the Supreme Court upheld the circuit court's narrow interpretation of Title VII wage discrimination complaints (*Ledbetter v. Goodyear Tire and Rubber Company* 2007; Green 2008; Goldvaser 2008).

Ledbetter's case demonstrates the significant limitations of the courts to use the EPA and Title VII to adequately address the gender pay gap and the need for Congress to enact legislation. The year the case was decided, House Democrats introduced and passed the Lilly Ledbetter Fair Pay Act. Senate Republicans blocked it, claiming it would harm businesses by increasing the number of frivolous lawsuits. When Democrats gained control of both chambers of Congress in 2009, they quickly approved the legislation and sent it to President Barack Obama; signing the bill into law was one of Obama's first acts as president. Reversing the *Ledbetter* ruling, the act amends the Civil Rights Act of 1964 so that the 180-day filing window resets with each new paycheck that reflects pay discrimination (Canales 2018).

According to experts, without a concerted effort to close the gender wage gap, women and men in the United States will not reach pay parity until 2059. For Black women, that parity will not come until 2133; for Latinas, it will take until 2206. Fortunately, there are a number of policy solutions that could hasten wage equality. For example, because women are more likely than men to hold minimum wage jobs, be harassed in the workplace, and take primary responsibility for caregiving in the home, laws that increase minimum wages, actually eradicate sexual harassment at work, and help balance work and family would narrow the gender pay gap (National Partnership for Women and Families 2022a).

Women in Professional Sports

As the gender pay gap garners more public interest, policymakers face greater pressure to eradicate it. The recent increased attention on the significant gender pay gap in professional sports has held a mirror up to gender inequality in the United States and sparked a national conversation. At the forefront of this exchange has been soccer.

The most watched soccer match in US history was the 2015 Women's World Cup final between the US Women's National Team (USWNT) and Japan, with twenty-four million people watching—22 percent more than watched the men's final the previous year. The second most-watched match was the Women's World Cup final four years later between the United States and the Netherlands, with more than twenty million people in the United States tuning in (DiCaro 2021). In addition to the record-breaking numbers of viewers, the women's team surpassed multiple world records in the sport. In 2019, it set a record for the most goals in a Women's World Cup match and in a tournament overall, as well as the most consecutive World Cup match triumphs. The USWNT also holds the record for the most Women's World Cup victories. The women's team won Olympic gold medals in 1996, 2004, 2008, and 2012. The US Men's National Team (USMNT) fared much worse: its best result was third place in the first Men's World Cup in 1930. More recently, the men's team lost in the round of sixteen in the 2014 cup; it did not qualify in 2018; and it has qualified for the 2022 cup to be held in Qatar. The last time the men's team won an Olympic medal was in 1904 (Masters 2020; Bonn 2022).

Even with the much greater success of the USWNT, there has always been a significant pay differential between the women's and men's teams. The 2015 USWNT received $2 million for winning the Women's World Cup, considerably less than the $9 million the USMNT took home the previous year despite only reaching the round of sixteen. In 2018, the French men's team received $38 million for winning the Men's World Cup; the following year, the USWNT won $4 million for winning the Women's World Cup (Steidinger 2020).

In 2016, members of the USWNT registered a complaint with the EEOC, claiming that the differences in compensation and working conditions between the women's team and the men's team constituted gender discrimination. Three years later, the USWNT filed suit against the United States Soccer Federation (USSF) for violating Title VII and the EPA by paying women thirty-eight cents for every dollar paid to the men, even though the women were held to the same practice and fitness expectations as the men. More notably, as the complaint stated, the women's team has outperformed the men's team while bringing in significant revenue for the USSF (Masters 2020). The USSF drew significant criticism for its initial claims that women's and men's teams and salaries are not comparable because men "are bigger, stronger, [and] faster" and the two teams do not perform equal work that requires equal skill, effort, and responsibility. In response to public outcry, the USSF tempered its language but continued to assert that any pay discrepancy was based on factors other than sex. In particular, the USSF has highlighted the different collective bargaining agreements the federation holds with the women's and men's teams (DiCaro 2021).

Many observers maintain that women in sports are paid less than men because they do not draw the same numbers of viewers or advertising sponsors; this is demonstrably not the case for women's soccer. During the 2015 Women's World Cup, the Fédération Internationale de Football Association (FIFA) signed twenty major sponsors, including Coca-Cola and Chevrolet. The final match of the cup drew as many viewers (twenty-four million) as the National Basketball Association (NBA) finals (Steidinger 2020). According to the *Wall Street Journal*, from 2016 to 2018, the USWNT brought in $50.8 million in ticket sales, compared with $49.9 million in ticket sales for the USMNT (DiCaro 2021).

In its 2019 suit, the USWNT asked for $67 million in back pay, the amount the players argue they would have been paid under the collective bargaining agreement the men had negotiated. In a significant blow to the women's team, a California federal district court dismissed their equal pay claim (DiCaro 2021). The team appealed, but before a decision was reached, in February 2022, after years of pressure from both the women's team and public opinion, the USSF agreed to pay $24 million to a group of dozens of current and former players. This was largely seen as an unspoken admission that the men's and women's teams had long been compensated unequally (Das 2022a). More important than this one-time payout was the USSF's promise of equal pay for the women's and men's teams moving forward. This promise came to fruition in May 2022 with their new collective bargaining agreements, in which for the first time, the USSF guaranteed that the men's and women's national teams will receive equal pay when competing in international matches and competitions. In another first-of-its-kind agreement—one that was actually initiated by the men's team's offer to share some of the World Cup bonus money with the women's team—the two teams will pool the unequal prize money payments from the FIFA World Cup and split it evenly among their members (Das 2022b). Unsurprisingly, women's movement activists were ecstatic about what they view as deservedly equal treatment between the men's and women's teams. As comedian and feminist Samantha Bee tweeted in response to the agreement, "Yay! Now do women in literally every other job" (May 18, 2022).

While gender inequality in soccer has recently garnered the most attention in the United States, women in other sports also face battles for equal pay, with mixed results. In tennis, as of 2007, all Grand Slam tournaments provide equal prize money for women and men; most other tennis tournaments still pay men substantially more prize money than women. At Ohio's Western and Southern Open in 2016, Roger Federer received $731,000 for winning the men's title; Serena Williams received only $495,000 for her victory in the women's title. By 2018, the pay gap in that tournament had widened: the women's overall winner Kiki Bertens won $501,976, compared with the $1,020,425 that the overall men's winner Novak Djokovic received. Similarly, in golf, the prize money for the Professional Golfers' Association Tour is much greater than the prize money for the Ladies Professional Golf Association. For example, in 2018, Patrick Reed won $1.98 million for a first-place finish in the Masters Tournament; Angela Stanford received $577,500 for winning the Evian Championship that year (Steidinger 2020).

In basketball, the average NBA salary is $5 million a year, which is typically fifty to seventy times higher than Women's National Basketball Association (WNBA) salaries. Prior to 2020, the average WNBA salary was $75,000 a year, with veteran players topping out at $113,500 and some rookies making only $40,000. Many WNBA players had to play for European teams in the off-season to make a living wage. The new collective bargaining agreement that the WNBA's Players Association negotiated in January 2020 nearly doubled the maximum league salary to $215,000. As a result of the new agreement, the average WNBA player will earn around $130,000 a year. Players also receive fully paid maternity leave and a $5,000 stipend for childcare each year (Steidinger 2020; DiCaro 2021). In addition to more fairly compensating female basketball players for the equal work they perform relative to male players, these salary improvements reflect the growing popularity of the WNBA. Formed in 1997, the WNBA averaged 7,716 fans in attendance at each game in its twenty-first season in 2018; the NBA did not attract crowds of this size until its twenty-sixth season (Steidinger 2020).

Conclusion

This chapter explored the progression of women's participation in the paid labor force, focusing on their unequal treatment in the workplace and how the various branches of government have addressed this discrimination. In 1964, Congress passed one of the most significant pieces of legislation in the fight for equal employment opportunities, the Civil Rights Act. In particular, Title VII prohibits discrimination on the basis of sex, race, color, national origin, and religion. Yet it was ultimately the executive branch and the courts that took the leading role in ensuring that antidiscrimination policies in the workplace were followed. The effects of Title VII on women's employment were not felt immediately after its passage, largely because the EEOC—the agency tasked with enforcing the statute—initially had few resources and showed little interest in rooting out sex discrimination in the labor market. But as the number of complaints increased, the government was forced to address the rampant sexual harassment and unequal pay structures that plagued women in the workplace.

Originally, courts were reticent to rule that sexual harassment constituted sex discrimination, in part because it could happen to both women and men. But by 1980, the EEOC had explicitly categorized harassment as a form of sex discrimination, and the courts followed suit. However, that does not mean that the problem abated. Recently, as a result of the #MeToo movement, women were energized to publicize the still all-too-common incidents of harassment in the workplace. In response, Congress passed a law in 2022 to prohibit forced arbitration in sexual assault and sexual harassment cases—an attempt to prevent companies from concealing accusations from the public and allowing serial predators to remain in the workplace. Legislators have made similar attempts to address the pervasive sexual misconduct in the military by moving the decision to prosecute such crimes out of the chain of command, which they hoped would lead to a greater number of assailants facing charges. As of this writing, no such legislation has passed.

Women make up almost half of the workforce, but are overrepresented in low-paying and low-prestige jobs. Congress initially addressed the gender pay gap in 1963 by passing the EPA. As this chapter demonstrates, the law has been severely limited in its efforts to abolish sex-based wage disparities. Congress passed the Lilly Ledbetter Fair Pay Act of 2009, which gives employees greater power to address sex-based pay discrimination. This only transpired in response to the courts' refusal to use existing law—the EPA and Title VII—to remedy wage discrimination based on sex. Although there are myriad laws prohibiting paying women less than men, the wage gap persists. On average, women earn 83 cents for every dollar paid to men; for women of color, this number is often lower. Still, there was a reason for hope in 2022 when it was announced that the US women's and men's national soccer teams will receive equal pay when competing in international matches and competition.

4

Balancing Work and Family Life

WOMEN ARE JOINING THE LABOR FORCE IN EVER-INCREASING NUM-bers, yet they are often still expected to be the primary caregivers in their families. Historically, it has fallen on women to find their own way to manage careers and families. Congress has enacted some legal protections for pregnant workers and employment benefits for new working parents, but current legislation is far from sufficient. Many women continue to face pregnancy discrimination in the workplace, most parents have a difficult time finding affordable quality childcare, and the United States remains the only industrialized country in the world without paid family leave at the national level.*

Women's Labor Force Participation

In 1950, women's participation rate in the United States labor force was 33.9 percent; by 1970, it had risen to 43.3 percent. Over those two decades, a pattern emerged. Women between the ages of sixteen and twenty-four were most likely to enter the workforce, with a noticeable drop in participation among women ages twenty-five to thirty-four.

---

*We understand that not all pregnant people identify as women, but because women have historically been the target of pregnancy discrimination and most of the policies and judicial rulings throughout the book speak of pregnant women, we also refer to pregnant women (Lewis 2021).

Comparing their participation rate by age, in 1950, the rate for the youngest working age group (sixteen to twenty-four years old) was 43.9 percent; for the next age group (twenty-five to thirty-four years old), it was 34 percent. By 1970, although the labor force participation rate had increased for all women, a gap remained between the rate for the youngest group (51.3 percent) and the next age group (45 percent). The primary reason for the decrease is that women typically left the labor force when they married or had their first child, which was most likely to happen for women ages twenty-five to thirty-four. For women ages thirty-five to fifty-four, the participation rate steadily increased as many women returned to the labor force after bearing and raising their children (Fullerton 1999).

Since the 1980s, women with young children have become increasingly likely to enter and remain in the nation's workforce. From 1967 to 2012, the percentage of mothers with children younger than eighteen who do not work outside the home declined from 49 percent to 29 percent (Cohn, Livingston, and Wang 2014). By 2019, the labor force participation rate for all women with children under eighteen was 72.3 percent. Of those women, mothers whose youngest child was between six and seventeen had the highest participation rate at 76.8 percent. The participation rate of mothers with children under six was 66.4 percent; for mothers with children under three, it was 63.5 percent. As these figures indicate, mothers have strong ties to the workforce, and their participation is linked to the ages of their children.

By 2019, only 28.6 percent of heterosexual married-couple families with children under eighteen conformed to the traditional image of the family with a "stay-at-home" mom and a dad in the labor force; in 64.2 percent of heterosexual married-couple families with children under eighteen, both parents were wage earners. Nearly one-quarter (24 percent) of the mothers were "solo moms," and in those families, 75.4 percent of them were employed (Geiger, Livingston, and Bialik 2019; US Department of Labor, Bureau of Labor Statistics 2021a).

Pregnant Women in the Workforce

Though the government has long favored private solutions for pregnant women, a series of lawsuits in the 1970s helped draw society's attention to the concerns of pregnant working women and ultimately opened the door for government policies intended to prevent discrimination against them. As the number of women in the labor force steadily increased in the second half of the twentieth century, legislators could no longer ignore the problems related to balancing pregnancy with employment, especially after passage of Title VII of the 1964 Civil Rights Act, the law prohibiting employment discrimination "based on race, color, religion, sex and national origin" (42 U.S.C. §2000e). Nevertheless, the courts initially held that treating pregnant employees differently from nonpregnant employees did not run afoul of the act, and it was largely left to individual employers to decide whether (and how) to accommodate pregnancy in the workplace (Piccirillo 1988).

In March 1972, the Equal Employment Opportunity Commission (EEOC) released new guidelines defining "disabilities caused by pregnancy" as "temporary disabilities" that must be included in the employer's insurance or sick leave policies (*Federal Register* 1972, 6837). This change had significant repercussions, as people suffering from disabilities linked to pregnancy, childbirth, miscarriage, or abortion became entitled to the usual benefits associated with a temporary disability. These guidelines addressed pregnancy protections in a gender-neutral fashion by treating disabilities resulting from pregnancy like other temporary disabilities. In this way, women employees were not singled out for special treatment. But the guidelines did not immediately translate into equal treatment for women and men in the workplace. A series of Supreme Court decisions in the 1970s directly challenged the EEOC's interpretation of the law.

In *Geduldig v. Aiello* (1974), the Court decided that California did not violate the Fourteenth Amendment's equal protection clause by denying insurance benefits to an employee for work loss resulting from her pregnancy. It upheld the right to exclude a pregnant woman from the state's disability benefit plan because, in its view, the exclusion was based on her pregnancy, rather than her sex. In *General Electric Company v. Gilbert* (1976), a majority drew a similar distinction between pregnancy and sex under Title VII. As in *Geduldig*, it ruled that excluding pregnant women from a company's disability plan was not discriminatory because there were women in the group of nonpregnant workers who did not face discrimination. The following year, in *Nashville Gas Company v. Satty* (1977), the high court held that the employer did not violate Title VII by denying sick pay to an employee on maternity leave. As these rulings indicate, the Supreme Court did not equate discrimination against pregnant women with sex discrimination. However, the public disagreed.

In response to these rulings, a coalition of more than 300 groups that called itself the Campaign to End Discrimination Against Pregnant Workers formed to lobby Congress to overturn the *Gilbert* decision and repeal discriminatory laws (Gelb and Palley 1987). As the coalition pointed out, since only women can become pregnant, the absence of legislation prohibiting pregnancy discrimination particularly harms women. In less than a year, Congress drafted legislation aimed at reversing *Gilbert*; in 1978, the Pregnancy Discrimination Act (PDA) passed with overwhelming support. An amendment to Title VII, the PDA prohibits discrimination based on pregnancy, directly acknowledging it as a form of sex discrimination. The new law followed the EEOC interpretation of Title VII and pregnancy by requiring employers with fifteen or more employees to treat pregnancy-related disabilities as they do other temporary disabilities. Employers who offered disability or sick leave policies would have to include coverage for all conditions related to pregnancy and childbirth.

The Courts and Preferential Treatment

The passage of the PDA began a much-needed conversation about pregnancy and employment. Women's rights advocates were largely united in their support of the antidiscrimination law but disagreed about how far legal protection for women should extend; thus, a debate ensued between feminists advocating special treatment for women and those promoting equal treatment. On one side, feminists favoring special treatment asserted that pregnancy presents unique obstacles for women in the workforce, obstacles that do not exist for men. For women to achieve equality, they argued, maternity benefits that recognize these unique needs are necessary. On the other side, equal treatment feminists argued that singling women out for special treatment would penalize them in the long run because employers would be apprehensive about hiring them if they believed they required more workplace benefits than men. Equal treatment advocates also feared that maternity benefits would reinforce the idea that a woman's primary responsibility is to care for her home and family (Huckle 1981; Williams 1984–1985; Taub 1985; Finley 1986; Symes 1987; Vogel 1990; Vogel 1995).

The courts entered the debate over special treatment versus equal treatment in the 1980s when an employee of the California Federal Savings and Loan Association was fired after taking maternity leave. Under California's 1978 Pregnancy Disability Leave Law, employers with five or more employees were required to provide pregnant women up to four months of unpaid leave and guarantee them a position upon their return. But when the employee tried to reclaim her job after eight weeks of leave, she found that the bank had hired a replacement and had no openings for a similar position. She turned to the California Fair Housing and Employment Commission, but before it could act, her employer, along with the California Chamber of Commerce and the Merchants and Manufacturers Association, filed suit in federal court. They argued that the California law violated the PDA's nondiscrimination principle because men with disabilities did not receive the same kind of benefits as pregnant women—that is, they could not take pregnancy leave. The California federal district court judge agreed and ruled in favor of the bank.

The ruling intensified the debate over preferential treatment, and women's organizations in favor of equal treatment, such as the National Organization for Women (NOW) and the Women's Rights Project of the American Civil Liberties Union, found themselves in a difficult position because they believed that any law advantaging women workers would ultimately lead to discrimination against them in the workforce. Although they ostensibly sided with the bank, they did not support repealing the California law; rather, they argued that its benefits should be extended to all temporarily disabled workers. Such a change would mean that pregnant workers would maintain job protection without being singled out for special treatment. On the other side of the debate, women's organizations, such as Coalition for Reproductive Equality in the Workplace and the 9 to 5 National Association of Working Women, voiced their opposition to the court's decision. These activists claimed that to achieve equality, women needed laws acknowledging that only they can bear children. The groups said that by granting pregnant women work-related privileges, the California law made women and men more equal by allowing both sexes to exercise their reproductive rights without fear of losing their jobs (Leo 1986; Radigan 1988).

The Ninth Circuit Court of Appeals reversed the district court, holding that the California pregnancy leave law violated the PDA (*California Federal Savings and Loan v. Guerra* 1985). Two years later, in *California Federal Savings and Loan v. Guerra* (1987), the Supreme Court upheld the circuit court, agreeing that by enacting the PDA, Congress had intended "to construct a floor beneath which pregnancy disability benefits may not drop—not a ceiling above which they may not rise" (285, quoting *California Federal Savings and Loan v. Guerra* 1985, 396). The high court ruled that the PDA did not preempt the California law because the intent of both was the same. Moreover, it said, the laws did not conflict because an employer could comply with both at the same time by providing disability leave and job protection to all employees, regardless of their sex.

Guerra did not end the debate over preferential treatment, and the courts have yet to articulate a consistent approach to pregnancy in the workplace. A Montana case that arose in the early 1980s underscores the courts' inconsistent approach to pregnancy and employment. In 1984, the Montana Supreme Court was asked to rule on the validity of the 1975 Montana Maternity Leave Act (MMLA) after an employee charged the Miller-Wohl Company with violating the act by firing her because she was unable to work during the early months of her pregnancy. The company allowed its employees to take sick days, but she was ineligible because she had been employed less than a year. The state labor commission upheld her claim. Meanwhile, the company, asserting it did not treat this female employee differently than men who failed to show up to work, turned to the Montana federal district court for relief, arguing that the MMLA violated the equal protection clause of the Fourteenth Amendment by giving pregnant women preferential treatment. The district court rejected Miller-Wohl's interpretation, holding that on the contrary, the MMLA placed women on an equal basis with men by eliminating pregnancy-related illnesses as a cause for terminating employment (*Miller-Wohl Company v. Commissioner of Labor and Industry* 1981). The court also recognized that by guaranteeing women's wages during pregnancy, the law "help[ed] support the family" (1267). Moreover, it ruled, the state law did not conflict with the PDA because an employer could comply with both simply by extending its sick day policy to men and women employees in their first year on the job. The Ninth Circuit agreed and dismissed Miller-Wohl's appeal (*Miller-Wohl Company v. Commissioner of Labor and Industry* 1982).

When the company sought relief from the labor commission's ruling in the Montana state court, the judge agreed that the MMLA discriminated against disabled nonpregnant women and men in favor of pregnant women and was preempted by the PDA. On appeal in the state supreme court, women's rights activists were divided on whether to support the lower state court ruling. In any event, the Montana Supreme Court reversed the court below, holding that while the law appeared to be gender neutral, it penalized women in a way it did not penalize men. Echoing the federal court, the state supreme court found that an employer could comply with the MMLA and the PDA by allowing all first-year employees to take sick leave (*Miller-Wohl Company v. Commissioner of Labor and Industry* 1984). Somewhat inexplicably, the high court vacated the state supreme court decision and, without explanation, ordered it to reconsider it in light of its ruling in *Guerra* (*Miller-Wohl Company v. Commissioner of Labor and Industry* 1987a). After reconsidering its opinion, the state supreme court said it saw no reason to reverse its judgment and reinstated its ruling in the plaintiff's favor, awarding her attorneys' fees (*Miller-Wohl Company v. Commissioner of Labor and Industry* 1987b). The employee ultimately won her suit and was awarded back pay and legal costs but the controversy over equal treatment versus special treatment remained unresolved (Fitzgerald 1988).

The Supreme Court continued to equivocate about the role of pregnancy in the workplace when it ruled on a woman's claim against Missouri for denying her unemployment benefits. The plaintiff's employer refused to reinstate her when she sought to return to work after her pregnancy leave. The state denied her claim for unemployment benefits, declaring her ineligible because she had left work because of her pregnancy rather than a reason directly attributable to the job or her employer. The Court decided that the state did not violate the 1935 Federal Unemployment Tax Act (FUTA), a law prohibiting the denial of unemployment compensation solely based on pregnancy, because pregnancy was only one of many reasons for denying a claim (*Wimberly v. Labor and Industrial Relations Commission* 1987). According to the Court's convoluted explanation, FUTA precluded treating pregnant women differently but did not mandate special treatment (Radford 1988).

As these cases demonstrate, the Supreme Court has ruled inconsistently on pregnancy in the workplace. Its decisions "range[d] from minimally endorsing the preferential treatment law in *Guerra* to refusing to express an opinion on the more far-reaching maternity leave policy in *Miller-Wohl* to narrowly construing the federal statute banning discrimination on the basis of pregnancy in *Wimberly*" (Mezey 2011, 173). In 2015, the Court revisited the issue when a former driver for United Parcel Service charged that the company violated the PDA by forcing her to take unpaid leave—and lose her employee medical coverage—rather than accommodate the pregnancy-related lifting restrictions recommended by her doctor. Its ruling adopted a middle ground between the pregnant worker and the employer. It held that to prevail in a lawsuit, a pregnant employee must show that her employer refused to accommodate her pregnancy-related medical condition while accommodating other employees who had similar medical conditions unrelated to pregnancy (*Young v. United Parcel Service, Inc.* 2015).

Women's rights advocates were hopeful after the Court's ruling in *Young*, believing that it would make it more likely that pregnant women denied workplace accommodations would win legal cases against their employers. They soon discovered that it is extremely difficult to prove that other employees are receiving accommodations denied to pregnant employees. In a review of dozens of discrimination cases in the wake of *Young*, the legal advocacy organization A Better Balance found that in over two-thirds of them, courts sided with employers that had denied pregnant workers accommodations (Bakst, Gedmark, and Brafman 2019). The judicial landscape after *Young* therefore remains muddled at best.

As advocates lose faith in the courts to uphold the rights of pregnant women, they have increasingly turned their attention to legislative bodies. Almost two-thirds of states have adopted pregnancy accommodation laws, but because the details of each law differ, there continues to be confusion about what constitutes pregnancy discrimination and accommodation. National lawmakers are hoping to clarify this through the Pregnant Workers Fairness Act, which would require employers to provide reasonable accommodations to employees who are affected by pregnancy, childbirth, or related medical conditions, unless those accommodations would cause the employer undue hardship. First introduced in 2012, the act cleared the House twice without being voted on in the Senate. Even as legislative support for the bill grew, many Republican lawmakers refused to vote for it without exemptions for religious organizations, fearing that employers would have to accommodate workers who have an abortion (Gupta and Petri 2021; Wiessner 2021). Still, the act passed in December 2022.

The Family and Medical Leave Act

The PDA was a victory for the women's movement, proving to be beneficial for many pregnant women in the workforce. Less progress has been made on the issue of family leave, and the United States remains the only industrialized country in the world without a national paid leave policy (OECD Family Database n.d.). In their struggle for the government to enact a national family leave policy, women's rights activists have largely adopted a gender-neutral approach by advocating policies that would advance the needs of families beyond work-related protections for pregnant women. With little agreement among members of Congress, issues of work-family balance have largely moved to state and local legislative bodies, as well as the executive branch. Moreover, a growing number of businesses have assumed the responsibility of providing paid leave and, in some cases, childcare, to their employees in the absence of a national public policy commitment.

As the number of employed women in the nation increased, Congress began to evince a greater interest in policies that offer more security to workers and their families. The Family and Medical Leave Act (FMLA) of 1993 (29 USC §2601), the first federal law to offer significant benefits to working families, affords qualified workers up to twelve weeks of job-protected unpaid leave for their own serious illness or injury or to care for a new child or family member with a serious health condition. As it became clear that many workers could not afford to take time off without pay, by 2022, eleven states and Washington, DC, as well as a growing number of cities, counties, and private businesses, have implemented paid family leave policies to cover the gap left by the federal legislation.

The first version of the FMLA, the Family Employment Security Act (FESA), was written in 1984 but never formally introduced in Congress. It provided workers up to twenty-six weeks of job-protected leave for their own disabilities or to care for a new child or a spouse or child who suffers from a serious illness or disability. Setting the precedent for future bills, the FESA's coverage was gender neutral and included disability leave and family leave for reasons other than the arrival of a new child. Most equal treatment feminists endorsed the proposed legislation, but not all activists supported this approach. Some still advocated special treatment for women, such as additional disability leave during pregnancy. Others worried that a more inclusive bill such as the FESA would face greater opposition in Congress than a bill that covered only a child's arrival in the family. After the demise of the Equal Rights Amendment in 1982 and the growing influence of the religious right during the Ronald Reagan administration, some activists sought a bill that would gain support from social conservatives who claimed to be pro-family. Legislation that centered on parents' ability to spend more time with their new children—as well as reinforced the idea that pregnant women need special treatment—was more likely to pass in the political climate of the 1980s, and many activists were eager for a success for the women's movement after several perceived losses (Elving 1995; Bernstein 2001).

Women's movement leaders played a vital role in placing family leave on the federal government's public policy agenda and on the public's radar (Bernstein 2001). After the initial bill was written, the coalition advocating family leave quickly grew to include organizations centered on children and seniors and around issues of labor, disability, and religion (Asher and Lenhoff 2001, 116; Sholar 2016a, chap. 2). In Congress, Representative Patricia Schroeder (D-CO), co-chair of the Congressional Caucus on Women's Issues and the most senior Democratic congresswoman, took the lead. Schroeder's seat on the Education and Labor Committee was a natural fit for the development of family leave legislation (Wisensale 2001). On April 4, 1985, she introduced the Parental and Disability Leave Act (PDLA) on the floor of the House. As with the FESA, the new bill was gender neutral in language and benefits. Adopting a generous approach to benefits, the bill applied to companies with a minimum of five employees; it allowed twenty-six weeks over a twelve-month period of job-protected leave for workers with temporary disabilities unrelated to work, as well as eighteen weeks over a twenty-four-month period of parental leave for the birth, adoption, fostering, or serious illness of a child. An earlier version was even more generous and applied to all employers, but it was later amended to limit benefits to companies with at least five employees (Kaitin 1994). Though the leave was unpaid, employers were required to continue health benefits for employees during it and guarantee a return to employment at their previous level of seniority and benefits.

The PDLA made little progress in Congress. It had no cosponsors when introduced, and the first subcommittee meeting did not take place until six months after its initial reading in the House. It eventually passed through two House subcommittees, but a companion bill never materialized in the Senate (Wisensale 2001). Still, its introduction in the House represented progress. It gave family leave proponents a specific policy goal to advocate and provided a template for lawmakers to build on in future legislative sessions. The following year, Schroeder and her Democratic colleagues introduced the Parental and Medical Leave Act of 1986. Like its predecessor, it called for twenty-six weeks of disability leave and eighteen weeks of parental leave. Over the course of the legislative session, the name of the bill was changed to the Family and Medical Leave Act (Radigan 1988). It was also revised to include stricter guidelines, with the total time for either medical or family leave limited to thirty-six weeks over a two-year period. Moreover, the size of covered companies was increased from five to fifteen employees, and a three-month or 500-hour qualifying term of employment was added. At the same time, coverage expanded beyond parents, allowing employees leave to care for a child, spouse, or parent with a serious illness or injury (Wisensale 2001). The bill was approved in several House committees and subcommittees but was never considered by the full House (Lenhoff and Bell n.d.).

As the movement for family leave gained momentum, the business community grew increasingly vocal in its opposition to what it dubbed an "unfunded mandate" that would open the door to greater government intervention and ultimately, they claimed, would cost businesses a large share of their profits. After the introduction of the PDLA in 1986, the US Chamber of Commerce urged its members to oppose it; consequently, numerous small business owners asked their members of Congress to vote against it. Similarly, the National Association of Manufacturers, the Society for Human Resources Management, and the National Federation of Independent Business directed resources toward defeating family leave legislation and encouraged businesses to contact their legislators to voice their concerns. In 1987, the Concerned Alliance of Responsible Employers formed and subsequently became the lead organization in the effort to defeat family leave legislation. Ultimately, business interests created an anti-FMLA coalition of forty-three groups, with a clear message that family and medical leave policies should be voluntary, not mandatory (Radigan 1988; Elison 1997; Asher and Lenhoff 2001; Wisensale 2001; Anthony 2008). To reinforce their view, they pointed out that over half the states and numerous companies already provided some sort of family and medical leave without a federal mandate (Friedman 1990; US Department of Labor, Women's Bureau 1993; Kelly and Dobbin 1999).

Family leave advocates were not deterred, especially as Democrats had gained a majority in both houses of Congress in the 1986 elections. In the first few weeks of the 100th Congress in 1987, Democrats again introduced family leave legislation in each house, and over the next three years, a family leave bill was introduced each legislative session and passed through committees and subcommittees with legislators continuing to debate company size, eligibility requirements, and generosity of benefits. As the number of covered companies and workers decreased, support from moderate Republicans increased. Even some conservative Republicans and the US Catholic Conference eventually came out in favor of the bill because they thought it might lead to fewer abortions if women were provided resources to better balance their work and family lives (Radigan 1988; Bernstein 2001).

In May 1990, the House passed a bill that provided twelve weeks unpaid family and medical leave during a twelve-month period to employees who had worked at least 1,000 hours in the previous year for a company with at least fifty employees. The leave could be taken to care for a new child, an employee's own health condition, or a child, spouse, or parent with a serious illness or injury. The following month, the Senate passed the House bill with no amendments, but President George H. W. Bush vetoed it (Lenhoff and Bell n.d.). In 1991, Congress again had the necessary votes to pass a family and medical leave bill. Recognizing that—as in 1990—the House did not have sufficient votes to override the veto they expected from Bush, lawmakers paused work on the policy for the remainder of the session. Because 1992 was a presidential election year, family leave advocates hoped that they could pressure Bush to sign the bill to win greater electoral support from the working families who would benefit most from the legislation. But in September 1992, he vetoed the bill again. To avoid drawing attention to his second veto of legislation that was growing in popularity, Bush reiterated his support for family leave on a voluntary basis while maintaining that government-mandated leave would harm business and limit economic growth. He urged Congress to pass legislation that would provide tax credits to businesses that voluntarily provided family leave to their employees (Wines 1992).

The prospects for family leave increased dramatically in 1993. Not only did Democrats maintain a majority in both houses of Congress following the 1992 elections, but Democrat President Bill Clinton—who had campaigned on the issue of family leave—won the presidency. On February 5, 1993, only a few weeks after taking office, he signed the FMLA into law, making it his administration's first major piece of legislation. In its final form, the act guaranteed twelve weeks of unpaid job-protected leave during a twelve-month period to eligible employees for the birth, adoption, or fostering of a child; the care of a child, spouse, or parent with a serious illness or injury; or the employee's own serious health condition. Unlike other countries that have separate programs for parental leave and leave to care for a sick relative, in the United States, these categories were grouped under the term "family leave." To qualify for leave under the law, employees must have worked at least 1,250 hours in the previous year for the same employer with fifty or more employees in a seventy-five-mile radius; only private companies with at least fifty employees, as well as all public agencies and local education agencies, are covered. Employers must continue to provide health benefits to their employees on leave but are permitted to deny leave to employees in the top 10 percent of the pay scale. If both parents work for the same employer, they must divide the twelve weeks of leave between them to care for a new child or a family member with a serious health condition.

While celebrating the passage of the FMLA, the activists who fought for it also hoped that it would be the first in a long line of family leave policies. Most wanted coverage for a greater number of workers and leaves that included wage replacement. To their dismay, in the decades since the FMLA became law, little has been done to expand its benefits. Since 1993, only a handful of amendments have been added to broaden coverage, and there has been no move toward paid leave in the FMLA.

In January 2008, President George W. Bush signed the National Defense Authorization Act for fiscal year 2008, creating new leave benefits for members of the armed forces and their families. Under this law, eligible employees can take up to twelve weeks of unpaid leave during a twelve-month period when a service member is on active duty. In addition, employees may qualify for up to twenty-six weeks of leave to care for a service member with a serious health condition. President Barack Obama later expanded these benefits in the National Defense Authorization Act for fiscal year 2010. In December 2009, the Airline Flight Technical Corrections Act clarified eligibility requirements for airline crew members, specifying they were eligible for FMLA leave if, during the previous twelve-month period, they worked or had been paid for at least 60 percent of applicable monthly guaranteed hours, which must total at least 504 hours. In December 2019, President Donald Trump extended twelve weeks of paid parental leave to federal employees, but that remains the only national paid leave policy.

After the benefit expansions of the 2000s, the Department of Labor (DOL) clarified that an employee may qualify for leave under the FMLA to care for the child of a same-sex partner (US Department of Labor 2010). Additionally, as part of the Obama administration's commitment to marriage equality, in 2015, DOL modified the definition of "spouse" under the FMLA to allow eligible employees in a legal same-sex marriage leave to care for their spouse (US Department of Labor 2015a). Despite this expanded coverage, by 2020, only about 56 percent of workers were eligible for FMLA leave. The remaining 44 percent do not qualify because of the size of their workplaces or insufficient employment tenure or hours worked (Brown et al. 2020). Even when they qualify for FMLA leave, many women find that the benefit comes with hidden costs.

Gender and Work-Life Balance

Most family leave advocates believed the passage of the FMLA a victory, viewing it as the federal government's long-awaited acknowledgment that it has a responsibility to help families achieve a better work-life balance. Many feminists also praised lawmakers' language that centered on gender equality, as the act stated its purpose was to "promote the goal of equal employment opportunity for women and men." Recognizing that "the primary responsibility for family caretaking often falls on women . . . and affects the working lives of women more than it affects the working lives of men," the law's drafters had instituted gender-neutral family leave to allow men to share caretaking responsibilities. In other words, as Deborah Anthony (2008) notes, the intent of the FMLA was to "alleviate a pattern of historic and unconstitutional gender discrimination" (473).

The act's commitment to expand gender equality in the workplace, a necessary first step, has fallen short of its stated goal, for regardless of their employment status, women continue to assume most caregiving responsibilities. As a 2012 survey of workers' experiences with the FMLA showed, female workers take 61.7 percent of caregiving leaves for a child (Glynn 2018; Armenia and Gerstel 2006; Klerman, Daley, and Pozniak 2012; Hess, Ahmed, and Hayes 2020). At first glance, results from a later 2018 FMLA Employee Survey seem to suggest that the caregiving gap may have closed, for women and men now report taking leave for the same reasons: 50 percent for their own health condition, 30 percent to care for someone else, and 20 percent for a new child. Upon closer examination, the gender gap in caregiving responsibilities becomes apparent. First, more women (18 percent) take leave than men (14 percent), even though more men are eligible for FMLA leave than women (64 percent versus 59 percent). Second, women's average leaves last thirty-four days, while men take twenty-one days on average. This difference is largely explained by women taking longer leaves for a new child (fifty-four days) than men (eighteen days) (Herr, Roy, and Klerman 2020; Brown et al. 2020). Taken together, these statistics suggest that women are still taking more time off for caregiving responsibilities than men are. Because fewer women qualify for FMLA leave, they are also more likely to take unpaid leave with no guarantee of reinstatement or exit the workforce entirely to address their caregiving duties.

When there is tension between a worker's job and family responsibilities, the worker's potential for career advancement is likely to suffer because of lower productivity and greater turnover (Glass and Estes 1997). A Pew Research Center (2019) study found that mothers are more likely than fathers to experience career interruptions because of their caregiving responsibilities: 42 percent of mothers and 28 percent of fathers have reduced work hours; 39 percent of mothers and 24 percent of fathers have taken significant time off; 27 percent of mothers and 10 percent of fathers have quit their jobs; and 13 percent of mothers and 10 percent of fathers have turned down a promotion. If workers take leave to maintain ties to their workplace, it is still possible their employers will view them as less committed to their jobs and offer them fewer opportunities for career advancement (Padavic and Reskin 2002). Because women take leave more often than men, it is more likely they will face such a stigma. Indeed, 26 percent of women say that family caregiving has negatively affected their ability to retain their jobs or advance in the workplace (Lenhart, Swenson, and Schulte 2019).

Gender Wage Gap and Family Responsibilities

Family responsibilities almost certainly explain part of the persistent gender gap in wages. Recent DOL figures show women's annual earnings are 82 percent of men's, with the wage gap generally larger for women of color (US Department of Labor, Bureau of Labor Statistics 2021d). Over a forty-year career, a woman earns over $400,000 less compared to her male counterpart; Black women typically lose over $900,000, Native American women over $1,000,000, and Latinas over $1,100,000 (Fins 2020). Because women leave the workplace—either temporarily or permanently—in higher numbers than men to fulfill caregiving responsibilities, they tend to have less work experience and fewer opportunities for promotion. They are also more likely to work part-time, which is typically accompanied by lower hourly wages and fewer benefits than full-time work (Bleiweis 2020).

A growing body of research has pointed to the effects of motherhood on wages, concluding that mothers earn less than women without children (Staff and Mortimer 2012; Jee, Misra, and Murray-Close 2019; Kleven, Landais, and Søgaard 2019). The FMLA allows many mothers time off work to care for their children. Yet this (unpaid) time away from work undermines women's earning potential. Similarly, because FMLA leave is unpaid, most couples decide that the partner with the lower salary—which, in a heterosexual relationship, is more likely to be the woman—should stay home to act as caregiver. Though the FMLA has been praised for its gender-neutral language, the law has done little to alleviate gender inequality. Women continue to take more time off work for caregiving purposes, reinforcing the idea that they should be the primary caretakers in the family and hurting them economically in both the short term and over the course of their careers. To advance equal opportunities for women workers, at a minimum, family leave policies must be expanded to include wage replacement.

Paid Family Leave

Since the passage of the FMLA in 1993, there has been an endless stream of proposals to expand the policy to help individuals reconcile their work lives with their family obligations. Over 35 million workers are employed at firms with either fewer than fifty employees or more than fifty employees outside the required seventy-five-mile radius; lowering the minimum employer size or location threshold of the FMLA would ensure that more workers are covered. About 20 percent of workers do not work full-time, which means they often do not meet the FMLA's hours-worked requirement. Women, who are more likely than men to work part-time or hold multiple part-time jobs, are especially hurt by this. Lowering the number of hours an employee must work before becoming eligible for leave would allow millions more employees in the private sector to access leave when they need it (Jorgensen and Appelbaum 2014; National Partnership for Women and Families 2020a).

Most caregivers (89 percent) care for a relative, but more than one-quarter of these family caregiver relationships fall outside of the FMLA's coverage: 8 percent of caregivers provide for a grandparent, 8 percent care for a parent-in-law, 7 percent care for a sibling, and 6 percent care for other relatives (AARP and National Alliance for Caregiving 2020). Broadening the definition of "family member" would ensure that a greater number of caregiving relationships would be covered under the FMLA. Removing the provision that forces spouses who work at the same company to divide their leave time between them would increase the total amount of caregiving that a family could undertake. Allowing both spouses to take the full amount of leave would also make it more likely that different-sex couples would have a more egalitarian division of caregiving labor (National Partnership for Women and Families 2020a). Activists have advocated for these types of revisions from the moment the FMLA was signed into law—with little success. But the most frequent recommendation to improve family leave policy in the United States has been wage replacement.

Only 23 percent of workers in the United States have access to paid family leave through their employers, which means that millions of workers are not receiving an income when the need to take leave arises

(US Department of Labor, Bureau of Labor Statistics 2021c). Consequently, many either take a shortened leave or forgo it altogether. A 2020 study showed that 7 percent of employees reported needing leave for a qualifying FMLA reason within the previous twelve months but ultimately took no leave. In comparison, 15 percent of employees said that they needed leave and took it. In other words, unmet need for leave among workers is about half as common as taking leave. Moreover, it is not spread evenly across all groups. Unmet need for leave is more common among low-wage workers, Black workers, women, and employees living in single-parent households (Brown et al. 2020).

The primary reason workers do not take needed leave is financial concern: 66 percent of employees with unmet need for leave report that they could not afford to take unpaid leave. More than half of workers who lost some or all their earnings during leave report that they would have taken a longer leave if additional pay had been available. This issue is especially pressing for low-income workers, as they are the least likely to have access to paid leave; only 12 percent of private-sector workers in the bottom quarter of wage earners have paid leave, while 37 percent of the top quarter of earners receive it (US Department of Labor, Bureau of Labor Statistics 2022). Such class-based factors are intertwined with race, ethnicity, and gender. Thus, Black and Latinx employees are less likely to have access to paid parental leave than white employees (Glynn and Farrell 2012; Gupta et al. 2018). Because people from marginalized groups are more likely to be low-income workers, it is often difficult for them to take uncompensated leave. Citing financial reasons, nearly one in four employed mothers returns to work within two weeks of giving birth (Lerner 2015). Among employees who do not receive full wage replacement during leave, two-thirds say that it is difficult to make ends meet while on leave. To compensate, these workers often limit their spending or tap into their savings. Almost a third of workers report they must borrow money, delay paying bills, or cut their leave short due to financial concerns. To cover lost earnings, 17 percent of workers—including 26 percent of low-wage workers—go on public assistance during their unpaid leave (Brown et al. 2020).

Women who return to their jobs after paid leave are 39 percent less likely to receive public assistance in the year following a child's birth than women who take no leave at all. In other words, women who receive paid family leave are more likely to be financially stable in the period following that leave than women who do not have access to paid leave (Houser and Vartanian 2012). Viewing the nation more broadly, the absence of paid family and medical leave costs workers and their families an estimated $22.5 billion in lost wages each year. In the family, women are the most negatively affected: they lose approximately $9 billion a year, while men's estimated losses are closer to $1.2 billion (Glynn 2020). The negative economic effects are often felt most acutely by people of color, as they are less likely to have savings or other forms of income while on leave. As a 2020 study noted, 45 percent of Hispanic adults and 52 percent of Black adults, compared with 23 percent of white adults, say that it would be difficult or impossible to cover a $400 unexpected expense without selling something or going into debt (Federal Reserve Board 2020). Adding wage replacement to family leave in the United States would lessen the financial burden on employees—especially those in the lowest quarter of earners—who take leave and increase the number of workers who take the leave available to them. Such changes would positively affect gender equality in the home and the workplace.

These data show that the FMLA has done little to improve the gender gap in unpaid labor, as women continue to do most of the care work and domestic labor and remain more likely than men to take family leave. Because of outdated gender norms, many men still feel pressure to prioritize being a financial provider over being a caregiver. Therefore, they often limit the amount of family leave they take from work—especially when that leave is unpaid (Rehel and Baxter 2015; Harrington et al. 2014). If leave were paid, both the number of men who take leave and the average duration of men's leave would undoubtedly increase (Appelbaum and Milkman 2011; Baum and Ruhm 2016). An added benefit of leave is that when new fathers take two or more weeks of parental leave, they are more likely to remain involved in their children's care for the first years of their lives (Nepomnyaschy and Waldfogel 2007; Petts and Knoester 2018). This contributes to increased gender equality in the home, as studies show that a more equitable division of labor and care work develops when fathers in two-parent heterosexual households take paid parental leave (Rehel 2014). Not only does this shifting distribution of duties challenge the idea that women are and should be the primary caregivers, but it also helps reduce the stereotype of women as the employees most likely to take leave.

The lack of comprehensive paid family leave disproportionately hurts women in the workforce. Their limited access to paid leave in the United States helps explain why their labor force participation has been declining since 2000, after peaking at 60 percent in 1999. Women are more likely than men to reduce their working hours or leave the workforce after the birth of a child, but when new mothers receive paid leave, they are more likely to remain in the workforce, work a greater number of hours, and see their wages increase (Houser and Vartanian 2012; Rossin-Slater, Ruhm, and Waldfogel 2013; Baum and Ruhm 2016). It is not surprising that 48 percent of women say that greater access to paid family and medical leave "would help a lot with managing work and family responsibilities." These numbers are even higher for women of color (Lenhart, Swenson, and Schulte 2019). Men can play a significant role in women's ability to maintain ties to the labor market. More men taking paid leave and assuming a greater share of the unpaid labor at home would facilitate women returning to work. This would have long-term effects on women's earning potential over the course of their careers. A study in Sweden found that each month of parental leave taken by a child's father increased the mother's wages by almost 7 percent (Johannson 2010).

In addition to improving gender equality, paid leave has a positive influence on the health and well-being of women and their children. If mothers can take at least twelve weeks of leave after giving birth, their children have a better chance of avoiding significant health or developmental problems in the first year of life because it is more likely they will be breast-fed and receive regular checkups and necessary immunizations (Berger, Hill, and Waldfogel 2005; Daku, Raub, and Heymann 2012; Jou et al. 2018). Mothers who take at least eight weeks of paid leave are less likely to experience postpartum depression and generally report better overall health than those without such opportunities (Chatterji and Markowitz 2012; Jou et al. 2018). Women who receive paid parental leave are also less likely to have low-birth-weight babies (Stearns 2015). Additionally, when job-protected paid leave is available, infant mortality rates decrease substantially (Tanaka 2005; Patton, Costich, and Lidströmer 2017).

Paid leave plays an important role in infant development because new mothers without it typically take less time off work after the birth of a child than mothers who receive paid leave (McGovern et al. 2000; Guendelman et al. 2014; Lerner 2015). As with gender equality in the home and workplace, men's access to and subsequent uptake of paid leave positively affects the health and well-being of mothers and children. When fathers take paid leave, new mothers have fewer postpartum health complications and report improved mental health (Persson and Rossin-Slater 2019). Furthermore, children's emotional stability and educational attainment are generally improved when fathers play a greater role in their lives (Lamb 2010).

The benefits of family and medical leave extend to businesses as well. Workplace flexibility and family-friendly policies can attract top talent in a competitive market, and companies that provide paid family leave have lower turnover rates than those without paid leave. These higher retention rates save businesses a significant amount of money, reducing costs of recruiting and training new employees. A company can spend between 5.8 percent and 213 percent of an employee's annual salary to find a suitable replacement, depending on the position and employee skill set (A Better Balance 2010; Boushey and Glynn 2012; Stroman et al. 2017). In addition to lower turnover rates, paid leave generally increases productivity, profitability, and employee morale (Appelbaum and Milkman 2013; Panorama and American Sustainable Business Council 2019). Overall, individual businesses that do not offer paid leave lose their competitive edge to companies that have successfully implemented paid leave benefits. These effects are also felt on the national level; the government estimates that the nation loses more than $500 billion of additional economic activity each year because of the absence of paid leave (US Department of Labor 2015b).

Recognizing the importance of wage replacement during leaves, activists have struggled for decades to attain it. Some organizations, such as NOW and the Fund for a Feminist Majority, even rescinded their support for the FMLA prior to its passage because they believed the unpaid benefits were too meager (Bernstein 2001). In the decades after its passage, there was little progress on leave policies at the federal level. When asked to attend the celebration of the FMLA's twentieth anniversary in 2013, Schroeder, sponsor of the first version of the law, said, "Are you kidding? I'm so embarrassed you haven't expanded this. What are we celebrating? It's still unpaid" (quoted in Voss 2015, 166). In the absence of national progress, many state and local governments have taken the lead on paid family leave.

State Paid Family Leave Policies

Before the FMLA was enacted, thirty-four states, Washington, DC, and Puerto Rico had adopted their own type of unpaid family leave legislation; the laws varied significantly in coverage and length of leave (US Department of Labor, Women's Bureau 1993). The focus had briefly shifted to the federal level when the FMLA passed, and legislators introduced almost twenty bills to expand the law nationwide between 1993 and 1999. In a Congress dominated by Republicans, these bills made little progress, and many family leave advocates eventually turned their attention to other issues or set their sights on pursuing paid leave policies at the state level. In 2001 alone, twenty-six states introduced paid leave legislation (Wisensale 2003). By 2016, over one-third of states were offering family leave benefits more generous than the FMLA, such as covering employees in small businesses and part-time workers, expanding definitions of family members, or allowing more than twelve weeks of leave (National Partnership for Women and Families 2016). While such expansions of family leave policies are beneficial to covered workers and their families, most research indicates that adding wage replacement to family leave would bring about the greatest benefit and best address gender inequity in the home and workplace. By 2022, about one-third of states provided some or all state employees paid parental leave, ranging from three to twelve weeks to care for a new child. An increasing number of cities and counties have also adopted paid leave policies for government employees. Eleven states and Washington, DC, have gone further, enacting paid family leave policies for nearly all workers.

California adopted its Paid Family Leave (PFL) insurance program for private-sector employees—the first of its kind in the United States—in 2002. Under the PFL, workers receive 60–70 percent of their average weekly wage, up to $1,540 a week in 2022, for eight weeks to bond with a new child, care for a family member with a serious health condition, or provide care while a family member is on active duty in the military. The program is funded by a 1.1 percent tax on employees' wages. For individuals in companies with at least twenty employees, the California Family Rights Act provides job protection (California Employment Development Department n.d.).

California paved the way for other states to enact their own versions of paid family leave, beginning with New Jersey in 2008. The New Jersey paid family leave policy provides employees up to twelve weeks of family leave to care for a new child, a family member with a serious health condition, or address issues related to domestic or sexual violence. The plan is funded by employees through a payroll deduction of 0.14 percent; employees on leave receive 85 percent of their average weekly wage, which is capped at $993 a week in 2022. Under the New Jersey Family Leave Act, workers in companies with at least thirty employees receive job protection (New Jersey Department of Labor and Workforce Development n.d.).

In 2013, Rhode Island became the first state to include job protection in its paid family leave program, which provides five weeks to bond with a new child or care for a family member with a serious health condition. In 2023, available leave time will increase to six weeks. Employees receive approximately 60 percent of their average weekly wage, up to $1,007 a week in 2022, funded by a 1.1 percent payroll deduction on employees (Rhode Island Department of Labor and Training n.d.). Like in Rhode Island, New York's program includes job protection for family leave. Passed in 2016, the New York policy allows employees twelve weeks to care for a new child or a family member with a serious health condition, as well as to address certain military family needs. During their leave, employees receive 67 percent of their average weekly salary, up to $1,068.36 a week in 2022, funded by a payroll deduction of 0.511 percent of employees' wages (New York State n.d.).

It took six years for New Jersey to become the second state to adopt paid family leave after California. It was another five years before Rhode Island became the third state to do so. The momentum behind paid leave was growing steadily throughout that period, and since the passage of New York's law in 2016, there has been a tidal wave of state-level legislation addressing the need for improved work-life balance. The District of Columbia's paid leave policy, adopted in 2017, was the first program completely funded by employers, who contribute 0.26 percent of the employees' wages. Workers can take up to twelve weeks of leave to care for a new child or a family member with a serious health condition. While on leave, employees receive 90 percent of their average weekly pay, capped at $1,009 a week in 2022. The District's Family and Medical Leave Act provides job protection for people at companies with at least twenty employees (District of Columbia Department of Employment Services n.d.).

In 2007, Washington state had been the second state after California to pass paid family leave, but the policy was never implemented because it lacked a funding mechanism. A decade later, Washington state adopted a revised bill with expanded coverage, providing employees 90 percent of their average weekly wage, up to $1,327 in 2022. They can take up to twelve weeks to bond with a new child, care for a family member with a serious illness or injury, or address certain military family needs. Leave is funded by a 0.6 percent premium on employees' wages; employers contribute approximately 26 percent of the premium, and employees contribute the rest. The policy includes job protection for workers who meet eligibility requirements related to the FMLA ("Washington Paid Family & Medical Leave" n.d.).

As a result of Massachusetts's 2018 law, workers can take up to twelve weeks for leave to care for a new child or a family member with a serious health condition and up to twenty-six weeks of military family leave. They receive 80 percent of their average weekly wage, capped at $1,084.31 in 2022; the plan is fully funded by the employees, at a premium of 0.12 percent of wages, and the leave is job protected ("Paid Family and Medical Leave Massachusetts" n.d.). Connecticut's law, enacted in 2019, is entirely funded by employees with a 0.5 percent premium on wages. It provides workers with up to twelve weeks of job-protected leave to care for a new child or a seriously ill or injured family member or to attend to certain military family responsibilities. Employees receive 95 percent of their average weekly wage while on leave, up to $840 in 2022 ("Connecticut Paid Leave" n.d.).

Starting in 2023, Oregon workers are entitled to take up to twelve weeks of job-protected paid parental or family leave, safe leave connected to domestic violence, or leave to care for a child whose school or childcare provider has closed due to a public health emergency. Under this plan, workers receive 100 percent of their average weekly wage, topped out at 120 percent of the statewide average weekly wage ($1,325.24 in 2022), funded by contributions from both employees and employers to cover the premium of 1 percent of wages (Oregon Employment Department n.d.). Enacted in 2020, Colorado's law will begin allocating benefits in 2024. Funded through employee and employer contributions totaling 0.9 percent of wages, the plan will provide workers 90 percent of their average weekly wage, topped off at $1,100, as well as job protection. They can take up to twelve weeks for parental and family leave, domestic violence safe leave, or leave related to military family responsibilities (Colorado Department of Labor and Employment n.d.).

In 2022, Maryland and Delaware passed paid family leave laws that provide twelve weeks of job-protected leave to care for a new child or a family member with a serious health condition, or to address certain military family needs. Maryland workers will receive up to 90 percent of their average weekly wage, capped initially at $1,000; benefits will begin in 2025. In Delaware, beginning in 2026, workers will receive up to 80 percent of their average weekly wage, capped initially at $900. Employees and employers will share the costs in each state (Brenner, Fant, and Arroyo 2022; Lynch and Salins 2022). In addition to the eleven states and District of Columbia that now mandate paid leave, in June 2021, New Hampshire became the first state to adopt a voluntary paid leave program. Beginning in 2023, all state employees automatically qualify for leave benefits and are exempt from paying premiums. Private employers and employees will retain the right to decide if they want to opt in and contribute premiums to the program that provides up to six weeks of leave at 60 percent pay (DeWitt 2021).

These state laws provide employees greater economic security while they are taking time from work to care for their families. Each state approaches the issue in a different fashion with respect to length and purpose of leave, source of funding, and level of wage replacement. As more states adopted paid family leave, the policies became more generous. Compared with the earlier state laws, the policies adopted since 2017 generally include more generous benefits, such as leave to care for a family member addressing issues of domestic violence or leave to care for a child whose school or childcare facility has closed in response to a public health emergency. All the policies enacted since 2018 include job protection. In recent years, the earliest states to adopt paid leave have also expanded their benefits to match this growing generosity. For example, California's initial law provided six weeks of leave and increased to eight weeks in 2020; similarly, New Jersey's leave time doubled from six to twelve weeks in 2020. Even with the increasing movement toward adopting family leave policies, this patchwork approach to legislation remains insufficient to meet the needs of families nationwide. To ensure that all workers have access to paid family leave, a federal law is necessary.

Federal Paid Family Leave

For more than two decades after the FMLA passed, there was little progress on the issue of paid leave at the federal level. State legislatures stepped in to fill the void, with most states introducing some type of paid family leave plan. There is still reason to hope for greater progress at the national level. The fact that eight states and the District of Columbia enacted paid leave between 2016 and 2022 demonstrates that momentum is increasing, potentially clearing the way for federal legislation. Similarly, public opinion in favor of paid leave continues to grow; at least three-fourths of voters across the political spectrum favor a national paid family and medical leave policy that covers all workers (National Partnership for Women and Families 2018; National Partnership for Women and Families 2020b).

During the 2016 presidential campaign, both the Democratic and Republican nominees spoke out in favor of paid family leave for the first time (Sholar 2016b). Moreover, support continues to grow in the business community. In March 2021, over 250 companies, ranging from Etsy to Patagonia to Spotify, sent an open letter to Congress urging lawmakers to pass paid leave legislation (PL + US [Paid Leave for the United States] n.d.). But perhaps the most telling indicator of things to come is the Federal Employees Paid Leave Act (FEPLA), passed in 2019, providing federal workers twelve weeks of paid parental leave to care for a new child (Brown et al. 2020). With over two million federal employees, this law can have a significant effect. But because the leave is limited to federal workers who welcome a new child, a substantial proportion of workers across the country are still deprived of the paid family leave they need.

In recent years, lawmakers have proposed several policies to address this problem, each of which would pose significant problems for workers. Some Republican legislators suggested allowing workers to tap into their Social Security benefits to fund up to three months of leave for new parents. Their proposals seek to avoid the need for new revenue to fund the benefit; workers who take leave would later delay or reduce future Social Security benefits (Miller 2019). A more recent bipartisan proposal would allow taxpayers to advance up to $5,000 in child tax credits on the birth or adoption of a child. To cover the funds, the parents would receive reduced child tax credits in each of the next ten years (Jagoda 2020). But the proposal to address the lack of paid leave that has attracted most of the nation's attention since 2013 is the Family and Medical Insurance Leave (FAMILY) Act. Introduced into every legislative session since 2013 by Senator Kirsten Gillibrand (D-NY) and Representative Rosa DeLauro (D-CT), the FAMILY Act (HR 804/S 248) would provide workers up to twelve weeks of partial income while on leave for their own serious health condition, to care for a new child or a seriously ill family member, or for military caregiving and leave purposes. By extending coverage beyond new parents, the act would provide leave to millions of workers in the United States who need to care for themselves and their families. Employees would earn up to 66 percent of their monthly wages, funded by both employee and employer contributions of 0.2 percent each. For a typical worker, the weekly contribution would be less than $2. Unlike most family leave proposals and policies, workers in all companies would be covered, regardless of their size (National Partnership for Women and Families 2021a).

The 2021 version of the FAMILY Act had over 200 cosponsors in the House and Senate, but its chances of passing remain slim (GovTrack

2021a; GovTrack 2021c). Most Republican lawmakers say that while they support the idea of paid family leave, they do not think it should be mandated by the government nor do they support funding it through new revenue sources. Therefore, their legislative proposals typically center on tax credits for businesses that voluntarily provide paid leave or plans that allow workers to postpone or borrow from future tax or retirement benefits to fund family leave. For most Republican lawmakers, the FAMILY Act is an expensive form of government overreach, and Democrats lack the votes to overcome their opposition in Congress.

Public support for government action on paid leave continues to grow—especially in the wake of the Covid-19 pandemic. During 2020, the first year of the pandemic, an estimated 2.3 million women and 1.8 million men in the United States left the workforce. Women were disproportionately affected because female-dominated industries such as education, health care, and hospitality were hit the hardest. Unemployment rates especially rose for women of color, younger women, and women with disabilities (Ewing-Nelson and Tucker 2021). In addition, the loss of reliable childcare and unpredictable school openings and closings have exacerbated the existing caregiving challenges predominantly assumed by women (UN Women 2020). In a January 2021 survey, 28 percent of women with children said they were out of work because they needed to care for their children who did not attend school or were enrolled in day care; only 12 percent of men with children gave this response (Rothwell and Saad 2021). Research supports these claims: a 2022 study of the 2020–2021 school year found that in districts with remote or hybrid learning, mothers' employment levels were much lower than in the year before the start of the pandemic. In those school districts, the gap between mothers' and fathers' employment was 4 percentage points greater compared with households in districts where children could attend school in person full time (Landivar et al. 2022). This combination of factors propelling women—especially women with children—out of the workforce has led analysts to dub the country's economic downturn its first "shecession" (Gupta 2020). It has also drawn renewed attention to the lack of policies to help workers address their caregiving responsibilities. Research into workplace policies during the pandemic reveals a clear trend of growing support among both employees and employers for a national paid leave public policy (PL + US [Paid Leave for the United States], Promundo, and Parental Leave Corporate Task Force 2021).

Childcare Policies

According to neoliberal economic principles, there is little room for the government to play a role in caregiving arrangements. In the United States, caregiving is typically seen as a private—and largely female— duty (Teghtsoonian 1993; Gornick and Meyers 2003). It is therefore not surprising that the nation lacks a comprehensive childcare system. What is remarkable is how close it had come to adopting an extensive federally funded program in the early 1970s.

Childcare centers in the United States can be traced back as early as the 1820s, though they were relatively rare at that time. They proliferated in the late 1800s primarily in response to the increasing number of poor, immigrant mothers who were forced into paid labor. Because society maintained that a woman's natural role was to care for her children in the home, families who needed outside childcare were stigmatized and often required to meet with social workers if they wanted to use the centers (Michel 1999). Thus began the enduring illusion that childcare outside the home is only needed as a response to dire circumstances, rather than a potentially valuable service for all families. Such a pattern fits with the development of social welfare programs in the United States more broadly.

During the Progressive Era in the late nineteenth and early twentieth centuries, the government addressed the changes brought by increased immigration and industrialization by regulating working conditions and reforming the health care and housing sectors. This marked a shift from its largely hands-off approach to economic issues up to then. In response to the Great Depression, which plunged millions into poverty in the 1930s, the New Deal delivered the country's first national social welfare programs. As with the earliest childcare centers, this social safety net was presented as a means of remedying the immediate economic crisis in the country, rather than an indicator of an enduring political ideology centered on the government's responsibility to support its citizens, least of all employed women. Most lawmakers continued to emphasize personal accountability and success based on individual merits, believing that the government should generally stay out of private family issues (White 2009; Jansson 2019). This perspective has largely guided the development of childcare policies in the United States, resulting in programs that are often available only to low-income families or during times of national crisis.

In the early twentieth century, relatives were still the most common source of childcare. But the Progressive Era saw an increase in the number of low-income single mothers—generally through widow-hood or desertion—and spurred the development of childcare (also known as daycare) centers. When the Great Depression struck, the Works Progress Administration (WPA) created daycare centers to pro-vide jobs for women. The idea of childcare outside the home was still largely considered atypical, as demonstrated by the fact that many child-care centers required mothers to prove that they had been abandoned to be eligible for their services. Moreover, the WPA program provided only eighteen months of assistance, for it had been created as a short-term solution to an immediate crisis; policymakers did not intend childcare outside the family to take the place of familial—and especially mater-nal—care permanently (Rose 1999).

When the United States entered World War II in 1941, many women joined the labor force to replace the men who were away at war. Rec-ognizing the crucial role women were playing in the war effort, the fed-eral government approved funding for states to build and staff afford-able childcare facilities for mothers with children under thirteen. Maternal employment increased significantly over the course of the war, but within a year of the war's end, the government withdrew fund-ing and most of the childcare centers closed. The state of emergency was over, and women were generally expected to resume their caregiv-ing roles in the home. For the next two decades, little attention was paid to childcare services because it was assumed that women—especially middle- and upper-class women—would remain out of the workforce to raise their children (Michel 1999; Herbst 2017). When the issue of the government's role in childcare was raised, it was typically in the context of low-income families. The most well-known program, Head Start, which provides childcare and early educational, health, and nutritional services to low-income children and their families, was created in 1965 as part of President Lyndon Johnson's War on Poverty. As the name suggests, the program centers on early intervention to address the needs of children from low-income families who were perceived to be at risk for falling behind once they started school (Zigler and Muenchow 1992). But in the early 1970s, lawmakers set out to broaden the scope of the program to make it available to all families who wished to use it, regardless of income.

In 1971, the Comprehensive Child Development Act (CCDA) passed with bipartisan support in the House and the Senate before being vetoed by President Richard Nixon. The CCDA would have provided federal funding for a national network of childcare centers and pre-school programs. The architects of the CCDA specifically designed it to be universally available, rather than only for low-income families. The government would have subsidized the costs so that tuition was based on income. Lower-income families would receive free services, while most middle-class households would pay a portion of the cost; families in the top 25 percent income bracket would pay the full fee. The program was based on a range of services; in addition to custodial care, the centers would provide meals, medical checkups, and educational programs. No family would be forced to use the services, but every family would have the option of doing so. When the bill arrived on Nixon's desk, it was unclear whether he would sign it. Indeed, he had ordered his staff to write a veto message and a signing message so that he could keep his options open. Proponents emphasized how the CCDA would foster development in low-income children and provide support to their families, help working mothers meet the challenge of balancing employment and family, and enable businesses to maintain a fully committed workforce. In the end, these arguments did not convince Nixon to sign the bill.

In what many consider a nod to the right wing of the Republican Party, Nixon said he vetoed the CCDA because it sounded too much like the communal policies of the Soviet Union and had the potential to weaken the American family. This may have been a way to placate Republicans who were unnerved by Nixon's upcoming trip to China to establish diplomatic relations with the Communist government. Moreover, by framing the bill as antithetical to American values, rather than something the government could not afford at the time, Nixon helped bury the whole idea of universal childcare. In the years immediately after the veto, members of Congress were inundated with letters demanding that they vote against legislation proposing government-funded childcare. This fervent condemnation was fueled by a widespread misinformation campaign that claimed such government programs would indoctrinate children, prevent parents from forcing their children to go to church, and allow children to sue their parents. While lawmakers later began to introduce more modest bills designed to permit low-income children to attend preschool or help their parents afford childcare, the United States has never come as close to implementing a universal childcare program as it did in 1971 (Klein 1992; Collins 2009).

In 1988, lawmakers again broached the subject of childcare with the Act for Better Child Care Services (ABC), a proposal that was markedly less comprehensive than the CCDA but would still make childcare more accessible to millions of families. The ABC would increase government funding to make childcare more affordable for low-income families and develop a system of resource and referral networks that would help states expand the number and variety of childcare services available to all families. Additionally, it would improve the quality of care by implementing minimum health and safety standards for childcare centers. To meet these requirements, states would receive federal funding for training, education, and salaries for childcare workers (Palley and Shdaimah 2014). The bill found bipartisan support in the House but did not gain traction in the Senate or with the president. Ultimately, lawmakers settled on a compromise to increase funding for childcare-related programs such as Head Start and the Child Care and Development Block Grant (CCDBG) Act of 1990, to largely provide subsidies to low-income parents to allow them to enter the workforce or participate in education and training activities (Klein 1992). In particular, the CCDBG has dedicated much of its funding to moving women off welfare and into the workforce.

In 1996, Clinton strengthened the government's efforts to remove women from the welfare rolls by signing the Personal Responsibility and Work Opportunity Reconciliation Act, a law that implemented work requirements and time limits on assistance for most welfare recipients. As part of this legislation, Congress created Temporary Assistance for Needy Families (TANF)—the new name for the program formerly known as Aid to Families with Dependent Children—and the Child Care and Development Fund (CCDF). Funded by the CCDBG and TANF, the CCDF became a single federal funding stream for states to provide financial assistance to low-income parents to access childcare (Palley and Shdaimah 2014).

Most government funding for childcare in the United States is aimed at low-wage workers. For families with higher incomes, the minimal assistance they receive is generally in the form of tax credits. In 1954, Congress revised the income tax code to allow divorced, widowed, and low-income women to deduct the cost of childcare so they could remain in the workforce. Over time, the deductions were extended to middle-class families as well. The day after Nixon vetoed the CCDA in 1971, the tax code was amended to expand the number of eligible families and increase deductions available for childcare and household service expenses. With universal childcare having been rejected because of its association with the Soviet Union, it is not surprising that the tax code changes centered on private solutions to middle-class families' childcare needs. The allowed deductions were larger for in-home care than for childcare centers, which encouraged parents who could afford it to hire domestic help instead of using daycare centers. The Nixon administration had hoped that such policies would both reinforce the idea that childcare is the responsibility of the nuclear family and provide domestic jobs for poor women who would be removed from the welfare rolls (Dinner 2010).

The nation's tax code continues to benefit families who pay others to care for their children in the form of a childcare tax credit, based on a family's income and the amount spent on childcare. In 2020, the childcare tax credit was worth up to $3,000 for one child under age thirteen and $6,000 for two or more children under age thirteen (US Department of the Treasury, Internal Revenue Service 2021b). In response to the Covid-19 pandemic, the American Rescue Plan increased the childcare credits to up to $4,000 for one child and $8,000 for two or more children in 2021 (US Department of the Treasury, Internal Revenue Service 2021a). Similarly, the Child Tax Credit, for couples earning up to $150,000 and single parents earning up to $112,500, was increased from $2,000 to $3,000 per child over the age of six for 2021. For children under the age of six, the credit increased from $2,000 to $3,600 for 2021. This credit is not earmarked for childcare, but parents are able to use it to help defray the cost of care. However, the increase in credits was a one-time enhancement in response to the Covid-19 pandemic; in 2022, the tax code reverted to the 2020 tax credit rules. President Joe Biden had proposed extending the extra credits as part of his Build Back Better agenda, but he was unable to secure the necessary legislative support (The White House n.d.).

The average annual cost of infant care in the nation ranges from $24,243 in Washington, DC, to $5,436 in Mississippi (Economic Policy Institute n.d.). For a toddler in daycare, the average cost is over $13,000 a year (Miller 2021). These figures indicate that in parts of the country, childcare can be more expensive than the average cost ($10,388) of in-state tuition at a public college (Powell, Kerr, and Wood 2021). It is not surprising that a 2021 Penny Hoarder survey of 2,000 parents found that 84 percent of them say they are either sometimes or often overwhelmed by the cost of childcare (Dow 2021). More than half (55.3 percent) of working families with children under the age of five report paying for childcare, meaning a significant portion of the population feels beleaguered by the costs of care (Malik 2019). Unlike most economically developed countries, the United States has done little to ease this burden. It is an outlier among countries in the Organisation for Economic Co-operation and Development (OECD), spending only 0.2 percent of its gross domestic product (GDP) on childcare for children two and under. The average OECD country spends 0.7 percent of its GDP on such care (Miller 2021).

There is broad bipartisan support for increased government action on childcare in the United States; three in four voters say elected leaders should prioritize childcare and early education. A substantial majority of 86 percent of voters—including 78 percent of Republicans—think the government should subsidize the cost of childcare and allow families to pay on a sliding scale, with the typical family paying about $45 per week (First Five Years Fund 2021). Seventy percent of voters want more government funding for childcare assistance and early childhood education. Though support is highest among Democrats (84 percent), 61 percent of independents, and 60 percent of Republicans also approve an increase. Seven in ten voters believe childcare payments should be limited to 7 percent of a family's income (Halpin, Agne, and Jain 2020). More than half (58 percent) of Americans favor providing universal pre-K for all children (*Yahoo News*/YouGov 2021). Even with such high levels of public support for childcare, legislative progress continues to stall.

A variety of factors have contributed to the government's inability or unwillingness to address the dearth of affordable quality childcare in the United States. Perhaps most notable is the persistent lack of a coordinated effort demanding such governmental action. From the earliest days of childcare centers, care outside the home was considered a last resort to be used under desperate circumstances by the poor and working classes. During the Progressive Era, a growing number of single mothers led to increased demand for childcare facilities. At the same time, many viewed single mothers as a symbol of societal breakdown that challenged the belief—especially among the middle and upper classes—that men should bear the financial costs of families and women should raise the children. As a result, many women activists fought for mothers' pensions that would allow them to stay home with their children instead of childcare assistance (Rose 1999).

In the 1960s, feminist groups generally viewed childcare as a right. Yet as the second wave of feminism progressed, divisions on the issue emerged. Many believed women's access to childcare was necessary for them to advance in the workplace, but some worried that advocating for childcare would bolster the idea that caring for children was primarily a woman's responsibility. There were also racial and class divisions that prevented the development of a unified movement to advocate for government-sponsored childcare. Some Black women were distrustful of a national childcare program, fearing that their children would be placed in low-quality care while their mothers were forced to work in low-paying jobs. Activists disagreed about the degree to which the childcare needs of working-class women should be prioritized over those of middle-class women (Dinner 2010).

Some feminists were reluctant to endorse more accessible childcare because they disapproved of the poor working conditions and low wages of childcare workers, who were mostly women (Zigler, Marsland, and Lord 2009). Such divisions based in race and class can undermine the ability of women's movements to influence policy outcomes (Michel 1999; Weldon 2006). Moreover, Michel (1999) argues that while feminist organizations such as NOW and the Feminist Majority generally supported women's increased access to quality childcare, it was never a legislative priority for them, perhaps because most upper-class women were able to afford it. Labor unions' presence in the fight for childcare has diminished since their height in the 1960s as well. Though they were heavily involved in the fight for the CCDA in the early 1970s, they have been largely absent from subsequent debates as their membership numbers continue to decline (Palley and Shdaimah 2014).

In response to the New Deal, a conservative movement emerged that largely opposes government intervention in businesses, workers' rights, and social welfare supports (Phillips-Fein 2009). It has often framed social programs as government overreach into the family, arguing that because it is a personal choice to have children, it is also a matter of personal (not governmental) responsibility to care for them. Since the earliest childcare centers were developed, the need for government-sponsored childcare has been stigmatized as an issue affecting only the poorest segments of society, rather than a necessity for a more universal working population. Childcare continues to be viewed through a partisan lens, with Republicans especially reticent to devote the amount of government money necessary to ensure that all families have access to affordable, high-quality care. Thus, government involvement in family policy in recent years has been limited, especially at the national level. While states have given more attention to the issue, the subnational efforts to address childcare needs reach only a fraction of Americans, and the benefits have been scant, with only Florida, Vermont, and Washington, DC, offering universal pre-K education (Palley 2010; Palley and Shdaimah 2014; New America 2020).

The lack of quality and affordable childcare affects all Americans, but it is especially problematic for women, who make up nearly half the nation's workforce and are held responsible for the bulk of childcare. This problem is exacerbated by the fact that most women workers do not have access to paid family leave. With the US political system designed to promote incremental change, only a unified movement with significant resources will be able to overcome the entrenched opposition to such social policies designed to help women achieve a better balance between work and family.

Conclusion

This chapter assessed women's ability to balance their responsibilities to their employment and their families, explaining how their increasing participation in the labor force resulted in policies addressing pregnancy and motherhood in the workplace. In 1972, the EEOC released guidelines stating that pregnancy discrimination was a form of sex discrimination. The courts initially ignored this interpretation, ruling that discrimination against pregnant women did not constitute sex discrimination because it was a woman's pregnancy, rather than her sex, that led to her unequal treatment. Likewise, the courts maintained that because there were typically women in the group of nonpregnant workers who did not face discrimination from an employer, pregnancy discrimination could not be based on sex.

Recognizing the limitations of the judicial branch—and responding to the public's growing outrage of the courts' rationale—Congress enacted the PDA in 1978 to prohibit discrimination in employment based on pregnancy. Although the act has benefited countless women in the workplace, advocates are calling for greater clarity in the law; court rulings in the four decades since the passage of the PDA have been inconsistent in their support for pregnancy discrimination claims. Approximately two-thirds of states have already enacted their own pregnancy accommodation laws, and in 2022, President Biden signed the national-level Pregnant Workers Fairness Act into law.

On the issue of family leave, legislators have been the primary actors. Before the passage of the FMLA in 1993, almost two-thirds of states had adopted some type of unpaid family leave legislation. The FMLA, which provides twelve weeks of unpaid leave to care for a new child or a family member with a serious health condition, as well as to address certain military family needs, was the first federal law to acknowledge a role for the government in ensuring work-life balance. After enacting the FMLA, Congress largely retreated from the discussion, despite the documented need for paid family leave to be made available to all workers. Instead, state and local governments have stepped in to remedy the inadequacies of the federal policy. Approximately one-third of states and over 100 cities and counties have adopted paid leave policies for government employees. Eleven states and the District of Columbia have enacted paid family leave for nearly all workers. In 2019, the Trump administration involved the executive branch by extending paid parental leave to roughly 2 million federal employees—to date the only national paid leave policy. Advocates have been trying to enact the FAMILY Act since 2013, but Republicans continue to decry it as fiscally irresponsible government overreach.

Childcare has long been considered a private responsibility in the nation. When the government has gotten involved, it has primarily been to help low-income families. Congress has passed a number of laws that allow tax credits for childcare, but they cover only a fraction of the high costs of quality childcare. Because women continue to bear the brunt of caregiving responsibilities, this oversight especially harms them, often forcing them to step back from the labor force. Recent research found that if affordable, high-quality childcare were available to everyone who needs it in the nation, the number of women with young children who work in full-time, year-round jobs would increase by about 17 percent. For women without a college degree, there would be an approximately 31 percent increase (National Women's Law Center and Center on Poverty & Social Policy at Columbia University 2021).

The lack of government-sponsored programs to address work-life balance has perhaps never been more important—or more visible—than as a result of Covid-19. As the pandemic propelled women out of the labor force in 2020 and 2021—because of business layoffs or closings and women's increased caregiving responsibilities as a result of closed schools and daycare centers—their participation fell to its lowest yearly rate (56.2 percent) in over three decades (US Department of Labor, Women's Bureau 2020; US Department of Labor, Bureau of Labor Statistics 2021b). In 2021, President Biden introduced a series of initiatives aimed at addressing the current imbalance. As part of its Build Back Better agenda, the Biden administration initially proposed paid family leave, universal pre-K programs, increased childcare funding, and an extension of the enhanced child tax credit. However, with no support from Senate Republicans and dissent within his own party, those programs were dropped. In a stripped-down version of the agenda, renamed the Inflation Reduction Act and enacted in 2022, climate change, health care and drug prices, and taxes took center stage (Luhby and Lobosco 2022; Zhou 2022). In what has become the norm in the United States, care work remains overlooked and undervalued. Until this changes, it is unlikely that lawmakers will adopt the sweeping reforms necessary to ensure that all families have the resources to achieve proper work-life balance. It also means that women will likely continue to be responsible for the majority of care work, for, as sociologist Jessica Calarco observes, "Other countries have social safety nets. The U.S. has women" (quoted in Peterson 2020).

5

Protecting Access to Contraception

WOMEN'S RIGHTS ADVOCATES HAVE LONG SOUGHT TO PROTECT access to safe and effective contraception. For over a century, the debate surrounding birth control has involved differing beliefs about the role of religion, morality, education, age, and cost. Notwithstanding a range of opinions, there is widespread approval of birth control in the nation, with 92 percent of the respondents in a Gallup Values and Beliefs Poll viewing it as "morally acceptable" (Brenan 2022).

Data collected in the National Survey of Family Growth 2017–2019 show that during these years, 65.3 percent of women ages fifteen to forty-nine were using contraception. Their usage varied by age, with 38.7 percent of women ages fifteen to nineteen relying on birth control and 74.8 percent of women ages forty to forty-nine using birth control (Daniels and Abma 2020). Affirming the widespread use of contraceptives overall, another study found that as of 2008, 99 percent of women ages fifteen to forty-four have used at least one type of birth control (Guttmacher Institute 2021a).

The benefits of birth control are widely reported. Assessing numerous studies, researchers at the Guttmacher Institute—an organization dedicated to "advancing sexual and reproductive health and rights" (2022a)—concluded that women are more likely to succeed in a range of areas, especially education and employment, if they can plan their childbearing. They believed that in order to do so, women must have "consistent access to effective and affordable contraception" (Sonfield et al. 2013; Guttmacher Institute 2020).

Family Planning Policy in the United States

Margaret Sanger, who coined the phrase "birth control," launched the modern US family planning movement, asserting "we claim that woman should have the right over her own body and to say if she shall or if she shall not be a mother, as she sees fit" (Sanger 1921). Sanger started the American Birth Control League (ABCL) at the first American Birth Control Conference in November 1921 in New York City; in 1942, the ABCL was renamed the Planned Parenthood Federation of America. At the conference, Sanger proclaimed, "our definite aim is to repeal the laws so that the medical profession may give women at their request knowledge to prevent conception" (Good 2021). As president of the ABCL, she played a key role in disseminating information about birth control to thousands of women and sought to educate public officials about the demonstrable toll pregnancies can take on women, including death, compromised health status, infant mortality, dependency, and more generally, the opportunity to become equal participants in the nation (Donley 2019). Celebrated for emphasizing the importance of family planning and the positive effect it has on women's lives, Sanger later became the source of much controversy as she was criticized for espousing racist and eugenicist views (Valenza 1985).

The US Food and Drug Administration (FDA) approved an oral contraceptive—the pill—in 1960. With its increasing popularity in the 1960s and 1970s, fueled by the feminist movement and women's consciousness of their expanding roles in society, the question of legal access to contraception was resolved by the Supreme Court in a trio of cases beginning in 1965. Mirroring the infamous 1873 Comstock Act—the federal law aimed at suppressing obscene literature, including material related to birth control—states enacted laws to block the distribution of birth control information and devices. With most state officials unwilling to ease access to birth control because of concerns that they would be charged with encouraging immoral sexual activity, women's rights advocates turned to the courts to challenge such laws, claiming they infringed on their constitutional rights.

The Supreme Court became involved in contraceptive policymaking when it reviewed the convictions of the executive director of the Planned Parenthood League of Connecticut Estelle Griswold and medical director Dr. C. Lee Buxton. They had been arrested for violating an 1879 Connecticut law prohibiting counseling married couples to use birth control to prevent conception. The two, whose aim was to test the legality of the Connecticut law, were each fined $100.

In *Griswold v. Connecticut* (1965), the Court invalidated the statute, declaring that the Constitution created a "zone of privacy," stemming from various protections of the Bill of Rights, that bars the government from invading "the sacred precincts of marital bedrooms." Such an intrusion, the majority said, is "repulsive to the notions of privacy surrounding the marriage relationship" (485). By holding that a married couple's use of contraception is protected from government regulation, *Griswold* formalized a constitutional right to privacy and established a doctrine that led to greater autonomy in sexual activity, childbearing, and childrearing. A few years later, in *Eisenstadt v. Baird* (1972), the Court further enhanced access to contraception by striking down a Massachusetts law prohibiting the distribution of contraceptive devices or materials to unmarried persons. Following the reasoning in *Griswold*, the majority held that the state must apply the same rules to married and unmarried individuals; a couple's right of privacy belongs to single persons as well. Perhaps laying the foundation for its landmark ruling on abortion rights decided less than a year later, it explained, "if the right of privacy means anything, it is the right of the individual, married or single, to be free from unwarranted governmental intrusion into matters so fundamentally affecting a person as the decision whether to bear or beget a child" (*Eisenstadt v. Baird* 1972, 453).

The next significant case to review government limits on birth control arose from a challenge to a New York law prohibiting the distribution of nonprescription contraceptives to minors under sixteen, allowing distribution only by licensed pharmacists, and banning advertising. In *Carey v. Population Services* (1977), the high court declared that contraception is a fundamental right and states must have a compelling reason to interfere with the decision "to bear or beget a child" (686). It concluded that the state failed to show a sufficiently compelling reason for imposing an age limit on access to birth control.

Title X and Birth Control

The Supreme Court's support for individual reproductive autonomy did not ensure its affordability—a significant hurdle for millions. Therefore, the federal government intervened with the hope that "family planning programs would promote the opportunities of children and families and thus drive economic growth" (Bailey 2013, 342; Bailey 2012). In 1969, a speech by President Richard Nixon reinforced the federal government's support for national family planning policies, linking them to its fight against poverty. Speaking about the Department of Health, Education and Welfare (HEW) and the Office of Economic Opportunity, he warned,

> their combined efforts are not adequate to provide information and services to all who want them. In particular, most of an estimated five million low-income women of childbearing age in this country do not now have adequate access to family planning assistance, even though their wishes concerning family size are usually the same as those of parents of higher income groups. It is my view, that no American woman should be denied access to family planning assistance because of her economic condition. I believe, therefore, that we should establish as a national goal the provision of adequate family planning services within the next five years to all those who want them but cannot afford them. This we have the capacity to do. (Nixon 1969)

A year later, Nixon signed the Title X Family Planning Program (42 USC §300)—the Family Planning Services and Population Research Act of 1970—helping secure access to birth control and reproductive health care for millions of women. Title X, the only federal program primarily focused on family planning services, permits the Department of Health and Human Services (HHS, the successor to HEW) to award contracts and grants "to public or nonprofit private entities to assist in the establishment and operation of voluntary family planning projects which shall offer a broad range of acceptable and effective family planning methods and services." It is intended "to enable individuals to determine freely the number and spacing of children" and requires services to be "provided to low-income individuals at no or reduced cost" (*Federal Register* 2016, 91852).

Title X presented an opportunity for abortion-rights opponents to weaponize contraceptive care against women seeking abortion care. By law, the statute explicitly precluded funding for family planning services to "be used in programs where abortion is a method of family planning" (*Rust v. Sullivan* 1991, 178). In February 1988, HHS had promulgated regulations to prevent Title X facilities from "provid[ing] counseling concerning the use of abortion as a method of family planning or provid[ing] referral for abortion as a method of family planning" (*Federal Register* 1988, 2945). Known as the Gag Rule, the regulation barred personnel in Title X–funded family planning clinics from discussing abortion with their patients under any circumstances, even when the patients requested the information; staff members were given elaborate instructions on how to respond to such questions and warned not to assist patients in locating abortion providers. In addition, the regulation mandated physical and financial separation between a provider's Title X facilities, personnel, and records and those of its abortion services.

In *Rust*, a case that had implications for abortion rights as well, the Supreme Court considered arguments that the regulation infringed on physicians' rights to freedom of speech under the First Amendment and created an undue burden on women's access to abortion. A majority believed women were no worse off than if the government had not funded the family planning program at all (Strasser 2017). It declared the regulation an acceptable means to denote the government's preference for childbirth and ensure that no federal aid goes to abortion through Title X funding. *Rust* set the stage for allowing restrictions on government-funded activities, "establish[ing] that the government could robustly regulate any program it funds and laid the groundwork for future state laws that require extensive separation between the funded organization and its abortion-providing affiliate" (Davidson 2019, 591).

Congress's later effort to repeal the Gag Rule failed when it was unable to secure the necessary votes to override President George H. W. Bush's veto. However, the rule remained in effect for only a brief time. In January 1993, President Bill Clinton issued a memorandum stating that Title X–funded clinics may provide abortion counseling and referrals as well as perform abortions if they do not rely on Title X funds to do so. Toward the end of the Clinton administration, on July 3, 2000, a new government regulation formally negated the Gag Rule and permitted physicians to offer pregnant women neutral ("nondirective") counseling about their options—including "prenatal care and delivery . . . adoption, and pregnancy termination"—as well as referrals to other providers, including those who perform abortions. Crucially, this modified the rule that abortion-related activities must be physically and financially separate from Title X activities, only requiring abortion providers to show that their finances are separate from their Title X programs (*Federal Register* 2000, 41269; Guttmacher Institute 2000).

Title X helped make family planning services and health care more available to people who could not otherwise afford to pay (Primrose 2012; Densmore 2018–2019). In 2015, there were nearly 4,000 Title X–funded health care centers in the nation, serving over four million clients; 90 percent were female, and 18 percent were nineteen or younger (Napili 2017; Frost et al. 2017). Title X funding has been relatively stable since about 2002. In 2019, there was approximately $286 million appropriated to it, with appropriations higher during most of the Obama years (US Department of Health and Human Services, Office of Population Affairs 2019). A 2019 Kaiser Family Foundation Poll found that the program has significant public support, with three-quarters of the American public believing it is important for the government to fund reproductive health care for low-income women in a program such as Title X (Kirzinger et al. 2019).

Private nonprofit family planning clinics, such as Planned Parenthood, play an integral part in fulfilling the nation's commitment to family planning services. In time, the organization became the face of family planning and reproductive care for millions of people in the United States (Primrose 2012). A frequent target of birth control and abortion opponents, Planned Parenthood was "the largest recipient of [Title X] funding" (*Politico*, July 16, 2017). The organization receives funding directly from the federal government and indirectly from state and local governments; its fifty-six affiliates around the country operate about 600 health care centers. A 2015 Congressional Budget Office analysis estimated that Planned Parenthood and its affiliates were awarded about $60 million a year in Title X funds (Napili 2017). Several studies indicate that its affiliates account for approximately 13 percent of Title X clinics, serving almost half (41 percent) of Title X patients (Frost et al. 2017; Napili 2017). As a Title X-funded agency, Planned Parenthood's clientele include vulnerable and underserved populations, providing needed health care to minority and low-income communities. Researchers at the Guttmacher Institute reported that "as of 2019, one-quarter of its patients are Black and one-third are Hispanic, and two-thirds of its patients have incomes at or below the federal poverty level" (Keller et al. 2020). Its clinics offer a broad range of FDA-approved contraceptive methods, as well as diagnosis and treatment of sexually transmitted infections, pregnancy testing, infertility treatments, HIV testing, and breast and cervical cancer screening, all at little or no cost to patients.

The 2010 elections swept abortion opponents into state and federal office and Republican-dominated state legislatures soon enacted volumes of anti-abortion laws. Paradoxically, abortion opponents also sought to limit women's access to contraception by curtailing spending on Title X contraceptive care programs, primarily within the Planned Parenthood network (Patton 2018). The organization, the nation's most well-known provider of family planning services, became a favorite target of state legislators who wanted to "prevent abortion providers from receiving any public funds, even for services wholly unrelated to abortion, simply because they provide abortions" (Davidson 2019, 581). Planned Parenthood's detractors characterized it as "the nation's leading abortion provider" (NPR, May 18, 2018). According to its 2016–2017 annual report, abortion services were only 3 percent of its medical services (Planned Parenthood 2016–2017; Kubak et al. 2019). Even though no federal dollars are advanced for the organization's abortion services, anti-abortion activists cite the "fungibility" theory to argue that when federal dollars, including Title X grants, are channeled to Planned Parenthood, "it frees up a private dollar, which then becomes available to cover the costs of abortion services or advance Planned Parenthood's abortion rights agenda" (Patton 2018, 303–304).

Opposition to Planned Parenthood kept mounting after 2010, with at least a dozen states placing restrictions on Planned Parenthood and other Title X recipients for reasons unrelated to their ability to provide Title X services. Collectively known as "defunding legislation," legislators were especially anxious to eliminate or sharply reduce funding to Planned Parenthood, even though their actions resulted in reduced services for the nation's predominantly low-income Title X clientele and their needs for family planning (*Federal Register* 2016, 91852). Most of these measures explicitly targeted Planned Parenthood; others used neutral language that was clearly aimed at the organization. In another attack, states restricted Planned Parenthood's funding by denying it reimbursement for treating patients in the Medicaid program (the joint federal-state program based on income in which the federal government provides most of the funding and the states administer it under flexible guidelines). This was a major blow, as Planned Parenthood received even more federal dollars from Medicaid than from Title X (NPR, May 18, 2018). Notwithstanding the provision of the Medicaid Act (Title XIX of the Social Security Act) that allows beneficiaries to select qualified providers of their choice for their treatment, states labeled Planned Parenthood clinics unqualified and refused to reimburse them or simply suspended their contract with the state (Eversman 2019). The lower federal courts remain divided on whether the law allows individuals to sue states for denying patients their choice of providers (Gilley 2019).

In December 2016, HHS promulgated a regulation to restrict a state's ability to defund Planned Parenthood by specifying that the only criteria for making a Title X award was the program's "ability to provide Title X services" (*Federal Register* 2016, 91855). The incoming administration dramatically changed the Title X funding process when, on April 13, 2017, President Donald Trump signed a bill reversing the December 2016 regulation, effectively ending Planned Parenthood's protection from state and federal defunding efforts (NPR, April 13, 2017). Welcomed by anti-abortion activists, the law was intended to return authority over Title X grants to state officials. At a White House closed-door signing ceremony, the head of an anti-abortion group proclaimed, "We expect to see Congress continue its efforts to redirect additional taxpayer funding away from Planned Parenthood through pro-life health care reform" (*New York Times*, April 13, 2017). After another attempt at defunding Planned Parenthood passed in the House of Representatives but failed in the Senate, the Trump administration followed through on the president's campaign promise to defund the organization by forcing it to terminate abortion care or forfeit Title X funding.

More generally, on March 4, 2019, HHS issued a regulation to strengthen the prohibition against using Title X funding for abortion as a method of family planning (*Federal Register* 2019, 7714). Critics charged "the primary goal of these regulations is to block the availability of federal funds to family planning providers, such as Planned Parenthood, that also offer abortion services with non–Title X funds and to prohibit sites that receive Title X funds from referring pregnant patients to other providers for abortion services" (Sobel, Salganicoff, and Frederiksen 2019). The proposed HHS regulation required that by March 4, 2020, Title X sites must maintain "clear physical and financial program separation from programs that use abortion as a method of family planning," including separate examination and waiting rooms, personnel, electronic and paper records, entrances and exits, phone numbers, and email addresses. It also prohibited grantees from using Title X funds to advocate for abortion rights. The regulation ostensibly allowed the site staff to determine what information to present to the woman, permitting personnel to discuss abortion care during counseling but barring them from providing encouragement or assistance even if the patient requests it. Despite the government's denial that the regulation was a gag rule, a Planned Parenthood official observed that "blocking doctors from telling a patient where they can get safe and legal care in this country is the definition of a gag rule," noting that it is irrelevant that the rule allows counseling if it does not permit referrals (NPR, May 18, 2018).

In addition to restricting Title X funding in the United States, Trump blocked US aid to health care providers around the world by expanding previous limits on them (Montes 2018). Known as the Global Gag Rule (or the Mexico City policy), the ban on funding was first imposed by President Ronald Reagan and then shifted back and forth between Democratic and Republican presidents, forcing health care clinics to choose between forgoing millions in US aid or abandoning their comprehensive family planning services, depriving millions of women around the world of birth control (Planned Parenthood 2021). In 2017, the Trump administration had not only restored the Global Gag Rule but tightened the restrictions on almost all global health assistance, including, for the first time, expenditures for HIV care (*The Lancet*, June 15, 2019). Ironically, as critics noted, if the policy forced clinics to close, "women's health will suffer and abortion rates will increase" (Behti 2019, 118; Kaiser Family Foundation 2020).

Aside from funding restrictions, the 2019 Trump administration regulation allowed Title X–funded clinics to exclude abortion providers entirely from lists of professionals offering abortion care; if they chose to include them, they could not identify them as such. In addition, it required facilities to refer all pregnant women to prenatal care sites, whatever their inclinations about continuing their pregnancy. Finally, the regulation allowed government funders to award Title X contracts to religiously based clinics that limit birth control exclusively to abstinence and fertility awareness programs (otherwise known as natural family planning or the rhythm method). Such Title X–funded clinics typically offer no artificial methods of birth control (that is, contraceptives) to their clients (*Mother Jones*, January–February 2020).

Using Title X funding as a cudgel, the 2019 regulation compelled Title X recipients to either abandon their abortion services or resign from the program. Reacting to the Trump administration's approach to Title X funding, the Maine Family Planning Program—the only statewide Title X grantee in Maine and a leading provider of abortion services—sued the federal government, arguing that the regulation limited women's access to family planning services and abortion care (Sobel, Salganicoff, and Frederiksen 2019; Relias Media 2020a). While its federal lawsuit was pending, on August 23, 2019, Maine withdrew from the program, abandoning a three-year Title X grant. Nearly a year later, a Maine federal district court judge upheld the regulation, finding that it does not bar Title X–funded clinic personnel from discussing abortion with their patients nor deny patients access to abortion services (*Family Planning Association of Maine v. US HHS* 2020).

Several providers also challenged the requirement that Title X clinics maintain a physical as well as a financial separation between their Title X–funded family planning programs and their abortion care. The federal courts were soon inundated with suits against the federal government by Democratic attorneys general in California, Washington, Oregon, Maine, Virginia, New York, and Maryland; altogether more than twenty states filed suit against the regulation (*Washington Post*,

October 4, 2021). In addition to the states, the American College of Obstetricians and Gynecologists (ACOG), the American Medical Association, several Planned Parenthood affiliates, and numerous civil rights groups either filed suit or submitted briefs, arguing that the regulation violated Title X and the First and Fifth Amendments of the US Constitution. Other states and anti-abortion groups also filed briefs, urging the courts to uphold the regulation.

The plaintiffs in the California federal district court case argued that the "rule will create daunting barriers to California women seeking timely, effective reproductive health care, impose medically and ethically unsound restrictions on Title X providers attempting to provide patient-centered care, and inflict severe public health consequences and costs on the State" (*California v. Azar* 2019, 969). Ruling for the plaintiffs, the federal judge blocked the regulation from going into effect, as did federal district court judges in *Oregon v. Azar* (2019) and *Washington v. Azar* (2019). The Oregon federal judge criticized the rule, declaring it "would create such a financial strain on Title X providers that, ironically, it would create a geographic vacuum in family planning that experts warn would lead to substantially more unintended pregnancies and, correspondingly, more abortions" (*Oregon v. Azar* 2019, 903). The court rebuked the government, saying, "at best, the Final Rule is a solution in search of a problem. At worst, it is a ham-fisted approach to health policy that recklessly disregards the health outcomes of women, families, and communities." The judge enumerated the constraints the regulation placed on health professionals, women, and counselors, proclaiming, "at the heart of this rule is the arrogant assumption that government is better suited to direct the health care of women than their medical providers" (902). Reviewing the evidence before him, he found that the regulation has negative consequences for women with respect to contraception and pregnancies, as well as early detection of cancer and HIV. He ended by charging that HHS was indifferent to such "negative health outcomes" because it was solely concerned with ensuring Title X funds will not "be used in programs where abortion is a method of family planning" (903).

The Ninth Circuit Court of Appeals overruled the Washington state, California, and Oregon district courts, holding that the regulation was consistent with federal law and the Constitution and was a reasonable interpretation of the statutory ban on Title X funds being available to "programs where abortion is a method of family planning" (*California v. Azar* 2020, 1073). Meanwhile, in *Mayor of Baltimore v. Azar* (2020), the Fourth Circuit Court of Appeals affirmed the Maryland federal district court ruling blocking the regulation (Relias Media 2020b).

While the federal courts were adjudicating challenges to the regula-tion, on August 19, 2019, several days before Title X grantees were required to submit "an assurance and action plan" to HHS, Planned Par-enthood formally withdrew from the Title X program, citing the rule prohibiting Title X–funded clinics from referring their patients to abor-tion providers (McCammon 2019). The decision cost the organization $60 million in federal funding (*New York Times*, August 19, 2019). Its critics expressed their pleasure that they had defunded Planned Parent-hood when it had declined to accept the Title X funds (*Politico*, Sep-tember 1, 2019). Ultimately, as a result of the Trump administration reg-ulation, over 950 Title X sites (including Planned Parenthood clinics, state health departments, and independent clinics) withdrew from the Title X network of programs, leaving at least one and a half million people deprived of Title X care and no Title X providers in half a dozen states (Relias Media 2020a; *Washington Post*, October 4, 2021). The decline in Title X services had a disproportionate effect on women of color in the nation. A 2017 study of Title X clients showed that 21 per-cent are Black or African American (compared with 13 percent in the US population) and 30 percent are Hispanic or Latinx (compared with 17 percent in the US population) (Gillette-Pierce and Taylor 2017).

Shortly after assuming office on January 20, 2021, President Joe Biden underscored the importance of the president's role in policymak-ing, echoing Nixon's words of over fifty years ago by proclaiming "women should have access to the healthcare they need." Affirming his administration's commitment to "support[ing] women's and girls' sex-ual and reproductive health and rights in the United States, as well as globally," Biden directed HHS to review all regulations, including those related to the Title X Rule, that restrict the use of federal funding for programs offering women the information they need to control their medical care. He ordered the agency to determine the best approach to substituting new regulations for those imposed by the Trump adminis-tration (Biden 2021).

The president graphically stated his goal was to "undo the damage Trump has done" (*Politico*, April 14, 2021). His administration soon announced it had started to roll back the 2019 regulation and revert to "the [year] 2000 regulations . . . to ensure access to equitable, affordable, client-centered, quality family planning services for all clients, espe-cially for low-income clients" (*Federal Register* 2021a, 19819). It charged that the Trump administration had precipitated the departure of one quarter of Title X providers, leaving some states with no providers. Moreover, it added, "as a result of the decrease in clients able to receive

Title X services, it is estimated that the 2019 Final Rule may have led to up to 181,477 unintended pregnancies" (*Federal Register* 2021a, 19815).

The litigation over the Trump administration regulation continued until, on May 17, 2021, the Supreme Court dismissed the pending cases, leaving it to the Biden administration to interpret the law (Howe 2021a). HHS soon proposed a new rule that would replace the 2019 Trump-era rule and remove limits on abortion referrals by Title X recipients. On October 7, 2021, HHS Secretary Xavier Becerra announced the Biden administration's policy change on Title X funding, declaring, "today more than ever, we are making clear that access to quality family planning care included accurate information and referrals—based on a patient's needs and direction" (*Federal Register* 2021b, 56144; *Washington Post*, October 4, 2021). Promising that the new Title X program will expand to serve more clients, HHS Assistant Secretary for Health Rachel Levine proclaimed, "advancing equity for all, including people of color and others who have been historically underserved, marginalized, and adversely affected by persistent poverty and inequality, is a priority for the Administration, including the Title X program and the Department" (US Department of Health and Human Services 2021). The new rule became effective on November 8, 2021.

The Affordable Care Act and Birth Control

In 2010, President Barack Obama sponsored legislation to expand access to health care, proposing the Patient Protection and Affordable Care Act (ACA), later known as Obamacare; the term was coined by his Republican opposition but embraced by him because, he said, "it indicates he cares" (*Washington Post*, September 2, 2012). The act was intended to distribute the benefits of health insurance to millions of uninsured and underinsured Americans. After much partisan rancor, with no Republican support, Obama signed it into law on March 23, 2010.

The first federal law to do so, the ACA established national requirements for health insurance coverage for private insurers and employers. It applied to employers with fifty or more full-time employees and directed that employer-provided group health care plans must cover a wide range of procedures and medications. Its passage was contentious, with extensive congressional debate over such issues as state expansion of the Medicaid program, fines on people who failed to sign up for a plan (the individual mandate), the extent of religious exemptions, and the relationship between abortion and contraception. At the same time, there were popular features such as eliminating exclusions for preexisting conditions, allowing minors to remain on their parents' insurance policies until age twenty-six, eliminating gender rating, and incorporating essential health benefits into private insurance policies (Nicelli 2017).

Controversy over women's reproductive health care played a significant role in the debate surrounding the ACA. Before its passage, state laws regulating insurance coverage for contraceptive care varied widely and, although many employers included such coverage in their employees' health care policies, without state oversight, the choice was left to the employers and insurance companies (Sonfield 2012; Sobel, Beamesderfer, and Salganicoff 2016; US Equal Employment Opportunity Commission 2000a). Numerous studies point to sex-based differences in insurance coverage, particularly with insurers refusing to pay women's contraception costs (Law 1998). With the passage of the ACA, the nation took a great step toward alleviating disparities in health care by increasing opportunities to obtain health insurance. Because they "suffer disproportionate rates of chronic disease and disability from some conditions, and often have high out-of-pocket health care costs . . . women in particular stand to benefit from these additional preventive health services" (Institute of Medicine 2011, 18). In addition to lowering women's health care costs, studies have shown that increasing women's access to contraceptive care leads to improved health outcomes in the nation (Sonfield 2012).

The ACA sought to redress gender inequities in the health care market in at least two ways: first, section 1557 of the act makes it illegal to discriminate on the basis of sex, pregnancy, and childbirth, thereby attacking the practice of gender rating in which health insurers charge women more than men; second, the Women's Health Amendment (WHA) advances women's equality in health care by requiring employers and insurers to cover women's preventive care and screenings with no co-payments or deductibles. Intended to remedy discrimination against women in the health care market, its chief sponsor pointed out that the WHA addressed the "punitive practices of insurance companies that charge women more and give [them] less in a benefit" (Donley 2019, 519–520; Nicelli 2017).

The amendment did not explicitly require employers to cover contraception but directed the Health Resources and Services Administration (HRSA), an agency within HHS, to specify the services that must be made available at no cost. HRSA turned to the Institute of Medicine (IOM) to compile a list of "family planning services that are provided to prevent unintended pregnancies including contraception (i.e., all

FDA-approved contraceptive drugs and devices, sterilization procedures) as well as patient education and counseling" (Institute of Medicine 2011, 102). Reflecting the IOM's finding that about half the pregnancies in the nation are unintended, on August 1, 2011, HRSA issued
the Women's Preventive Services Guidelines to implement its recommendations, including no-cost access to birth control, popularly known
as the contraception mandate (Wood 2017; Donley 2019; Kimof 2019).
In May 2015, to resolve disputes over the methods of birth control covered by the ACA, the Obama administration specified that insurance
plans must include at least one of the eighteen FDA-approved methods
of birth control without cost-sharing (Becker and Polsky 2015, 1210).

With prescription contraceptives "among the most widely used
medical services in the United States, by eliminating the cost sharing
provisions from women's health care plans, the contraception mandate
led to large reductions in total out-of-pocket spending on contraceptives" (1204). Overall, according to studies of women's spending on
various forms of birth control, the ACA contraception mandate led to
significant savings, especially for the pill, one of the most common
forms of birth control (Guttmacher Institute 2021b). Before the ACA,
it was estimated over one-third of women's health care expenses were
spent on contraception (Planned Parenthood 2020). After the ACA's
passage, a study estimated more than 61 million women received cost-
free FDA-approved contraceptives, resulting in $1.4 billion a year in
out-of-pocket savings on the pill alone (Becker and Polsky 2015, 1209;
The Intercept, July 9, 2020). Another study of almost two thousand pri-
vately insured women found that between 2012 and 2014, 67 percent
paid nothing for the pill (Sonfield et al. 2015).

By 2015, more than 62.4 million women were accessing contraceptive care and other preventive services without cost sharing through the
ACA, with "the average woman sav[ing] $269 a year on birth control"
(Donley 2019, 522). A government analysis released in May 2015 estimated that because of the ACA's no cost requirement, over 55 million
women have insurance coverage for preventive services without cost-
sharing (US Department of Health and Human Services, Assistant Secretary for Planning and Evaluation 2015). Cecile Richards, president of
Planned Parenthood, summed up the benefits of the ACA for women, saying, "birth control is basic preventive health care for women. The Affordable Care Act ensures that women can access birth control without co-
pays, no matter where they work, just like any other kind of preventive
care" (*Washington Post*, January 1, 2014). Despite the ACA's successes in
furthering gender equity in health care through the contraception man-

date, millions of unemployed women, women working in small companies, and those employed by temporarily exempted "grandfathered" companies failed to receive the benefits of no-cost contraception.

Much of the controversy over the contraception mandate revolved
around the extent to which private employers may circumvent the
requirements of the law by claiming that it violated their constitutional
right to the free exercise of religion under the First Amendment; the
courts were soon inundated with lawsuits over the conflict between
women's birth control needs and the claims of religiously affiliated
businesses and organizations. Seeking to lower the flood of demands for
exemptions, HRSA created the "church exemption" from the start, automatically excusing churches and houses of worship from complying
with the mandate. To qualify for this exception, organizations must have
the purpose of inculcating religious values, primarily employ and serve
individuals who share their religious faith, and qualify as nonprofit
groups under the federal tax code (McNulty and Moser 2019). Over the
objections of religious leaders, this categorical exemption did not
extend to nonprofit religiously affiliated institutions that employ or
serve individuals of different faiths (Sonfield 2012). Availing themselves of the "church exemption became the goal of the non-church religious organizations" (Griffin 2016).

Opponents of expanding the religious exemption argued that millions of women should not be deprived of medically necessary health
care benefits merely because of their employers' religious beliefs. In discussing the rule granting the automatic religious exemption, HHS Secretary Kathleen Sebelius defended the government's policy, maintaining
that "it strikes the appropriate balance between respecting religious freedom and increasing access to important preventive services" (*New York
Times*, January 20, 2012). Furthermore, she noted, the administration had
already accommodated objections from church-affiliated institutions by
extending their deadline for compliance with the law until August 1,
2013, a year after other employers.

Religious leaders were dissatisfied with the administration's offer of
accommodation, arguing that the exemption was too narrow and the one-
year delay was meaningless. The Catholic Church took a leading role in
advocating to broaden the religious exemption, arguing that forcing religiously affiliated institutions and Catholic-owned businesses to facilitate
artificial means of contraception infringed on their religious liberty. A
spokesperson for the United States Conference of Catholic Bishops said,
"we can't just lie down and let religious freedom go" (*New York Times*,
January 29, 2020). Church leaders who had personally lobbied Obama to

broaden the exemption expressed anger at the administration, with Arch-
bishop Timothy M. Dolan of New York charging, "in effect, the president is saying we have a year to figure out how to violate our consciences" (*New York Times*, January 20, 2012).

Attempting to placate the religious leaders, in February 2012,
Obama proposed a compromise that would grant nonprofit religiously
affiliated institutions, such as schools, hospitals, and charities, the right
to permit their women employees to obtain coverage directly from their
insurers or third-party administrators (if self-insured) at no charge to the
institution. Some religious leaders appreciated Obama's proposal; Dolan
called it "a first step in the right direction," and leaders of the Catholic
Health Association were also pleased (*Washington Post*, February 10,
2012). But it was not well received by all religious leaders. The president of a Catholic university in Florida criticized the plan, noting that
because the university underwrites employee and student health plans,
it still contributes to activities it condemns. In his words, Obama's strategy amounted to "a fig leaf of a political compromise that's trying to
have it both ways, to mollify women's groups and so-called centrist
Catholics" (*Washington Post*, February 11, 2012). He predicted that the
struggle was just beginning and the religious faithful would turn to the
courts to protect their right to exercise their religion. Catholic leaders in
other parts of the nation also objected to the administration's proposed
accommodation. Among them was Bishop David Zubik of Pittsburgh,
who wrote "the Obama administration was essentially saying 'to hell
with you,' particularly to the Catholic community by dismissing our
beliefs, our religious freedom and our freedom of conscience" (*Lubbock*
[Texas] *Avalanche-Journal*, February 3, 2012).

Not surprisingly, the controversy became an issue in the 2012 presidential election, with Democrats generally advocating for limited religious exemptions and characterizing their position as support for
women's rights. On the other side, Republicans portrayed the law as an
unconstitutional infringement on religious liberty. A Senate vote on a
Republican-sponsored amendment on March 1, 2012, allowing religious
employers to refuse to cover contraceptive care in their health insurance
policies, narrowly failed in a 51–48 vote, with three Democrats joining
forty-five Republicans (*New York Times*, March 1, 2012).

HHS specified the parameters of the religious exemption in final
regulations issued on July 2, 2013, following submission of hundreds
of thousands of comments during the public comment period (*Federal
Register* 2013, 39870). The rules exempted religious employers—
namely, churches and houses of worship—from covering contracep-

tive care entirely and allowed religiously affiliated nonprofits with faith-based objections to contraceptive care to arrange for their health plan insurers to "provide separate payments for contraceptive services for plan participants without imposing any cost-sharing requirements on the eligible organization, its insurance plan, or its employee beneficiaries." These entities would not be required "to contract, arrange, pay, or refer for such coverage." They could simply self-certify their exemption by submitting a two-page Employee Benefits Security Administration Form 700 to their insurers or third-party administrators, declaring their unwillingness to pay for birth control on religious grounds; the insurers would inform the recipients and arrange coverage for them (Sonfield 2013, 11).

The ACA went into full effect on January 1, 2014, requiring covered employers to offer health care plans that include ten "essential health benefits." Most, such as "mental health and substance use disorder services," "preventative and wellness services and chronic disease management," and "emergency services," were gender neutral and noncontroversial; however, the list included "pregnancy and maternity services," over which significant controversy arose (Nicelli 2017, 41–42). The attacks on the contraception mandate by religiously affiliated institutions attracted the nation's attention, especially as the number of lawsuits increased. The plaintiffs in these cases claimed that including contraception in their employee health insurance plans, even indirectly, violated their religious freedom. In addition to the litigation brought by these organizations, there were disputes over whether secular for-profit corporations could legally opt out of covering women's contraceptive care in their employee benefit packages on the grounds that their owners had religious or moral objections to contraception (Lupu 2015).

In 2014, the Supreme Court agreed to decide whether the religious exemption must apply to such owners, consolidating rulings from the Third and Tenth Circuit Courts of Appeals in *Hobby Lobby Stores, Inc. v. Sebelius* (2013) and *Conestoga Wood Specialties Corporation v. Secretary of the United States Department of Health and Human Services* (2013). These courts had reached opposite conclusions about whether the mandate violated the religious beliefs of business owners who objected to funding specified types of contraceptive care. The owners of these two closely held for-profit corporations, Hobby Lobby and Conestoga Wood Specialties, complained that paying for certain methods of contraception would make them complicit in facilitating the demise of a human embryo. They stressed that enforcing the mandate and requiring them to offer contraception coverage would infringe on their sincerely held religious beliefs and violate their right to free exercise under the Religious Freedom Restoration Act (RFRA) (42 USC §2000bb) and the First Amendment's free exercise clause (FINDLAW 2016).

Clinton had signed RFRA into law on November 16, 1993. It prohibits the federal government from "substantially burden[ing] a person's exercise of religion" unless it "is in furtherance of a compelling government interest" and "is the least restrictive means of furthering that compelling governmental interest" (Lupu 2015; Hersh 2018). The primary impetus for enacting RFRA was the Supreme Court's ruling in *Employment Division Department of Human Resources of Oregon v. Smith* (1990), in which it affirmed the decision of an Oregon state agency to deny unemployment benefits to two Native American drug rehabilitation counselors who were discharged for ingesting peyote. The high court rejected the employees' defense that they were following the beliefs of their Native American Church, declaring the free exercise clause does not excuse people from obeying a generally applicable law, such as a drug prohibition.

Concerned that *Smith* weakened individuals' rights to the free exercise of religion, Congress sought to limit government restraints on religion (Laycock and Thomas 1994; Lupu 2015). Approved by an overwhelming majority in Congress, the law initially covered states as well as the federal government. But in *City of Boerne v. Flores* (1997), the Court decided that while RFRA applied to the federal government, Congress lacked the authority to apply it to the states. Since then, more than half the states have enacted their own versions of RFRA, holding state and local governments to the same standards as the federal government. Ironically, RFRA was initially supported by the American Civil Liberties Union (ACLU) and other progressive groups. But since 2013, they have expressed concern that most of the state laws modeled after the federal RFRA were intended to justify opposition to same-sex marriage (Bazelon 2015; Lupu 2015).

The Hobby Lobby and Conestoga owners and their families, who belonged to Christian denominations opposing abortion, maintained that RFRA shielded them from providing the types of contraception that they claimed interfered with their religion (Dabrowski 2014; Samar 2015). The family members believed that emergency contraception—otherwise known as Plan B or generically as morning after pills—and intrauterine devices, all on the FDA-approved list, are akin to abortion because they prevent the implantation of a fertilized egg, a view most scholars say has "little scientific support" (Bazelon 2015; *PBS Newshour,* October 11,

2017). By forcing them to include such contraceptives in their employee health insurance plans, they contended that the government infringed on their sincerely held religious beliefs.

The Court affirmed that the for-profit entities fall within RFRA's definition of a "person" entitled to the exercise of religion (*Burwell v. Hobby Lobby Stores, Inc.* 2014). A majority agreed that compelling the plaintiffs to cover all FDA-approved contraception methods or face millions of dollars in fines placed a substantial burden on their religious exercise. The justices were not persuaded by the Obama administration's argument that it would be too difficult to decide the governing religion in a publicly traded corporate giant, saying such an issue would be unlikely to arise and, in any event, "the companies in this case before us are closely held corporations, each owned and controlled by members of a single family" (717). The majority also rejected the Obama administration's argument that the companies had failed to produce evidence that any employee would use one of the disapproved methods. The Court declared that under RFRA, the judiciary's only role was to determine whether a law or policy substantially interfered with the plaintiffs' ability to conform their businesses to their religious beliefs, not the reasonableness of the beliefs. Given the severe financial penalty (as much as $100 a day for each employee) the government might assess on them if they denied contraceptive care coverage to their employees, it held the mandate placed a substantial burden on the plaintiffs' religious beliefs (Corbin 2016).

In RFRA litigation, if a court finds a challenged law places a substantial burden on the plaintiffs, it must determine whether the government has a compelling interest in the law and whether it has chosen the least restrictive means to fulfill the interest. The high court was skeptical that the government even viewed its interest as compelling because the ACA allowed several exceptions, such as small or grandfathered companies. In the end, the majority simply assumed the government's interest in women's access to birth control was compelling and turned its attention to inquiring whether it could use a less restrictive policy to satisfy this interest. The Court concluded that there were less restrictive policies, suggesting that rather than require the employer's insurance company to cover the cost of contraceptives to which it objected, the federal government might pay for them—a small amount compared with the cost of the ACA. Such an arrangement would satisfy the government's interest in providing women's contraception care while removing the burden on the owners' religious exercise. It noted that this accommodation was already in place for religiously affiliated institutions through the self-certification process by which their insurers "provide plan participants with separate payments for contraceptive services without imposing any cost-sharing requirements on the employer, its insurance plan, or its employee beneficiaries" (*Burwell v. Hobby Lobby Stores, Inc.* 2014, 682–683). Such a policy "achieves all of the government's aims while providing greater respect for religious liberty" (692). Based on these considerations, the opinion held that because the government had not chosen the least restrictive option to further its interest in women's contraceptive care, the ACA contraception mandate violated the companies' right to free exercise under RFRA.

The Court dismissed as too far-fetched the administration's warnings that closely held corporations such as these could mount religious objections to innumerable medical interventions, such as blood transfusions and immunizations. The majority was satisfied the government could devise an accommodation to preserve the religious liberty guaranteed by RFRA while safeguarding the ACA's commitment to women, concluding that requiring these companies to provide the birth control to which they objected did not conform to the standards set under RFRA. The majority emphasized its ruling was limited to closely held family businesses, avoiding the question of how to determine a corporation's faith (Lupu 2015; Brown et al. 2019). In explaining how the government might craft a policy to reconcile the aims of the ACA and RFRA, the Court glossed over such issues as forcing women to reveal their preferred contraceptive methods to their employers, assuming insurers would be receptive to establishing a separate policy to cover contraception costs, and Congress's willingness to appropriate funds for women's contraceptive care.

To implement the *Hobby Lobby* ruling, the Obama administration extended the existing religious accommodation (currently available to religious nonprofit organizations) to allow closely held for-profit companies whose owners had religious objections to contraceptive coverage to submit a two-page form to the government. Not satisfied, religiously affiliated entities continued to challenge the contraception mandate in court, stressing that simply asking for an accommodation made them complicit in actions contrary to their religious faith (Green 2015; Sepinwall 2015). The plaintiffs in these cases demanded automatic exemptions from the mandate, arguing that no matter how limited their role in procuring contraception, the administration was forcing them to condone birth control in violation of their religious beliefs. Most appellate courts rejected such claims, holding that merely asking for the accommodation did not infringe on their religious tenets (Denniston 2015; American Civil Liberties Union 2021a; Green 2015).

The high court further enmeshed itself in the contraception mandate controversy when, a few days after announcing *Hobby Lobby*, it granted Wheaton College, a Protestant denominational college in Illinois, an emergency injunction (*Wheaton College v. Burwell* 2014). The college had filed suit in 2013, arguing that submitting Form 700 would violate its right to religious exercise under RFRA. In an unsigned order, the Supreme Court had granted the school a temporary injunction, deciding that it could satisfy its obligation under the ACA by notifying HHS in writing that "it is a non-profit organization that holds itself out as religious and has religious objections to providing coverage for contraceptive services" (958). A dissent by the three women justices (Ruth Bader Ginsburg, Elena Kagan, and Sonia Sotomayor) pointed out that in *Hobby Lobby*, the Court had cited the "self-certification procedure" that allowed organizations to opt out of contraception coverage with the insurer responsible for the costs as an acceptable resolution of the conflict between religious exercise and women's health needs. They also objected to permitting Wheaton College to refuse to identify its insurer in its request for the accommodation, leaving it to the government to ferret out the entity responsible for the cost of the coverage.

In a subsequent opinion, the Seventh Circuit Court of Appeals clarified that Wheaton believed that merely notifying the government "triggers" the eventual coverage of contraception to employees and students and embroils it in a sinful act. During the oral arguments in the circuit court, the school admitted that it objected to furnishing the name of its insurer precisely to make it more difficult for the government to arrange the accommodation (*Wheaton College v. Burwell* 2015; *Harvard Law Review* 2016).

In response to the Court's decision in *Wheaton College*, in July 2015, the administration further accommodated religious entities by releasing rules making the two-page form optional and permitting them to simply state their objections to the contraception mandate by writing directly to HHS, indicating their religious opposition to some or all methods of birth control and identifying their insurer; HHS would take responsibility for notifying the insurer as well other government agencies (Sepinwall 2015). Under this plan, whatever the notification method, the insurer or third-party administrator would assume the financial liability for the mandate without imposing costs on the employees or the company and would notify employees that the company is not administering or funding their birth control coverage. The Court's reformulation of the accommodation in *Wheaton College* was still unsatisfactory to some religious nonprofits, and they continued to challenge the ACA contraception requirement, charging that notification of any sort violates their religious beliefs because it enables contraception coverage. With most appellate courts rejecting their arguments, they turned to the high court.

In November 2015, the Supreme Court announced it would consolidate seven cases from four circuits (the Third, Fifth, Tenth, and District of Columbia) that had affirmed the government's position. The Second, Sixth, Seventh, and Eleventh Circuit Courts of Appeals, which were not involved in the litigation, had also ruled in favor of the administration, rejecting the plaintiffs' argument that the accommodation imposed a substantial burden on the exercise of their religion. In these cases, the lower courts "consistently cut through the rhetorical posturing to identify the real focus of the objections," that the plaintiffs simply refused to comply with the ACA's mandate; only the Eighth Circuit Court of Appeals supported the religious entity (Sepinwall 2015; McNulty and Moser 2019; American Civil Liberties Union 2021a).

On May 16, 2016, in an unsigned opinion, the eight-member Supreme Court essentially withdrew from the controversy, remanding the cases to the lower courts and instructing the parties to agree on a resolution that "provides seamless access to cost-free contraceptives" but allows religious entities to bypass notification, making the insurer responsible for the notification and coverage in a separate policy (*Zubik v. Burwell* 2016, 1560–1561). The Court rationalized its actions by explaining that after the oral arguments in March 2016, it had asked for supplemental briefs and the religiously affiliated entities had signaled they would consent to an arrangement in which their health care plan would not include contraceptive coverage and their insurer, on its own initiative, would provide birth control coverage through a separate policy. They offered this as a compromise, they said, because it allowed them to avoid playing any role in covering birth control that violates their religious tenets. Because the government affirmed that such an arrangement "was feasible," the Court had directed the parties to implement it.

The nonprofit institutions soon made it clear their offer came with stringent conditions essential to "satisfying their religious convictions." First, they said, "contraception coverage could only be provided by their insurers if 'there are two separate health insurance policies . . . with separate enrollment processes, insurance cards, payment sources, and communication schemes'"; second, "employees must affirmatively opt in to any such plan, rather than being automatically enrolled." The government argued that imposing such conditions would deprive women of health care benefits and "result in predictable and significant harm to thousands of women" (Griffin 2016; Schwartzman, Schragger, and Tebbe 2016). On January 9, 2017, in the waning days of his tenure, the Obama administration announced it could not reconcile the two sides and would return to the existing arrangements. With this pronouncement, "the Court's attempt at fashioning a compromise was now officially dead" (McNulty and Moser 2019, 109).

In returning the cases to the lower courts, the Supreme Court had emphasized that it was not expressing any views on their merits and "nothing in this opinion, or in the opinions or orders of the courts below, is to affect the ability of the Government to ensure that women covered by petitioners' health plans 'obtain, without cost, the full range of FDA approved contraceptives'" (*Zubik v. Burwell* 2016, 1560–1561, quoting *Wheaton College v. Burwell* 2014, 959). It hastened to add it was also offering no opinion about the parties' arguments with respect to RFRA. With no guidance from the high court, the parties remained at odds before the November 2016 election (Hersh 2018).

According to a Pew Research Center (2016) national poll, most Americans agreed with the Obama administration's position on the contraceptive mandate: 67 percent of respondents believed that "employers who have religious objections to the use of birth control should be required to provide birth control coverage," with only 30 percent disagreeing; the remaining 3 percent gave no answer. Despite the public's support for employer-funded contraceptive care coverage, in the view of judicial scholar Lyle Denniston (2016), "the entire future of the ACA, including its birth-control mandate, may now depend upon who wins the presidential election this year and which party has control of Congress when it reassembles in 2017."

The Supreme Court's exhortation notwithstanding, the parties failed to arrive at a compromise and with Trump in office and the newly gained Republican majorities in the House and Senate, his administration focused much of its attention on dismantling Obamacare. It devoted a great deal of its effort to weakening the contraception mandate, in part motivated by Trump's desire to appease the religious faithful who thought they were under siege and had overwhelmingly voted for him. In signing an order singling out the contraceptive mandate on May 4, 2017, at a White House ceremony, the president promised "we will not allow people of faith to be targeted, bullied or silenced anymore" (*New York Times*, October 6, 2017).

The order directed executive branch agencies to "consider issuing amended regulations . . . to address conscience-based objections" to the mandate (Executive Order 13798 2017). Pointing to representatives of the Little Sisters of the Poor (an order of Catholic nuns who were plaintiffs in the *Zubik* litigation) in attendance, Trump announced they had "sort of just won a lawsuit" and declared that "with this executive order, we are ending the attacks on your religious liberty" (*New York Times*, May 29, 2017). The Little Sisters, a religious organization long involved in litigation against the mandate, believed that "deliberately avoiding reproduction through medical means is immoral" (*Little Sisters of the Poor v. Pennsylvania* 2020, 2376). In their view, merely submitting a form to the government forces them to take part in providing contraception and infringes on their religious faith.

Trump's Executive Order was set in motion when, on October 6, 2017, the Department of Justice (DOJ) issued a guidance to federal agencies and DOJ attorneys, spurring them to privilege religious exercise over the enforcement of antidiscrimination laws, particularly in the employment sector. The same day, the administration issued two interim rules broadening eligibility for exemptions to the contraceptive mandate on moral as well as religious grounds (*Federal Register* 2017a, 47838; *Federal Register* 2017b, 47792). The Trump administration justified its approach to the exemptions, designated the "conscience exemptions," in part by rejecting the Obama administration's stance that the government has a compelling reason to provide cost-free contraceptive coverage to women. It proclaimed that "the Government's legitimate interests in providing for contraceptive coverage do not require us to violate sincerely held religious beliefs while implementing the Guidelines." The government, it added, was also not required "to violate sincerely held moral convictions in the course of generally requiring contraceptive coverage" (*Federal Register* 2018, 57605). The interim regulations eliminated the accommodation process crafted during the Obama administration and simply exempted all employers who objected to birth control because of their religious beliefs or their moral principles. No longer did employers have to certify that they objected to covering birth control in their employee health plans, nor did they have to inform the government they would cease providing the coverage. The "exemptions allow[ed] any employer (whether for-profit or non-profit) to deny employees insurance coverage for contraception for nearly any reason" (onlabor.org, April 21, 2021).

An HHS press release acknowledged women would lose coverage for birth control, including contraceptives prescribed for medical conditions under the new rules, but maintained they might only involve about 200 employers and "will not affect over 99.9% of the 165 million women in the United States" (US Department of Health and Human Services 2017). In a letter dated December 5, 2017, the ACLU urged the administration to "rescind" the rules, charging they will "allow virtually any employer or university to deprive women of contraceptive coverage, harming them and their health and well-being" (American Civil Liberties Union 2017). The organization objected to the finding that certain birth control methods, such as the morning after pill, are abortifacients and "not in the best interests of women and society." In response, an HHS spokesperson made no mention of the impact of the regulations on women, declaring that the government is now "focused on guaranteeing religious freedom and conscience protections for those Americans who have a religious or moral objection to providing certain services based on their sincerely held beliefs" (*PBS Newshour*, October 11, 2017).

In proposing these rules, the administration privileged religious faith over women's health care needs, its actions affecting women in the nation differently depending on their state of residence. Some states, such as California, required all employers (except churches) to cover contraceptive care with no co-payments; others, such as Iowa, entitled employees to birth control coverage if their health care plans included prescription drug coverage but it was silent on cost-sharing (Sobel, Salganicoff, and Gomez 2018). The two Trump HHS interim rules, which became effective immediately, were quickly challenged in three states (Pennsylvania, Massachusetts, and California). On December 15, 2017, the Pennsylvania federal district court judge issued a nationwide injunction against the rules and reinstated the policy prior to October 6, 2017 (*Pennsylvania v. Trump* 2017). She found the Trump administration rules inconsistent with the ACA because, in her view, the law only granted HRSA the right to define the types of necessary services but had not authorized it to exempt individuals from compliance with the mandate; nor did she agree that RFRA required the administration to adopt the two regulations. In addition, she concluded, the Trump administration had likely violated federal law by failing to adhere to the notice and public comment provisions required in the regulatory process under the Administrative Procedure Act (APA). In a suit filed by Democratic attorneys general in California, Delaware, Maryland, New York, and Virginia, a California federal district court also put the regulations on hold in thirteen states and the District of Columbia while the lawsuit challenging them continued; the Ninth Circuit Court of Appeals affirmed the district court in *California v. Azar* (2018).

With the injunctions in place, the Trump administration was unable to implement the new policy. The status of the Pennsylvania case became uncertain when, on November 7, 2018, HHS issued final regulations, replacing the interim rules. Essentially reiterating the interim rules, the final rules broadly exempted all nonprofit (including religiously affiliated colleges and universities with student health plans) and for-profit entities (regardless of their size and whether they were closely held or publicly traded) from complying with the contraception mandate based on religious objections. They also allowed nonprofit entities and closely held companies to opt out of the mandate by raising moral objections. Moreover, the regulations released the employer from having to furnish notice of noncompliance to the government and, in some cases, even to affected employees. Among other things, the moral exemption raised concerns about its boundaries. As an attorney in the Pennsylvania attorney general's office noted, it "could in theory allow an employer who objects to women in the work force, for instance, to remove itself from providing contraception" (*New York Times*, May 6, 2020). The Trump administration justified extending the exemption to moral beliefs because "moral convictions are protected in ways similar to religious beliefs," when the convictions are those (1) that a person "deeply and sincerely holds"; (2) "that are purely ethical or moral in source and content"; (3) "but that nevertheless impose . . . a duty"; (4) and that "certainly occupy . . . a place parallel to that filled by . . . God in traditionally religious persons," such that one could say the "beliefs function as a religion" (US Department of Health and Human Services 2018).

With both exemptions in place, thousands of women employees and students were deprived of the no-cost contraceptive care they had been receiving. In announcing the final regulations, an HHS press release acknowledged the exemptions might affect as many as 127,000 women employees in a year (US Department of Health and Human Services 2018). HHS also "estimate[d] that the cost of losing contraception is $584 per woman per year" (Sobel, Salganicoff, and Rosenzweig 2018).

The Pennsylvania judge also blocked the final rules from going into effect with a nationwide injunction issued on January 14, 2019; she accepted the states' (Pennsylvania was joined by New Jersey) contention that the ACA requires employers to cover preventive care and screenings, which, according to HRSA, includes no-cost FDA-approved contraception. The judge also agreed with the states that the regulations would harm them because women would have to draw on state and local resources to compensate for the loss of coverage under their employers' plans and they would injure women whose health suffered with the inevitable increase in unintended pregnancies (*Pennsylvania v. Trump* 2019). On July 12, 2019, the Third Circuit Court of Appeals affirmed the lower court judge in *Pennsylvania v. President United States* (2019). The Supreme Court agreed to review the circuit ruling to consider whether the administration had exceeded its authority under the ACA in creating the two exemptions. Not initially a party in the suit, the high court allowed the Little Sisters of the Poor to join the case after it began and the case was titled *Little Sisters of the Poor v. Pennsylvania*. The states claimed that HRSA exceeded its authority under the ACA by carving out exceptions to the contraceptive mandate. The government responded that the ACA granted broad discretion to HRSA to interpret the act, including its exemptions.

On July 8, 2020, the Court announced its opinion in *Little Sisters of the Poor v. Pennsylvania* (2020), focusing on the limits of HRSA's authority under the ACA. The majority rejected the challengers' arguments, holding that "HRSA has virtually unbridled discretion to decide what counts as preventive care and screenings. But the same capacious grant of authority that empowers HRSA to make these determinations leaves its discretion equally unchecked in other areas, including the ability to identify and create exemptions from its own Guidelines" (2380). This authority, it added, extended to fashioning the exemptions. The Court noted that the ACA did not specify that women had access to free birth control coverage; Congress instead gave HRSA almost total control over the mandate.

The justices exhibited little concern about how the opinion would affect women, simply echoing the government's position that they would not be harmed. Although the dissent stressed that "between 70,500 and 126,400 women would immediately lose access to no-cost contraceptive services," the majority noted that the government "dispute[d] that women will be adversely impacted," adding that in any event, "such a policy concern cannot justify supplanting the text's plain meaning" (2381). The Court's stated concern that women receive adequate contraceptive care was belied by the fact that it allowed the employers' religious and moral objections to contraception to thwart their health care needs. Some justices seemed surprised that women would not simply accept their employer's point of view about birth control and look for contraceptive coverage elsewhere. The opinion was also silent on its effect on low-income wage earners who would be deprived of contraceptive care if their employers maintained it violated their consciences (*Health Affairs*, March 23, 2021). Critics should direct their concerns about depriving women of birth control to Congress, the Court proclaimed, for failing to specify contraceptive coverage in the law.

Because the text of the statute was clear, the majority declared, it did not have to address whether RFRA affected the conscience exemptions; Clarence Thomas and Samuel Alito emphatically asserted that the Court should have held that RFRA required the government to establish the religious exemption. The opinion ended with a paean to the Little Sisters, extolling it for "hav[ing] engaged in faithful service and sacrifice, motivated by a religious calling to surrender all for the sake of their brother" and their "commit[ment] to constantly living out a witness that proclaims the unique, inviolable dignity of every person, particularly those whom others regard as weak or worthless." It praised the administration for finally devising "a solution that exempts the Little Sisters from the source of their complicity-based concerns—the administratively imposed contraceptive mandate" (*Little Sisters of the Poor v. Pennsylvania* 2020, 2386).

In determining that the government had the authority to exempt the Little Sisters from the contraceptive mandate, the Court did not address the states' argument that the regulations violated the APA; it returned the case to the lower courts to consider the APA claims. Kagan and Stephen Breyer, who agreed HRSA had the statutory authority to grant the exemptions, predicted that the lower courts would find them too broad because they allowed publicly traded for-profit corporations and employers with moral scruples against contraception to be excused from compliance with the contraception mandate. Moreover, they noted, in its zeal to safeguard religious faith, the administration had turned a blind eye to women's needs for contraceptive care that HRSA had deemed necessary when the rules were first promulgated.

The White House press secretary applauded the decision, calling it "a big win for religious freedom and freedom of conscience" (Reuters, July 8, 2020). Pennsylvania's attorney general released a statement, saying, "while I am disappointed with much of the majority opinion, I am pleased the Court allowed our challenge to the Administration's overly broad rules to proceed. We now return to the lower courts to address whether the exemptions are arbitrary and capricious. This fight is not over" (*CBS 21 News*, July 8, 2020). Ironically, the Little Sisters, the public face of the religious objectors, had always been exempted from providing birth control coverage to their employees, for their benefits were part of a church plan that was exempt from the mandate (*The Intercept*, July 9, 2020).

In July 2020, before the Supreme Court announced its opinion in *Little Sisters of the Poor*, Biden had stressed his intention to withdraw the 2018 regulations, maintaining that "as President, I will reverse President Trump's rollbacks of the Affordable Care Act, including his efforts to deny women access to health care, and work to restore the Obama-Biden policy that was in place before the U.S. Supreme Court decided *Hobby Lobby*. We should be expanding, not diminishing, access to health care—especially in the midst of a health crisis" (Biden 2020). Health care advocates urged the administration to go further than merely negating the Trump regulations; they sought enhanced access to reproductive health care for the entire nation (North 2020). But the Biden administration has been unable to achieve its goal of swiftly reversing the conscience exemptions because of the lengthy procedure involved in promulgating new regulations that include complying with the requirements of the APA.

On August 16, 2021, HHS, the Department of Labor, and the Internal Revenue Service released a joint document to address questions about the administration's plans to revoke the Trump regulations. Labeled a FAQ, in response to a question about changes to the 2018 final regulations, the document stated, "The Departments intend to initiate rulemaking within 6 months to amend the 2018 final regulations and obtaining public input will be included as part of the Departments' rulemaking process" (US Departments of Labor, Health and Human Services, and Internal Revenue Service 2021). More broadly, responding to complaints that women were being denied coverage entirely or forced to pay for their contraception, the Biden administration expressed concern with the insurance companies' compliance with the contraceptive mandate. In June 2022, administration officials reminded health insurers of their responsibility to provide contraceptive services (at least one form of each of the eighteen FDA-approved birth control methods).

Conclusion

This chapter highlighted the interactions among Congress, the courts, and the executive branch in formulating and implementing contraceptive care policies, focusing on the two programs that sought to expand access to family planning—Title X and the ACA. Most women in the United States have relied on contraception at some point in their lives, primarily to prevent unwanted pregnancies. The chapter discussed US family planning policies, explaining that for over a century, women's rights advocates struggled to remove government restrictions on their access to birth control. The legal barrier to state bans on disseminating information and contraceptive devices and material effectively ended when the Supreme Court formalized a constitutional right to privacy in *Griswold v. Connecticut* (1965). Soon the high court removed most of the remaining legal barriers to contraception. Women were able to obtain contraception, but for many, the cost was prohibitive.

The federal government's first effort to extend contraceptive care was the 1974 Title X Family Planning Program, a program to expand access for the nation's low-income women. Title X eventually became embroiled in the controversy over abortion rights and the status of Planned Parenthood, a key Title X agency. Republican efforts to defund Planned Parenthood at the state and federal levels led to restrictions on Title X recipients, resulting in diminished services for poor women, depriving many of their needed contraceptive care.

The ACA, expanding access to medical insurance coverage, also became embroiled in debates over women's reproductive rights. The contraceptive mandate, a key provision of the act, required most employer-funded insurance policies to provide no-cost contraceptive care for their employees. With the support of the Trump administration, religiously affiliated employers sought exemptions, challenging the mandate as an infringement on their religious liberty. In *Little Sisters of the Poor v. Pennsylvania* (2020), the Supreme Court agreed, privileging religious freedom over the contraceptive mandate. Once in office, the Biden administration announced its intention to reverse Trump administration regulations and renew the promise of no-cost contraceptive care to millions of working women.

6

Pursuing
Abortion Rights

ABORTIONS WERE WIDELY ACCESSIBLE TO WOMEN IN THE UNITED
States from colonialism until the mid-1800s, following the English
common law principle that abortion was legal until quickening (the
point at which a woman feels the fetus move, usually occurring between
sixteen and twenty weeks of pregnancy). In the 1860s, states began to
enact abortion regulations, propelled in part by male doctors who
sought to limit competition from midwives and other quasimedical
practitioners. Other reasons for restricting abortion during this time
were rooted in the effort to increase the birth rate of white Protestant
(that is, nonimmigrant) women and minimize female autonomy. By
1910, abortion had become illegal in all states, including before
quickening (Mohr 1978; Reagan 1998; Center for American Progress,
August 8, 2013).

Even when illegal, abortions were not uncommon because "preventing women and girls from accessing an abortion does not mean they
stop needing one . . . [and a ban does] nothing to reduce the number of
abortions, it only forces people to seek out unsafe abortions" (Amnesty
International 2021). Studies estimate that when abortion was illegal and
precise numbers were difficult to obtain, the number of illegal or self-
induced abortions in the 1950s and 1960s ranged from 200,000 to 1.2
million a year (Gold and Donovan 2017). Illegal abortions endangered
all women, with a disparate effect on poor and minority women who
"paid a steep price for [the] illegal procedures" (Gold 2003).

By 1973, because of state reform movements, seventeen states had
either abolished their abortion laws or expanded exceptions, easing

access to abortion care. Women's rights advocates, struggling to make abortion more accessible and safer nationwide, hoped the courts would advance their goal by striking down a Texas law criminalizing abortion except to save the woman's life. The Supreme Court agreed, and, in a 7–2 vote, held in *Roe v. Wade* (1973) that a woman's decision to terminate her pregnancy was protected by her right of privacy, derived from the liberty component of the due process clause of the Fourteenth Amendment and formalized in *Griswold v. Connecticut* (1965). But, it added, although the right is fundamental (and requires a compelling state interest to restrict it), it is not absolute and must be balanced against the state's interest in protecting maternal and fetal health.

Critical to the decision was the Court's finding that the reference to "person" in the Fourteenth Amendment does not include the unborn and its refusal to adopt the view that life begins at conception. The majority rejected the state's argument that its interests in maternal health and fetal life are compelling throughout pregnancy, instead holding that each becomes compelling as the pregnancy progresses. To reconcile the state's authority to regulate abortion with a woman's right to terminate a pregnancy, the Court adopted a trimester approach based on the principle that the regulations must vary with the stages, or more specifically, the trimesters, of pregnancy. Applying the trimester framework, a majority reasoned that a state cannot limit abortion to protect women's health during the first trimester because, with the rate of maternal mortality, an abortion is safer than carrying the pregnancy to term. At the start of the second trimester, the state's interest in women's health becomes compelling and it may regulate the procedure, but only to safeguard their health. The government's interest in potential life becomes compelling at the last trimester when the fetus is viable, that is, it can exist outside the womb. During this trimester, the state can ban abortions entirely unless they are essential to maintain women's lives and health. Because the statute did not distinguish among the stages of pregnancy, it was declared unconstitutional.

The Post-*Roe* Decade

While *Roe* established a constitutional right to abortion care, states (chiefly Pennsylvania, Ohio, and Missouri) continued to devise ways to restrict access, contending that their laws were aimed at safeguarding women's health. In the first decade after *Roe*, the Supreme Court largely rebuffed these efforts, striking laws banning certain abortion methods and imposing hospitalization requirements. In such cases, it scrutinized the regulations, weighing the government's justifications for them, rather than simply accepting its assertions.

Despite its commitment to abortion rights during this time, the Court allowed states to limit access for minors. Establishing that minors have a right to privacy, it nevertheless upheld laws requiring parental consent or at least notification if they included a judicial bypass that allowed them to seek court approval for the procedure. With the Court's acquiescence in limiting minors' rights, by 2020, thirty-seven states required at least one parent to be notified or consent to the procedure, with some requiring both notification and consent (Guttmacher Institute 2022d). The high court also permitted state and local entities, as well as the federal government, to bar public funds for abortions for indigent women, agreeing that they are not constitutionally obligated to provide funding. Recognizing that the policies make it more difficult for poor women to obtain abortions, a majority held that denying them funding did not infringe on their constitutional rights because the laws neither created nor affected their indigency (Mezey 2011).

One of the first congressional battles over abortion—one with continuing effects until the present—revolved around the Hyde Amendment, adopted in 1976. Named after Representative Henry Hyde (R-IL), it restricted the use of federal dollars for abortions for women enrolled in Medicaid—the federal-state medical assistance program for low-income people. Hyde revealed that his real goal was to limit access to abortion, saying, "I certainly would like to prevent, if I could legally, anybody having an abortion, a rich woman, a middle-class woman, or a poor woman. Unfortunately, the only vehicle available is the . . . Medicaid bill" (quoted in Boonstra 2007; *Rewire.News*, June 21, 2019). As originally approved, it only excepted an abortion necessary to save the woman's life. In 1993, Congress modified it to include exceptions for pregnancies resulting from rape or incest (Poggi 2005). While the amendment does not preclude states from spending their own funds, only sixteen states have taken that route (Guttmacher Institute 2022e).

Since its passage, the Hyde Amendment has been approved each year as a rider to a congressional appropriations bill, and it remains in force to block federal expenditures of funds for abortions. Initially applied to restrictions on Medicaid funding for abortions, it soon expanded to broadly apply to all federally funded programs, including government health insurance programs as well as the Title X family planning program. It also prohibits the use of federal money for abortions for veterans, federal employees, and residents of Washington, DC, as well as women in the military, federal prisons, and the Peace Corps (Salganicoff, Sobel, and Ramaswamy 2021). In 1980, the Supreme Court ruled on a challenge to the Hyde Amendment to determine whether states participating in the Medicaid program must fund medically necessary abortions when the amendment blocks federal reimbursement (Patton 2018). The Court upheld the government's choice to prefer childbirth over abortion because it reasonably relates to its legitimate interest in protecting potential life (*Harris v. McRae* 1980).

Democratic women in Congress unsuccessfully introduced legislation to repeal the Hyde Amendment in 2015 and again in 2019 (*Mother Jones*, March 31, 2021). President Joe Biden, who had initially voted for it in 1976, reversed himself as presidential candidate in 2019, saying, "circumstances have changed" (*Washington Post*, June 7, 2019). As president, Biden omitted the amendment from his fiscal year 2022 budget proposal (*Washington Post*, May 28, 2021). In July 2021, the House-passed package of spending bills also did not include the amendment. Representative Barbara Lee (D-CA) exclaimed, "finally, the right to reproductive freedom has been recognized by the majority of Democrats" (*Time*, July 29, 2021). Senate Democrats supported the House measure but the amendment remained in place because there were not enough votes to repeal it.

Diminishing Abortions Rights

In the decade after *Roe*, as a number of states sought to limit access to abortion care, they enacted laws, collectively known as informed consent laws, that they claimed were intended to protect women's health; such laws mandated counseling sessions, waiting periods (typically twenty-four or forty-eight hours), and physician warnings of abortion harms. Whatever their intent, the laws made abortions less accessible to women (Donovan 1980; Kapp 1982; Kramer 2018). In ruling on challenges to these regulations, the Supreme Court assessed the state's contention that its aim was to promote women's health rather than to simply persuade them to reject abortion as an option. In *City of Akron v. Akron Center for Reproductive Health* (1983), for example, a majority held the twenty-four-hour waiting period was detrimental to women's health because it led to scheduling delays that increased their risk. It characterized the provision requiring a physician to describe to her "in detail the anatomical and physiological characteristics of the particular unborn child at the gestational point of development at which time the abortion is to be performed" and advise her of the physical and emotional risks of abortion as "a parade of horribles" that was not intended to inform but to influence her choice against abortion. Similarly, a majority in *Thornburgh v. American College of Obstetricians and Gynecologists* (1986) struck down provisions of a 1982 Pennsylvania law that required a twenty-four-hour waiting period and a physician's lecture.

By the end of the 1980s, anti-abortion activists increasingly turned to state and local public officials to restrict access to abortion care, hoping the justices appointed by Republican presidents Ronald Reagan and George H. W. Bush would vote to overturn *Roe*—or at least permit stricter abortion regulations. Both sides of the abortion debate anticipated that the Court would determine the future of abortion rights in a ruling on a Missouri law that directly challenged *Roe* (*Webster v. Reproductive Health Services* 1989). In a fractured opinion, a three-justice plurality refused to overturn *Roe* but broadly criticized it, particularly characterizing the trimester framework as "rigid" and "unworkable in practice" (*Webster v. Reproductive Health Services* 1989, 518). The justices explicitly invited states to restrict abortion rights, strongly implying that the Court's subsequent rulings would "modify and narrow *Roe*" (*Webster v. Reproductive Health Services* 1989, 521; Dellinger and Sperling 1989; Kendis 2019).

Their invitation prompted numerous legislatures to further limit women's access to abortion to challenge the Court's commitment to *Roe*. One such Pennsylvania law included a waiting period and a prescribed physician's speech, mirroring the provisions declared unconstitutional in *Akron* and *Thornburgh*, as well as a provision requiring a woman to notify her husband of her planned abortion and furnish her provider with proof of the notification. In *Planned Parenthood of Southeastern Pennsylvania v. Casey* (1992)—one of the most closely watched abortion rights cases—the Court satisfied neither side of the debate with a three-justice joint opinion declaring support for *Roe* while charting a new course for evaluating restrictions on access to abortion. Disappointing the anti-abortion activists, the joint opinion reiterated *Roe*'s holding that a woman's decision to terminate her pregnancy is constitutionally protected by the substantive component of the due process clause of the Fourteenth Amendment. In a significant admission, the opinion recognized that *Roe* heightened women's agency, declaring "the ability of women to participate equally in the economic and social life of the Nation has been facilitated by their ability to control their reproductive lives" (*Planned Parenthood of Southeastern Pennsylvania v. Casey* 1992, 856).

Reviewing its prior rulings on abortion rights, the joint opinion restated *Roe*'s central tenets, identifying its three "essential" elements: the state may not unduly interfere with a woman's choice to abort a pre-viable fetus; the state may restrict abortion after viability, but must allow exceptions for the woman's life or health; and the state's interest in maternal and fetal life begins at the start of pregnancy and is present throughout. After declaring its commitment to *Roe*, the joint opinion replaced its fundamental rights analysis with a more deferential standard of review, known as the undue burden test. The effect of the new standard was to relieve the government of its obligation to show it had a compelling interest in an abortion regulation.

Casey signaled the Court's willingness to allow states more leeway to restrict women's access to abortion care (Jordan 2015; Cohen 2018; Ziegler 2018). It collapsed the first two trimesters into a previability stage, during which the state's interest in protecting potential human life entitled it to regulate abortion as long as it did not impose an undue burden on a woman. An "undue burden," the opinion clarified, "is a shorthand for the conclusion that a state regulation has the purpose or effect of placing a substantial obstacle in the path of a woman seeking an abortion of a nonviable fetus" (*Planned Parenthood of Southeastern Pennsylvania v. Casey* 1992, 874). In drawing the line at viability, the opinion reaffirmed the Court's commitment to effectuating *Roe*'s "most central principle" (*Planned Parenthood of Southeastern Pennsylvania v. Casey* 1992, 871), but echoing *Webster*, it underscored the state's interest in fetal life throughout the pregnancy. In the third trimester, now known as the postviability stage, the state was permitted to restrict and even prohibit abortion, if it retained exceptions for the woman's life or health.

Applying the new standard, the joint opinion upheld the physician's prescribed lecture and twenty-four-hour waiting period, overturning *City of Akron* and *Thornburgh*. The justices acknowledged that a waiting period may impose a burden on some women, particularly those who must travel long distances to medical facilities, but they did not view it as an undue burden. Several studies have underscored that forcing women to travel greater distances leads to higher costs, a greater likelihood of emergency room visits for follow-up care, and poorer mental health (Fuentes and Jerman 2019). The opinion dismissed the impact of these restrictions that make abortions more inconvenient, riskier, and more expensive.

The plurality opinion took a different view of the spousal notification provision, persuaded that women usually have good reasons to avoid informing their husbands of their intended abortion. Rejecting the state's argument that the law was not unduly burdensome because it would affect only a small fraction of Pennsylvania women, the opinion found that it could impose an undue burden on the women for whom it is relevant, that is, married women who do not want to notify their husbands of their upcoming abortions (Kendis 2019). Two other justices praised the joint opinion for reaffirming *Roe* but criticized it for diminishing the right to abortion as a fundamental right and allowing states greater latitude to regulate it. The remaining two disapproved of it for failing to overturn *Roe* but commended it for expanding the state's authority over fetal life and adopting a less rigorous standard to evaluate abortion regulations (Jordan 2015).

A Focus on Methods of Abortion

While *Casey* settled *Roe*'s immediate future, the battle over abortion rights continued to rage in state legislatures and Congress. Anti-abortion activists, encouraged by the Court's increasing willingness to restrict access to abortion care, initially focused their attention on laws limiting types of procedures (Donaldson 2018). A popular target was a rarely used method—primarily performed late in the second trimester or in the third trimester—called dilation and extraction or intact dilation and evacuation, also known as D&X. The D&X differs from the commonly used second trimester method, dilation and evacuation (D&E) (Lohr 2008; Donovan 2017). Physicians prefer to use the D&X procedure in certain circumstances because it avoids the use of sharp instruments and minimizes infections, excessive blood loss, and uterine damage that can severely compromise a woman's health or future fertility. In 2000, only 0.17 percent of 1.3 million abortions performed that year used the D&X method (Finer and Henshaw 2003). Despite its rarity, the procedure was frequently singled out by anti-abortion activists and politicians to embargo (Kaiser Family Foundation 2019).

The discord over the D&X procedure—called partial-birth abortion by abortion opponents and late-term abortion by abortion rights proponents—was brought to public attention in the early 1990s when Congress restricted its use. President Bill Clinton vetoed the law, believing it unconstitutional because it did not include an exception for the woman's health as *Casey* required. By the late 1990s, most states had enacted such laws, with courts generally striking them down because they were unconstitutionally vague or imposed an undue burden by risking the health of a woman for whom the procedure was safer (Mezey 2011). In 2000, the Supreme Court ruled on a Nebraska law, applicable throughout a woman's pregnancy, that revoked the license of a doctor who illegally performed a D&X; the law included an exception to save the woman's life but not her health. In *Stenberg v. Carhart* (2000), its first major abortion rights decision in eight years, it concluded the statute was unconstitutional because it lacked a health exception. The state argued that the D&X is never necessary because there are safe alternatives to it. The Court disagreed, citing medical evidence in the record that it is often the safest method to preserve a woman's health and fertility. The majority believed the statute itself "create[d] a significant health risk" (938) by forcing a woman to undergo a more dangerous procedure under the guise of protecting her health.

Following George W. Bush's election in 2000, House Republicans introduced a bill to curb the use of the D&X procedure, relying on a president who ran on an anti-abortion platform to sign it into law. Their first effort passed the House in 2002 but failed in the Democratic-controlled Senate. The next year, with Republicans in the majority in the Senate, Congress approved the Partial-Birth Abortion Ban Act (PBABA) of 2003, barring providers from intentionally performing a D&X abortion that is not essential to save the woman's life. When the law was challenged, the outcome of the case seemed likely when the majority opinion began by declaring that laws "express[ing] profound respect for the life of the unborn are permitted if they are not a substantial obstacle" (*Gonzales v. Carhart* 2007, 146). Unlike the Nebraska statute, which was unconstitutionally vague because it did not describe the banned procedure in sufficient detail, the majority concluded that the PBABA precisely delineated the "anatomical landmarks" of the fetus as it leaves the woman's body. Moreover, it held, Congress unmistakably identified the illegal conduct as applying only to physicians who "deliberately and intentionally" perform the procedure.

Citing *Casey*, the Court considered whether the purpose and effect of the law imposed an undue burden on a woman with a previable fetus and determined that Congress had a legitimate purpose in passing it: first, to demonstrate its respect for human life, including the unborn; second, to preserve the integrity of the medical community by preventing its members from engaging in repugnant acts; and third, to single out a method of abortion that much of society considered equivalent to infanticide. Because the congressional testimony reflected significant disagreement among medical experts about whether the D&X procedure was ever necessary to protect a woman's health, the Court believed the law does not require a health exception. In the face of such "medical uncertainty," it said, Congress may legitimately believe that omitting a health exception would not jeopardize women's health, especially because other abortion methods were available.

Gonzales revealed the high court's receptivity to limitations on access to abortion care and, by accepting Congress's justification for the PBABA without subjecting it to more rigorous analysis, the ruling signaled that the Court would "accept a state's purported reasons for passing abortion restrictions at face value," and in doing so, encourage antiabortion advocates to continue their efforts (Cohen 2018, 180). Not surprisingly, by 2021, twenty-one states had banned the D&X abortion, allowing an exception only to save the woman's life (Bernstein 2008; Mirakian 2008; Guttmacher Institute 2022c).

Abortion Statistics

There is a plethora of studies that examine the rate of abortions in the United States and the characteristics of the women receiving them. One widely cited study estimates almost one-quarter (24 percent) of US women between eighteen and forty-five will have an abortion by age forty-five (Jones and Jerman 2017). The data also show that most abortions are performed early in pregnancy; in 2018, slightly more than three quarters (77.7 percent) were done at or less than nine weeks' gestation, with the vast majority (92.2 percent) performed at or less than thirteen weeks (US Department of Health and Human Services, Centers for Disease Control and Prevention 2020a; *New York Times*, December 14, 2021). According to a report from the Kaiser Family Foundation (2019), the rare woman who undergoes an abortion late in her pregnancy typically does so for medical reasons, such as "fetal anomalies or maternal life endangerment."

A Guttmacher Institute report based on its fifth national survey of abortion patients represents one of the most comprehensive studies of the characteristics of women obtaining abortions in the United States. The study indicated that, in 2014, 60 percent of women receiving abortions were in their twenties and 25 percent in their thirties; almost 70 percent had high school or some college education, and about 23 percent had college degrees; 45 percent of the women were married or living with someone, 54 percent were not cohabitating when they became pregnant, and 59 percent had had at least one birth. Comparing abortion recipients by race and ethnicity, 39 percent were white, 28 percent were African American, 25 percent were Hispanic, and 6 percent were Asian or Pacific Islander. Perhaps the most striking characteristic was that 75 percent of women receiving abortions in 2014 lived in poverty or near poverty: 49 percent lived below the federal poverty line, and 26 percent had incomes within 100 to 200 percent of poverty (Jerman, Jones, and Onda 2016, table 1; Guttmacher Institute 2019).

With the heated debates over abortion policies, pollsters have been gauging support for abortion for almost five decades. Depending in part on the wording of the question, the surveys indicate views on abortion are nuanced. They have been quite stable, with most respondents supporting abortion rights, while also accepting restrictions under some circumstances; few want it prohibited in all cases. In a broadly worded question, a Pew Research Center survey of US adults in April 2021 reported 59 percent believed abortion should be "legal in all/most cases," and 39 percent think it should be "illegal in all/most cases." Pew concluded that "while Americans' support for legal abortion has fluctuated somewhat in recent years, it has remained relatively consistent in the past five years" (Pew Research Center 2021).

A Gallup poll of registered voters conducted in May 2021 also found that most respondents support the right to abortion: 32 percent thought it should be "legal under any" circumstances; 48 percent believed it should be "legal only under certain" circumstances; 19 percent stated it should be "illegal under all" circumstances, and 2 percent had no opinion (Gallup 2021). Similarly, a Monmouth University survey of US adults, conducted in September 2021, showed 33 percent of respondents felt abortion should "always be legal," 29 percent said it should be "legal with limitations," 24 percent wanted it to be "illegal with exceptions," 11 percent thought it should be "always illegal," and 2 percent said they did not know. Based on these results, Monmouth characterized the American people as "largely pro-choice, although many would accept some limitations on abortion access" (Monmouth University Polling Institute 2021).

A Proliferation of State Abortion Regulations

Many public officials, spurred by anti-abortion activists, seek to restrict access to abortion by "construct[ing] a lattice work of abortion law, codifying, regulating and limiting whether, when and under what circumstances a woman may obtain an abortion" (Guttmacher Institute

2022b). The 2010 election led to Republican dominance in most state legislatures, producing a flurry of such abortion restrictions nationwide. By 2020, twenty-nine states were characterized as hostile to abortion rights, with only sixteen considered supportive, and the remainder somewhere in the middle. According to these data, nearly forty million women of reproductive age lived in states hostile to abortion rights (Nash 2019).

About a dozen states, primarily in the Northeast and West, had strengthened abortion rights by allowing abortions up to viability, expanding professionals permitted to perform abortions, requiring funding by the state Medicaid program, and protecting clinic staff and patients' privacy. Most states, though, primarily in the South and Midwest, moved to restrict access to abortion (Nash et al. 2018; Nash et al. 2019; *The Hill*, January 8, 2020). They adopted a variety of measures, including mandatory counseling, ultrasound imaging and other testing, waiting periods, parental involvement, funding restrictions, structural clinic modifications, gestational limits, informed consent, and physician licensing (Djavaherian et al. 2017; Kubak et al. 2019; Guttmacher Institute 2022b).

Anticipating the Court's increasing hostility to abortion rights, twenty-six states were preparing to severely restrict or ban abortion: about half had enacted laws, known as trigger laws, that would make abortions illegal when *Roe* is overturned by the high court; others were relying on anti-abortion laws that predated *Roe* (some enacted in the 1800s); and others introduced constitutional amendments to deny access to abortion except in very limited conditions (Atkins 2021; Brown 2021; Nash and Cross 2021). In the states considered hostile to abortion rights, anti-abortion laws were in part fueled by grassroots activism, supported by national groups such as the National Right to Life, the Susan B. Anthony List, Alliance Defending Freedom, and Americans United for Life; they produced research, wrote model legislation, and provided litigation support as well as funding for political campaigns of anti-abortion public officials (*Washington Post*, May 18, 2019). After the 2016 election of President Donald Trump, who had pledged to curb access to abortion and appoint federal judges committed to overturning *Roe*, their efforts gained momentum. An official of Susan B. Anthony's List presciently observed: "*Roe v. Wade* is on the ropes. I think both sides know it" (*The Hill*, January 8, 2020).

By the middle of 2021, state legislatures had passed ninety anti-abortion measures, more than in any year since *Roe* was decided; most expressly conflicted with *Roe* and *Casey*'s viability standards (Nash and Naide 2021). Almost fifty years had elapsed since *Roe* first identified viability at about twenty-four weeks as the stage of pregnancy when, the Court had said, the fetus was "presumably" capable of living outside the womb. The widely shared medical view today is that viability still occurs around twenty-four weeks (American College of Obstetricians and Gynecologists 2017; *Politico*, May 17, 2021; Danielsson 2022). Doctors often describe viability as "a bit of a moving target," and "in many hospitals, 24 weeks is the point at which doctors will take steps to save the life of a baby born prematurely [which] generally means extreme medical intervention . . . followed by a lengthy stay in a neonatal intensive care unit" (Danielsson 2022). Moreover, they indicate that babies born before twenty-three weeks stand almost no chance of survival (*Washington Post,* January 17, 2017).

Contending that viability begins earlier, states such as Arizona, Iowa, and Kentucky drew the line at legal abortions at twenty weeks. Other states adopted even more stringent standards. Versions of such legislation, popularly known as heartbeat bills, were approved in North Dakota, Oklahoma, Georgia, Kentucky, Louisiana, Tennessee, Texas, and Ohio. The 2019 Georgia law even took the unusual step of allowing women to be prosecuted for abortion care once a heartbeat became detectable. Most states singled out abortion providers for punishment, rejecting the politically unpopular tactic of penalizing the woman (*The American Prospect*, June 16, 2016).

Anti-abortion activists and legislators adopted the term "heartbeat bill" because of its political impact rather than its descriptive value, reminiscent of the partial birth abortion rhetoric in the 1990s. Such laws ban abortions when some cardiac activity is detected, with the fetal age calculated from the first day of the woman's last menstrual period. Citing the impact of the term "fetal heartbeat," a doctor specializing in obstetrics and gynecology at a San Francisco hospital called it "an intentional obfuscation," explaining that "hearing the word heartbeat plays on people's emotions . . . when in fact what it does is effectively ban abortions for many people, because many people don't even know they're pregnant at six weeks" (*Wired*, May 14, 2019). Moreover, as other physicians and scientists have observed, it is misleading to call the electrical activity at six weeks a heartbeat. The executive director of an abortion rights group in Texas contends such laws are "intentionally written to evoke an emotional response," adding that they are actually "just a ban on abortion at six weeks' gestation, which is two weeks after a missed period" (*Texas Tribune*, September 2, 2021). According to the head of a fetal care center at a Miami Children's hospital, "at six weeks of pregnancy, an ultrasound may detect a little flutter in the area that will become the future heart of the baby," clarifying that "this flutter happens because the group of cells that will become the future 'pacemaker' of the heart gain the capacity to fire electric signals" (*LiveScience*, September 1, 2021).

Republican governors vied with each other to characterize their state's laws as the most extreme. In 2019, Georgia's Brian Kemp announced his was "the toughest abortion bill in the country" (*Huffington Post*, May 7, 2019). After signing the Tennessee bill, Governor Bill Lee called his state's law "arguably the most conservative, pro-life piece of legislation in the country" (ABC News, July 13, 2020). States restricted access to abortion through a variety of measures: Mississippi, West Virginia, Arkansas, and Texas banned D&E abortions, thereby effectively eliminating most second-trimester abortions. The federal government and nearly half the states prohibited women from obtaining prescriptions for medication abortions through telemedicine appointments. Arizona and Indiana banned abortions motivated by sex or race selection; Indiana, Louisiana, Ohio, and North Dakota barred women from having abortions for reasons of fetal abnormalities (Kubak et al. 2019; *Washington Post*, March 5, 2018). The federal courts frequently blocked such laws, but in *Preterm-Cleveland v. McCloud* (2021), the Sixth Circuit Court of Appeals upheld the Ohio law prohibiting doctors from performing a previable abortion when they know a woman is seeking it because of fetal Down syndrome. A divided court held that women do not have an absolute right to a pre-viability abortion and the Ohio law does not impose an undue burden on them. The majority emphasized the limits of the opinion, indicating it would only apply to a woman who told her doctor she wanted an abortion because of Down syndrome. The dissent criticized the ruling, accusing the majority of turning the statute "into a don't ask, don't tell law" (551).

States also reinforced their informed consent requirements, directing physicians to present a prescribed script of misleading and medically dubious statements to their patients. South Dakota, for example, ordered physicians to tell women of the elevated risk of depression and suicide afflicting women following abortions. Mississippi and Texas required abortion providers to warn patients they would develop breast cancer, and in Texas and North Carolina, physicians were obligated to perform ultrasound tests on women and describe the images to them in detail (Sanger 2008; Kramer 2018). As these laws proliferated, abortion rights activists continued to seek relief in the courts, arguing they conflicted with the right to abortion as affirmed in *Roe* and *Casey*. Courts often agreed and struck down the laws before they went into effect, but a sizable number remained on the books (Guttmacher Institute 2022f).

TRAP Laws

In the early 2010s, anti-abortion activists allied themselves with state and local officials, seeking to impose substantial impediments to abortion care, ostensibly to protect women (Jerman, Jones, and Onda 2016; Kubak et al. 2019). One set of such laws, called targeted regulations of abortion providers, or TRAP laws, were depicted by their proponents as "health-justified restrictions on abortion" (Greenhouse and Siegel 2016, 1432; Cohen 2018). Anti-abortion activists and their legislative allies preferred TRAP laws, because unlike laws that explicitly conflicted with *Roe*, they appeared reasonable on their face and purported to further the state's interest in women's welfare.

Modeled on laws drafted by the anti-abortion group Americans United for Life, TRAP laws sharply diminished access to abortion care by creating "a catastrophic tidal wave of targeted regulations against abortion providers" (Donaldson 2018, 257). In proposing the regulations, most legislators were aware they would be "unattainable for many abortion providers" and would result in "forcing large numbers of abortion clinics to close their doors" (Greenhouse and Siegel 2016, 1430). Abortion rights advocates contended these "onerous and irrelevant licensing requirements . . . have nothing to do with protecting women and everything to do with shutting down clinics" (Gold and Nash 2013, 7). They contended that TRAP laws constituted an admission by anti-abortion activists that straightforward attacks on abortion rights are less effective in preventing abortions than these more oblique tactics of regulating providers (Greenhouse 2020).

Such laws primarily singled out medical personnel and clinics, placing stricter limits on them than on other medical facilities (Kubak et al. 2019). More than half the states, primarily in the South, adopted TRAP laws, with most including structural standards on abortion facilities that required making them comparable to ambulatory surgical centers. They directed facilities performing abortions to conform to physical and staffing regulations typically designed for more complex surgical procedures, forcing clinics to close because the extensive alterations were beyond their resources (Guttmacher Institute 2022f). The provider-focused laws obligated doctors performing abortions to obtain privileges at local area hospitals so they could admit and diagnose patients on an emergency basis. In challenging the admitting privilege requirement, abortion rights advocates noted that abortions lead to very few complications and rarely necessitate emergency room referrals (Gold and Nash 2013). As one medical professional put it, "abortion is actually as safe as, or safer than, colonoscopy and has complication rates similar to outpatient plastic surgery or dental surgery." Another noted, "it's at least ten times safer than the risk of going forward with the pregnancy" (Reuters, December 11, 2014). Similarly, the author of a leading study on abortion complications determined they "are extremely rare" and the procedure is safer than "wisdom tooth extraction and tonsillectomies" (Reuters, July 11, 2018).

One study, published in 2015, gathered data on almost 55,000 abortions from women participating in the fee-for-service sector of California's Medicaid program between 2009 and 2010; the researchers' aim was to assess the number and type of complications that occurred up to six weeks after an abortion procedure. Their analysis showed only 2.1 percent of the abortions resulted in women seeking emergency room care or a return to the abortion facility, and, of those, most were for minor issues. The authors concluded "the complication rate is much lower [for abortions] than that found during childbirth" (Upadhyay et al. 2015, 181). While states defended TRAP laws on the grounds that they benefit women, this study and others suggest that such laws are not justified by medical need and, on the contrary, by leading to fewer personnel and clinic closures, result in higher costs and greater travel time to the nearest facility (Upadhyay et al. 2015; Kubak et al. 2019; Guttmacher Institute 2022f).

By 2013, with abortion rights activists mounting legal challenges to TRAP laws, the lower federal courts had adopted two approaches to determining whether such abortion regulations imposed undue burdens on women, each claiming fidelity to *Casey*. The Seventh and Ninth Circuit Courts of Appeals used a balancing test in which they required states to present evidence the regulations furthered their interest without penalizing women, that is, they weighed the benefits of the law against its burdens, striking down laws with insubstantial benefits (Kendis 2019). Rejecting this balancing methodology, the Fourth, Fifth, and Sixth Circuit Courts of Appeals applied the more deferential rational basis test, affording the state greater latitude to regulate abortions. These courts merely asked whether the regulation had a rational basis and whether it imposed an undue burden on women seeking abortions, that is, whether it created a substantial obstacle to an abortion (Cohen 2018; Kendis 2019).

The law drawing the most national attention was the Texas TRAP law, titled "Relating to the regulation of abortion procedures, providers, and facilities; providing penalties" (HB 2), signed into law by Texas Governor Rick Perry on July 18, 2013 (Ziegler 2018). It required, among other things, that abortion clinic doctors have active admitting privileges at nearby hospitals (within thirty miles of the facility) or face criminal penalties. Although it did not include a statement of purpose, state officials asserted it was intended to protect women's health and safety. Texas Planned Parenthood affiliates and abortion care providers filed suit, arguing HB 2 created an undue burden on women's access to abortion. They largely prevailed in the district courts, with the judges finding the law did not advance women's health. The courts cited evidence of significant clinic closures necessitating greater travel time and cost and concluded that it imposed a substantial obstacle on women seeking abortions. The Fifth Circuit Court of Appeals reversed the lower courts, finding HB 2 served a legitimate purpose by reasonably furthering the state's interest in safeguarding patient health and, even if it had led to fewer available clinics, it was not unduly burdensome because only 17 percent of women in Texas might have to travel over 150 miles to an abortion facility (Haksgaard 2017).

On June 27, 2016, the last day of the Supreme Court's 2015–2016 term, it announced its ruling on HB 2 in *Whole Woman's Health v. Hellerstedt* (2016). The high court explicitly approved the more liberal balancing approach that directed "courts [to] consider the burdens a law imposes on abortion access together with the benefits those laws confer" (2309). Turning to the evidence in the record, the majority cited empirical studies and expert testimony showing that the admitting privileges requirement in HB 2 was superfluous because abortion is a safe procedure with little risk. Despite the state's contention that the law advances women's safety when complications arise, the Court agreed with the district court that it does not make women safer because there are no health concerns the law alleviates. The majority noted that the state failed to produce evidence of a single woman whose health had been improved by the law.

Noting a substantial number of clinic closures that would result in increased travel time and costs, the Court found the law erected a substantial obstacle to women's access to abortion. It held that the lower court had correctly balanced the burdens imposed by the Texas law against "the virtual absence of any health benefit" and concluded that HB 2 placed an "undue burden" on Texas women (2313). The majority also noted that the record showed abortion facilities were well regulated before HB 2 and abortions are less dangerous than other procedures, such as colonoscopies, childbirth, and liposuction, which are not subject to ambulatory surgical center constraints. As with the admitting privileges section of the law, the Court concluded that forcing clinics to close placed a heavy strain on the remaining facilities in the state, as testified to by an expert witness and supported by "common sense." The dissenting justices objected to the majority's endorsement of the balancing test and its willingness to allow lower court judges to engage in fact finding and override the legislature's judgment.

The decision made substantial inroads into the legality of TRAP laws, with federal courts striking them down in Alabama, Wisconsin, Mississippi, Oklahoma, Indiana, Texas, and Virginia (Donaldson 2018). Its most important contribution was to allow reviewing courts to weigh the benefits and burdens of such laws to determine how they affected women's health and their access to abortion care (Cohen 2018).

A year after the Texas law was enacted, Louisiana passed a TRAP law, Act 620, called the Unsafe Abortion Protection Act, made effective on September 1, 2014. It was strikingly like HB 2, requiring physicians who perform abortions to have "active admitting privileges" at hospitals no farther than thirty miles from the facility where the abortion is performed. As in Texas, the plaintiffs claimed that Act 620 did not serve a legitimate interest and placed a substantial obstacle on their patients' ability to obtain previable abortions. The state argued the plaintiffs had not proved the law was unrelated to a legitimate state interest or created an undue burden. The district court judge explained that the Fifth Circuit explicitly rejected the balancing test as part of the undue burden analysis and does not allow district courts to examine the effect of the challenged regulation on such conditions as poverty—which may make it more difficult for women to access abortion care—because the law did not create the conditions. Nevertheless, he expressed concern that Act 620 prompted clinic closures that adversely affected Louisiana women seeking abortions and therefore placed a substantial obstacle in their path.

The circuit court reversed, returning the case to the district court. Because the high court had decided *Hellerstedt*, the district court judge was able to balance the benefits of the law with its burdens. In doing so, he concluded that it played no role in advancing abortion safety and that clinic closures imposed a heavy burden, especially on poor women and women of color. The appeals court reversed the lower court. Required by *Hellerstedt* to balance benefits with burdens, the circuit court held the state had shown the law was a real benefit and did not impose a burden on women because it did not prevent doctors from obtaining admitting privileges and allowing the clinics to remain open.

With the two Trump appointees on the Supreme Court—Neil Gorsuch replacing Antonin Scalia, who had died in early 2016, and Brett Kavanaugh replacing the retired Anthony Kennedy, who had voted with the majority to strike the Texas TRAP law—the significance of the case was apparent to all. Anti-abortion activists anticipated the Court would uphold the Louisiana TRAP law and move a step closer to overturning *Roe*. They were buoyed by the fact that over 200 members of Congress submitted a brief urging it to affirm the Louisiana statute and reconsider *Roe*. Most eyes were on John Roberts because the chief justice had dissented in *Hellerstedt* but might be reluctant to rule in favor of a law virtually identical to one the Court recently declared unconstitutional. Observers speculated on whether his commitment to precedent and the Court's institutional integrity would overcome his opposition to abortion rights (*The Hill*, June 21, 2020; Kay and Kolbert 2020). Roberts's questions during the oral arguments centered on the degree to which the Court was bound by its decision in the Texas case (*The Hill*, March 4, 2020).

Another unusual characteristic of the case revolved around the issue of the plaintiffs' standing, that is, their legal ability to bring suit. Even though Louisiana had not raised standing objections, the Court allowed the state to file a late petition, arguing that abortion providers lacked standing to challenge the law because the doctors' financial stake in the litigation conflicted with the interests of the women they purported to represent in the lawsuit. They contended by challenging laws such as Act 620, physicians sacrificed women's health and safety. Denying standing would have a dramatic effect in expanding state authority over abortion because providers are the primary challengers to abortion regulations. Because legal standing by abortion providers had been a well-settled principle and the majority had not accepted this stance in the Texas case, abortion rights supporters considered it an ominous sign that it permitted the state to raise it now (Winkler 2020).

On June 29, 2020, the Supreme Court announced its decision in *June Medical Services v. Russo* (2020), reiterating the familiar legal standard that a law erecting a substantial obstacle to a woman seeking an abortion is invalid. The Court was not persuaded that the statute did not affect the availability of abortion doctors and clinics in Louisiana. Instead, it found that the state had not shown Act 620 advances abortion safety, provides substantial health benefits, or furthers health outcomes. It summed up by declaring the "findings and the evidence that underlies them are sufficient to support the District Court's conclusion that Act 620 would place substantial obstacles in the path of women seeking an abortion in Louisiana" (2130). Because it imposed an undue burden on Louisiana women, the Court held that the law violates the Constitution. Concurring in the judgment to strike it, Roberts reiterated he still believed the Texas TRAP law was valid, but the principal question the Court had to address here was whether the doctrine of stare decisis (adhering to precedent) required it to abide by its opinion in the Texas case. Because the Louisiana law mirrored the Texas law, he acknowledged that "absent special circumstances [the Court must] . . . treat like cases alike" (2134). On these grounds, he voted to hold Act 620 unconstitutional.

While he agreed that the decision to strike Act 620 was correct, Roberts rejected the balancing test, as did the four dissenting justices. He charged that the majority in *Hellerstedt* had incorrectly interpreted *Casey*'s undue burden standard to require "that courts consider the burdens a law imposes on abortion access *together* with the benefits those laws confer" (*June Medical Services v. Russo* 2020, 2135, quoting *Whole Women's Health v. Hellerstedt* 2016, 2309, emphasis added). But, he argued, because *Casey* had only focused on the burdens imposed by the Pennsylvania law, it did not set a precedent for employing a balancing test. In *Casey*, he said, the joint opinion did not assess the benefits of the law, only evaluating it to determine whether it erected a substantial obstacle. In his view, balancing the benefits of a law against its burdens would lead to arbitrary results.

After the ruling, anti-abortion groups contended that the balancing test was invalid because a majority—five justices, including Roberts— had opposed it. They urged the Court to accept their position because it would allow states greater leeway to enact abortion regulations (Greenhouse and Siegel 2016; Greenhouse 2020; Lithwick 2020). *June Medical* left lower courts in a quandary about whether they should continue to apply the balancing test, whether they should simply accept a state's assertion about the benefit of a law, and what type of burden they should consider unduly burdensome (Kendis 2019). They were divided about the effect of Roberts's concurring opinion, some treating it merely as a statement of his views, others characterizing it as the new legal standard for evaluating the constitutionality of abortion laws (CNN, April 14, 2021).

Medication Abortions

Medication abortions have become the most common method of abortion in the nation, estimated to account for 54 percent of all reported abortions in 2020. A medication abortion is often confused with emergency contraception. The latter is mostly available over the counter (that is, without a prescription) and works primarily by delaying or preventing ovulation from occurring. Often called the morning after pill or Plan B, emergency contraception is approved by the Food and Drug Administration (FDA) for use within seventy-two hours of unprotected sex or contraceptive failure (*Healthline*, April 21, 2021; *Healthline*, August 19, 2021).

Also called a self-managed abortion, a medication abortion consists of two drugs: mifepristone, or RU-486, that blocks receptors for the hormone progesterone, needed for the pregnancy to progress, and misoprostol—a total of four pills taken twenty-four to forty-eight hours after mifepristone—that stimulates contractions to empty the uterus. Considered safe and effective for up to ten weeks, "the pregnancy is terminated successfully 99.6% of the time, with a 0.4% risk of major complications, and an associated mortality rate of less than 0.001 percent (0.00064%)" (Kaiser Family Foundation 2022; Chen and Creinin 2015). RU-486 was developed by French scientists in 1980 and approved in 1988. At the time, the French health minister pointed to the magnitude of this decision, saying, "from the moment government approval for the drug was granted, RU-486 became the moral property of women, not just the property of the drug company" (Collins 2022).

The FDA approved mifepristone for sale as a method of early abortion in the United States in 2000. The agency initially required women to appear in person at specially certified hospitals, medical facilities, or providers' offices to obtain the pill; depending on state regulations, they were allowed to ingest it elsewhere. The second medication, misoprostol, was available as a routine prescription at a local pharmacy and could be taken at home. On March 29, 2016, the agency increased access to medication abortions by revising the labeling for mifepristone, affirming its safety, and raising eligibility from seven weeks to ten weeks of gestation. Despite the acknowledged safety record and federal approval of medication abortions, over half the states have restricted access to them, including bans on telehealth appointments and mail delivery. Many women have still been able to secure the pills through the internet from other states or international sources (Jones and Boonstra 2016; *Axios*, June 23, 2022).

The Covid-19 pandemic, surfacing in early 2020, affected women's access to abortion. At the start of the pandemic, the FDA waived the in-person requirement for most drugs; mifepristone (for abortion care) remained the only one of the 20,000 FDA-regulated drugs that required a patient to obtain it from a certified provider in person (American Civil Liberties Union 2020b). When the FDA refused ACOG's request to suspend the rule for mifepristone, the organization filed suit. On July 13, 2020, a Maryland federal district court judge issued an injunction, holding that enforcing the FDA rule imposed an undue burden on women seeking abortions, increasing their risk of contracting Covid-19 by traveling to a medical office to receive the pill (*American College of Obstetricians and Gynecologists v. United States FDA* 2020a). The Fourth Circuit Court of Appeals rejected the Trump administration's request for a stay, and, on October 8, 2020, the Supreme Court returned the case to the district court judge, ordering him to reconsider his position. On December 9, 2020, he reaffirmed his earlier ruling, finding that pandemic conditions had worsened (*American College of Obstetricians and Gynecologists v. United States FDA* 2020b).

The Trump administration again sought a stay from the high court, hoping the latest appointee, Amy Coney Barrett, nominated in part for her well-publicized anti-abortion views, would help form a majority to support the government. On January 12, 2021, without argument, the Court reinstated the FDA rule requiring in-person acquisition of mifepristone (*Food and Drug Administration v. American College of Obstetricians and Gynecologists* 2020). Roberts, the only justice to explain his reasoning, ignored its effect on women and said the decision was based on whether the lower court judge had improperly substituted his judgment for the FDA's in assessing public health needs during a pandemic. Sonia Sotomayor dissented, characterizing the policy as "an unnecessary, unjustifiable, irrational and undue burden on women seeking to exercise their right to choose" (585). She ended by hoping the incoming Biden administration would revisit it.

On April 12, 2021, the Biden administration's acting FDA commissioner Janet Woodcock announced that the agency approved the change that would allow a person to obtain a prescription for mifepristone through a telehealth appointment and have the pill mailed. She cited studies showing women's safety was not improved when they received the pill in person and the new approach would lessen the threat of being exposed to the virus. But the FDA's reversal may not have affected laws in the nineteen states that prohibited the use of telemedicine to prescribe the medication for abortion purposes. Regardless of the FDA's policy change, those states still required the pills to be taken in the presence of certified medical personnel (*Politico*, April 12, 2021; McShane 2021). On December 16, 2021, the FDA announced that it was permanently eliminating the in-person requirement, allowing patients to get prescriptions through telemedicine appointments and acquire mifepristone at pharmacies or by mail order. Signaling a likely confrontation between the federal government and states intent on restricting access to abortion care, Texas and over a dozen states have enacted laws banning mail delivery and requiring in-person pick up of the drug. Ultimately, the courts will decide which side will prevail in a dispute between the states and the federal government over US mail delivery and the FDA's authority to regulate public health (*Washington Post*, December 16, 2021; *New York Times*, December 16, 2021).

Challenging *Roe*

State efforts to restrict access to abortion care continued to proliferate, spurred by the new Supreme Court majority that included the three Trump appointees, selected in part because of their perceived receptiveness to government limits on abortion; most had committed themselves to stare decisis during their Senate confirmation hearings. To achieve their long-sought goal of eliminating the right to abortion, anti-abortion groups worked with state legislators to enact laws to make abortion inaccessible in their states. Most states imposed criminal penalties on the provider who performed an illegal abortion; an Arkansas law held the woman undergoing the abortion criminally liable as well.

As the Supreme Court's 2020–2021 term ended, it had still not indicated whether it would review a 2018 Mississippi law banning almost all abortions after fifteen weeks. Signed by Governor Tate Reeves on March 19, 2018, the Gestational Age Act (HB 1510) prohibits an individual from performing an abortion on a fetus over fifteen weeks "except in a medical emergency or in the case of a severe fetal abnormality" (LegiScan 2018). When signing the bill, the governor stated, "we are saving more of the unborn than any state in America" (*New York Times*, March 20, 2018). The state's only abortion clinic quickly filed suit and the federal courts blocked the law as a "ban on abortion" that conflicted with *Roe*'s viability standard (*Jackson Women's Health Organization v. Dobbs* 2019).

On May 17, 2021, after deliberating for nearly a year, the Court granted the state's request to evaluate the law, limiting its review to the single question of whether it is unconstitutional to prohibit all previability abortions (*Dobbs v. Jackson Women's Health Organization* 2021; *New York Times*, July 22, 2021). In urging it to accept the case, Mississippi's attorney general had assured the Court that "the questions presented in this petition do not require the court to overturn *Roe* and *Casey*" (*New York Times*, July 29, 2021). Once the case was placed on the docket, the state's brief argued *Roe* was "egregiously wrong" and the Court should overturn it, abolish the viability framework, and allow states to control their residents' access to abortion (*Washington Post*, July 22, 2021; CNN, September 20, 2021). The brief extravagantly charged that "*Roe* and *Casey* are unprincipled decisions that have damaged the democratic process, poisoned our national discourse, plagued the law—and in doing so—harmed this Court" (*Washington Post*, July 22, 2021).

Dobbs was scheduled for oral arguments on December 1, 2021 (Howe 2021b; *Politico*, September 20, 2021). Anti-abortion activists were heartened, believing the Court's decision to review the Mississippi law signaled that it was favorably disposed to their view; they eagerly awaited a ruling to explicitly overturn *Roe* and *Casey* and allow states to restrict abortions, with few, if any, exceptions. Alternatively, they wanted it to eliminate viability as a dividing line for permitting abortion restrictions. The head of one of the groups applauded the Court for accepting the case, saying, "states should be allowed to craft laws that are in line with both public opinion on this issue as well as basic human compassion, instead of the extreme policy that *Roe* imposed" (*Politico*, May 17, 2021). Abortion rights advocates also assumed the decision to review the Mississippi law did not bode well for women's access to abortion care (*The Hill*, May 22, 2021). A proponent of abortion rights cautioned, "alarm bells are ringing loudly about the threat to reproductive rights" (*Politico*, May 17, 2021). She ominously warned, "if *Roe* falls, half the states in the country are poised to ban abortion entirely" (*Washington Post*, July 22, 2021).

The Texas Heartbeat Act

As the Mississippi case proceeded, all eyes watched to see if the high court would allow the Texas Heartbeat Act (SB 8) to take effect on September 1, 2021, as scheduled. The law prohibited a physician from performing an abortion when there is a "detectable" fetal heartbeat, defining a heartbeat as "cardiac activity or the steady and repetitive contraction of the fetal heart." It permitted an exception for "a life-threatening physical condition [that] places the woman in danger of death or a serious risk of substantial impairment of a major bodily function" but not for pregnancies resulting from rape, incest, or sexual abuse, nor for fetal abnormalities (*New York Times*, November 26, 2021).

Distinct from other anti-abortion laws in the nation, SB 8 relied on a novel enforcement scheme, intended to preclude federal court review. Counseled by anti-abortion groups, the state sought to avoid the fate of other states in which courts declared abortion restrictions unconstitutional in suits brought against a state officer with the authority to enforce the law—typically an attorney general or health commissioner (Kitchener 2021b). To prevent such actions, SB 8 explicitly bans state officials from enforcing the law, thus shielding them (and the state) from suit. Instead, it authorizes individuals to file "private civil actions" in a Texas state court in any county against anyone who "knowingly engages in conduct that aids or abets the performance or inducement of an abortion, including paying for or reimbursing the costs of an abortion through insurance or otherwise . . . regardless of whether the person knew or should have known that the abortion would be performed or induced."

In addition to providers, possible defendants ranged from clinic staff members, rape counselors, acquaintances, family members, neighbors, volunteer clinic escorts, contributors to an abortion fund, and taxi drivers; the pregnant woman is explicitly immunized from suit. SB 8 incentivizes such actions by awarding a successful plaintiff, who does not need to have a link to the abortion or been harmed by it, at least $10,000 in damages plus legal fees and costs; the law does not permit prevailing defendants to recover their costs from the plaintiffs. Damages are available to multiple plaintiffs for each "illegal" abortion. The law permits suits to be brought four years after the abortion and it is irrelevant if the abortion was legal when it is performed if it is later found illegal (LegiScan 2021; *Spectrum1* [Austin], May 18, 2021; *The Guardian*, May 19, 2021; *Texas Tribune*, May 19, 2021; *New York Times*, July 9, 2021; Holley and Solomon 2021; *New York Times*, December 10, 2021).

The bill's supporters frankly admitted they aimed to decrease access to abortion in the state by making a wide range of individuals, especially providers, fearful of the crush of litigation to which they may be subjected (Holley and Solomon 2021). Researchers at the Texas Policy Evaluation Project at the University of Austin estimated SB 8 would block more than eight in ten women in Texas from accessing abortion care. Assessing potential defendants in addition to providers and clinics, their study of abortion patients in 2018 concluded that most patients receive "logistic or financial support" from others, including family and friends (White et al. 2021).

Commenting on its dramatic effects, observers stated, "if SB 8 takes effect, it will not take long for state courts to end all legal abortion services in Texas" (Lithwick and Stern 2021). The head of the Center for Reproductive Rights (CRR) charged "the state has put a bounty on the head of any person or entity who so much as gives a patient money for an abortion after six weeks of pregnancy" (*Washington Post*, July 13, 2021). An official of the Texas Right to Life organization acknowledged that "the enforcement mechanism" of the law is designed to make it difficult to prevent a private citizen from filing an SB 8 lawsuit, saying, "how do you stop an undefined enforcer?" (Kitchener 2021a).

Abortion care providers challenged the law in a Texas federal district court on July 13, 2021, naming various state officials, including a judge, a court clerk, the attorney general, and public health officials as defendants. Citing the role of private individuals in enforcing the law, the state argued that the suit named the wrong defendants. A scheduled hearing in the district court was stayed by the appeals court. The providers then sought an emergency order from the Supreme Court to stop the law before it took effect or at least to allow the district court hearing to continue (Lithwick and Stern 2021). The high court refused the emergency request and, in a brief unsigned order, released just before midnight on September 1, 2021, a majority agreed with the state that the providers had sued the wrong defendants. It acknowledged that the plaintiffs had "raised serious questions regarding the constitutionality of the Texas law," but decided the case "presents complex and novel antecedent procedural questions on which they [the plaintiffs] have not carried their burden" (*Whole Woman's Health v. Jackson* 2021a, at 1). Aware that the six-week limit on legal abortions expressly conflicted with *Roe* and *Casey*, the justices nevertheless allowed it to remain in effect, emphasizing that in doing so, they were not expressing an opinion about its constitutionality.

The chief justice disagreed, disturbed the Court was allowing the state to benefit from its unique enforcement mechanism. He believed it should bar the law from taking effect to permit the federal courts to determine the legality of the state's tactic. Sotomayor, writing for herself and the two other Democratic-appointed justices (Elena Kagan and Stephen Breyer), characterized the decision as "stunning," calling it a "flagrantly unconstitutional law engineered to prohibit women from exercising their constitutional rights and evade judicial scrutiny." She accused the majority of "silently acquiesce[ing] in a State's enactment of a law that flouts nearly 50 years of federal precedents" because of "procedural complexities of the State's own invention" (*Whole Woman's Health v. Jackson* 2021a, at 8).

On September 2, 2021, Biden called the Court's refusal to stay the law an "unprecedented assault on a woman's constitutional right" and promised a "whole-of-government" response (*The Guardian*, September 2, 2021). Soon, almost a dozen states announced they were considering following Texas's lead and enacting laws modeled after SB 8. An Arkansas state senator indicated he would introduce a copycat bill, and the governor of South Dakota said her state would review its abortion laws "to make sure we have the strongest pro-life laws on the books" (*Washington Post*, September 4, 2021).

With the law in effect and millions of Texas women deprived of their constitutional right to abortion care, the Fifth Circuit Court of Appeals refused to schedule arguments in the case until December at the earliest. On September 23, 2021, the providers returned to the Supreme Court (filing a petition for certiorari before judgment) without waiting for a ruling from the circuit court. They asked the high court to decide "whether a State can insulate from federal-court review a law that prohibits the exercise of a constitutional right by delegating to the general public the authority to enforce that prohibition through civil actions" (*Washington Post*, October 22, 2021; Howe 2021c; Howe 2021d).

While the Court considered their request, abortion rights advocates awaited action by the Department of Justice (DOJ), and, on September 6, 2021, Attorney General Merrick Garland announced that "the Justice Department urgently explores all options to challenge Texas SB 8 in order to protect the constitutional rights of women and other persons, including access to an abortion" (*Everything Lubbock*, September 6, 2021). Three days later, Garland announced that DOJ filed suit in a Texas federal district court, claiming "the United States has the authority and responsibility to ensure that no state can deprive individuals of their constitutional rights through a legislative scheme specifically designed to prevent the vindication of those rights" (US Department of Justice 2021). The complaint stated, "it takes little imagination to discern Texas's goal—to make it too risky for an abortion clinic to operate in the State, thereby preventing women throughout Texas from exercising their constitutional rights, while simultaneously thwarting judicial review" (*Politico*, September 9, 2021).

After another hearing in federal district court, the judge issued a 113-page opinion, singling out the private enforcement policy that allowed the state to evade judicial review by the federal courts. He ordered it to inform state clerks and judges of his order and publish it on its website. The judge concluded by dramatically condemning the law for preventing women from exercising their constitutional rights, declaring he would not allow it to do so (American Civil Liberties Union 2021c; *Politico*, October 6, 2021). Texas immediately appealed to the Fifth Circuit, and within two days, a three-judge panel permitted the law to go back into effect. Shortly thereafter, on October 14, 2021, the circuit court also denied DOJ's request to reinstate the lower court order (American Civil Liberties Union 2021b). The Biden administration sought emergency review in the Supreme Court, and, on October 22, 2021, the high court declined once again to halt the law but agreed to decide both cases without waiting for a Fifth Circuit opinion and scheduled arguments for November 1, 2021 (American Civil Liberties Union 2021d). Although the cases implicated women's access to abortion, neither would revolve around the constitutionality of abortion rights. In the federal government's suit, the Court would decide the extent of its authority to block the state from enforcing SB 8; in the providers' suit, it would evaluate the state's novel enforcement scheme. Texas asked the Court to stay out of the controversy, adding that if it chooses to delve into the merits of the cases, it should overturn *Roe* and *Casey* and abandon the constitutional right to an abortion (Howe 2021c; Howe 2021d).

Numerous briefs were submitted before the oral arguments. The head of an anti-abortion group extolled SB 8, saying, "it is time to restore this right to the people and update our laws." A brief from prosecutors and judges warned that on the contrary, SB 8 was "perhaps the most blatant attempt to subvert federal authority since the Jim Crow era" (*Washington Post*, October 30, 2021). In the action brought by the DOJ suit, Texas contended SB 8 did not foreclose judicial review because defendants can raise their constitutional objections to it in state court. The newly confirmed US Solicitor General Elizabeth Prelogar emphasized the law's unusual nature, saying, "Texas's position is that no one can sue, not the women whose rights are most directly affected, not the providers . . . and not the United States" (*Washington Post*, November 1, 2021).

On December 10, 2021, the Supreme Court ruled on the Texas providers' challenge to SB 8, deciding only the narrow question of whether it could be challenged in federal court and, if so, who are the proper defendants. Ignoring the underlying constitutional question of women's rights to abortion care, the opinion in *Whole Woman's Health v. Jackson* (2021b) embodied a tutorial on sovereign immunity, the doctrine shielding states from suit in federal court but permitting them against state officials under the legal fiction they do not equate to suits against the state (*Ex parte Young* 1908). Speaking for a divided Court, Gorsuch emphasized that the question of "whether S. B. 8 is consistent with the Federal Constitution—is not before the Court. Nor," he said, "is the wisdom of S. B. 8 as a matter of public policy" (*Whole Woman's Health v. Jackson* 2021b, at 14). Ironically, a day before the high court announced its opinion, a Texas state court judge held that the enforcement mechanism of SB 8 violated the Texas constitution but inexplicably refused to grant the plaintiffs' request for an injunction (*Van Stean v. Texas Right to Life* 2021).

In a narrow victory for abortion rights supporters, eight justices agreed to allow the providers to sue four state executive licensing officials—and only those four—who appeared to have the authority under state law to discipline doctors for violating SB 8. Gorsuch cautioned that it might appear as if these four officials have the requisite power but it is up to the Texas courts to interpret the statute to verify it (*Whole Woman's Health v. Jackson* 2021b). He underscored the federal courts' limited authority over the states, dramatically declaring that allowing all the defendants named in the case to be sued would be a "violation of the whole scheme of our Government" (at 5). Warning of the danger if federal judges intervene in cases between "private parties" that properly belong in the state courts, he asked, "what would stop federal judges from prohibiting state courts and clerks from hearing and docketing disputes between private parties under other state laws?" (at 17)

The three Democratic-appointed justices and Roberts said they would have interpreted the law to allow the plaintiffs to sue the state attorney general as well as state court clerks to prevent them from accepting SB 8 lawsuits. Roberts stressed the "clear purpose and actual effect of S. B. 8 has been to nullify this Court's rulings" and warned that if it allows state legislatures to "annul the judgments of the courts of the United States, and destroy the rights acquired under those judgments, the constitution itself becomes a solemn mockery" (at 45). Thomas wrote separately to declare that he would have denied the plaintiffs the right to sue any of the state officials in federal court.

Sotomayor emphasized the harm to women, especially those unable to travel for abortion care out of state. "For the many women who are unable to do so, their only alternatives are to carry unwanted pregnancies to term or attempt self-induced abortions outside of the medical system." She sharply criticized the majority for not "put[ing] an end to this madness months ago, before S. B. 8 first went into effect. It failed to do so then, and it fails again today" (at 47–48). She stressed that "the Court effectively invites other States to refine S. B. 8's model for nullifying federal rights [and] . . . . thus betrays not only the citizens of Texas, but also our constitutional system of government" (at 47).

An associate at the Guttmacher Institute criticized the ruling, declaring it "unconscionable" that the Court permitted the law to remain in place. The head of In Our Own Voice: National Black Women's Reproductive Justice Agenda warned the ruling indicates "it is open season on women's rights and lives," with most of the harm directed at women of color (*Washington Post*, December 10, 2021).

An officer of Texas Right to Life was pleased that the high court allowed SB 8 to continue to limit access to abortion. An adviser to another anti-abortion group proclaimed the ruling "directly results in saving more pre-born human lives" (*Washington Post*, December 10, 2021).

On December 10, 2021, in an unsigned opinion, over Sotomayor's dissent, the high court simply dismissed DOJ's suit against Texas, holding the United States did not have legal authority to sue and the Court should not have agreed to review its claim in the first place (*United States v. Texas* 2021).

Even though eight justices agreed that the four licensing officials were at least possible defendants and four urged the district court judge to promptly resolve the issue, Gorsuch remanded the case to the Fifth Circuit, which refused to return the case to the district court for a ruling. The state argued that the four licensing officials were not proper defendants, and the appeals court held it would allow the state supreme court to resolve the matter, ensuring more months of delay. There was even a suggestion that one of the appellate court judges wanted to delay a decision on SB 8 until the end of June when she believed the Supreme Court would decide *Dobbs* and overturn *Roe* and *Casey* (*Washington Post*, January 22, 2022).

.The controversy over the legal status of SB 8 finally ended on March 31, 2022, when the Texas Supreme Court unanimously ruled that under Texas law none of the four licensing officials are empowered to enforce the law and cannot be sued in federal court (*Texas Tribune*, March 12, 2022; *Austin-American Statesman*, March 11, 2022). An official at one of the anti-abortion groups applauded the ruling, calling it "a big victory for the TX Heartbeat Act," adding, "the law will continue saving thousands of lives" (*Washington Post*, March 11, 2022). A CRR official lamented that "the sliver of this case that we were left with is gone" (*New York Times*, March 12, 2022). Emboldened by the events in Texas, the governor of Oklahoma signed a six-week abortion ban into law, modeled after the enforcement provisions of SB 8 (CNN, May 3, 2022). Even before the final disposition of the Texas law, Missouri had enacted a version of SB 8 that allowed private suits against any individual who helps a Missouri resident secure an out-of-state abortion; it also outlawed the distribution and possession of medication abortion pills in the state (*Washington Post*, March 3, 2022).

The Supreme Court Decides *Dobbs*

Most polls reveal that the American public has consistently opposed overturning *Roe* and allowing lawmakers to terminate or drastically restrict women's access to abortion care. With the widely publicized coverage of the Court's review of the Mississippi and Texas laws, the nation became even more aware that *Roe* was in jeopardy. In addition to questioning respondents about their views on abortion, a May 2021 Gallup survey asked whether *Roe* should be overturned. It reported that 58 percent believed it should not be, 32 percent wanted it overturned, and 10 percent had no opinion (Gallup 2021). The results of a *Washington Post*–ABC News poll conducted in November 2021 showed 60 percent of registered voters thought the Court should uphold *Roe*, with only 27 percent wanting the Court to overturn it. When specifically questioned about the Texas law, 65 percent said the Court should reject it, with only 29 percent agreeing it should be upheld. More generally, 75 percent believed the decision about whether a woman should have an abortion should be left to the woman and her doctor, with only 20 percent wanting it regulated by law (*Washington Post*, November 16, 2021).

With the courts embroiled in deciding whether SB 8 should be shielded from federal court review, on December 1, 2021, the Court heard oral arguments in the Mississippi case ("Transcript of Supreme Court Oral Arguments in *Dobbs v. Jackson Women's Health*" 2021). The attorneys for the providers argued that the Court has never revoked a constitutional right and the special justification needed to overturn a fifty-year precedent is lacking. Most justices appeared skeptical of the command to follow stare decisis, with Kavanaugh reciting numerous cases where it had overturned earlier rulings. The three justices supporting abortion rights expressed concern that overturning *Roe* would lead to criticism that the Court is a political institution, not a body making principled legal decisions. They stressed the danger of losing legitimacy among the public if it simply reversed past rulings with the appointment of new personnel. Sotomayor summed it up by asking whether the Court will "survive the stench that this creates in the public perception that the Constitution and its reading are just political acts? I don't see how this is possible" (*The Hill*, December 1, 2021).

The six Republican-appointed justices (Roberts, Gorsuch, Kavanaugh, Amy Coney Barrett, Clarence Thomas, and Samuel Alito) stated they thought *Roe* was wrongly decided and the viability standard was an arbitrary distinction that could easily be abandoned; most gave the impression they favored the Mississippi law and would overturn *Roe* and *Casey* outright. Possibly seeking to explore a compromise to retain *Roe* while upholding the Mississippi statute, Roberts questioned why the line should be drawn at viability, rather than at fifteen weeks, suggesting that fifteen weeks gave a woman enough time to decide to have an abortion. The other five justices believed the Court would be forced to choose between affirming *Roe* and *Casey* and overturning them entirely; they did not leave much doubt about which direction they would take.

Barrett asked why safe haven laws permitting mothers to abandon their newborns at hospitals or fire stations without penalty do not solve the problem of imposing unwanted parenting requirements on women. The two attorneys defending abortion rights cited the unique health risks posed by pregnancy, especially the disproportionate effect of maternal and infant mortality rates on women of color and poor women, particularly in Mississippi. They warned that women's equality will be diminished if the state removes their agency over their pregnancy and forces them to give birth against their will. They continually stressed that women's right to liberty, grounded in the Fourteenth Amendment, guarantees their right to exercise autonomy over their bodies. Kavanaugh questioned why, since the Constitution does not specify abortion rights, the Court should not be neutral and allow each state to regulate abortions; the state solicitor general agreed that such a resolution would be appropriate. Prelogar insisted that the Court cannot allow state legislatures to decide whether to "honor" a fundamental right. In response to questions about viability, the two lawyers defended it as a logical, "objectively verifiable" place to draw the line on access to abortion and if the Court removes the viability standard, states will hasten to impose earlier limits with no principled way to determine their constitutionality. They believed it likely states will ban abortion throughout the entire pregnancy and return to a pre-*Roe* model of permitting only narrow exceptions to save a woman's life.

Anticipating the Court's ruling, Republican-led states (those with Republican governors or legislative majorities), such as Arizona, Florida, Idaho, Kentucky, and Oklahoma, had passed legislation mirroring the Mississippi law and banning abortions at fifteen weeks; most contained no exceptions for pregnancies caused by rape or incest (*Mother Jones*, April 22, 2022). A Louisiana Senate committee approved a bill to make abortion a homicide and hold the woman criminally responsible as well as the provider (*Washington Post*, May 13, 2022).

Waiting for the high court to announce its decision took on an added drama when on May 2, 2022, a first draft of an opinion written by Alito and circulated to the justices on February 10, 2022, was leaked to the press by a court insider (*Politico*, May 2, 2022). The ninety-eight-page opinion was signed by the five Republican-appointed justices, including the three appointed by Trump; only Roberts did not join them. The origin of the leak, the first ever in modern Court history, remains unknown, and it is unclear who benefited from it.

In a stark dismissal of the Court's adherence to the doctrine of stare decisis, the opinion boldly stated that "*Roe* was egregiously wrong from the start" and "must be overruled" (*Politico*, May 2, 2022). It emphasized that, contrary to *Roe*'s premise, there is no constitutional right to abortion. It is not explicitly protected in the text of the Fourteenth Amendment's due process clause, Alito said, nor is it implicitly protected in the Constitution by virtue of being "deeply rooted in the Nation's history and traditions" when the amendment was adopted in 1868. He distinguished abortion from other privacy rights implicit in the due process clause, such as the right to interracial and same-sex marriage and contraception. Alito concluded by affirming that "the Constitution does not prohibit the citizens of each State from regulating or prohibiting abortion," and we "return that authority to the people and their elected representatives" (*Politico*, May 2, 2022).

Alito left little doubt that he believed the government's authority to restrict or ban abortions would be virtually limitless. Because abortion regulations are distinguishable from sex-based laws, he argued, they are not entitled to heightened scrutiny and must be given a "strong presumption of validity" and upheld if states have a "rational basis" to think they serve a "legitimate interest." In other words, he instructed reviewing courts to apply minimal scrutiny—the least rigorous form of review—in determining whether to uphold an abortion regulation. Applying this standard to the Mississippi law, the majority had no difficulty finding the fifteen-week limit rationally related to the state's interest in "preserv[ing] prenatal life at all stages of development" (*New York Times*, May 3, 2022).

The opinion noted that twenty-six states had submitted briefs asking the Court to overturn *Roe*, reinforcing earlier reports that in the absence of *Roe*, twenty-six states had been poised to ban abortion in 2021 (Nash and Cross 2021; *Washington Post*, May 3, 2022). Although state laws will differ (some will have fifteen-week bans, some will have

six-week bans, and some will incorporate SB 8 enforcement mechanisms), it was estimated that a decision to overturn the fifty-year-old
precedent will lead to a loss of reproductive autonomy for 52 percent of
US women of childbearing age (*Washington Post*, June 24, 2022).

Abortion rights advocates vigorously condemned the draft opinion.
They challenged Alito's historical analysis that abortion was illegal in
the nation until *Roe*, stressing that it was legal under common law until
quickening and that it was made illegal for a number of reasons, having more to do with physicians' desires to drive out competition from
unlicensed midwives and less to do with protection of potential life.
Others criticized the opinion for failing to meaningfully acknowledge
"its impact both on women and on the constitutional understanding of
sex equality as it has evolved in the past half-century" (Greenhouse
2022). They objected to Alito's dismissal of the constitutional right to
abortion based on his view of the rights that existed in the 1860s when
women were not full citizens, having no right to own property or vote.

Some critics emphasized that his narrow view of constitutional
rights undermined the significance of the Fourteenth Amendment in
establishing Black women's sexual autonomy, ending their sub-
servience to white slave owners (*Mother Jones*, May 4, 2022). They
pointed out that he disregarded the relationship between race and
maternal mortality, especially in Mississippi, where Black women were
118 times more likely to die from a pregnancy-related death than from
an abortion (*New York Times*, June 26, 2022). Leaders of other racial
minority groups, such as Asian Americans, Latinas, and Pacific
Islanders, also condemned the draft, one characterizing it "as a direct
and pernicious assault on people of color"; another more broadly
assailed it "as an attack on racial justice, economic justice, and equality" (*Washington Post*, June 25, 2022).

Abortion rights supporters challenged Alito's reliance on an opinion
in which the Court had allowed a state workers' disability plan to exclude
pregnancy benefits by distinguishing pregnancy from sex, a ruling that
was essentially nullified by the 1978 Pregnancy Discrimination Act. More
broadly, they were shocked at his blasé approach to pregnancy, including
his contention that adoption was readily available to pregnant women
who sought to avoid childrearing. They criticized the opinion for its off-
hand assertion that restricting or banning abortion would not affect
women's status in society and insistence—which they declared was
demonstrably wrong—that society had eradicated all difficulties associated with pregnancy with passage of pregnancy discrimination laws,
maternity leave, childcare, and pre- and postpartum health care.

Abortion rights advocates were particularly incensed that Alito frequently cited the works of Sir Matthew Hale, a seventeenth-century English jurist who was known for sentencing women to death for practicing witchcraft, believing marital rape was justified, and declaring that women are inherently untruthful when claiming rape (Hasday 2022). Finally, most were skeptical of Alito's assurances that the Court would be content to stop at abortion and refrain from eliminating other privacy rights based on the Fourteenth Amendment, none of which, they noted, are in the text or "deeply rooted." Some feared the United States would move toward a nationwide ban on abortion with Congress creating a right of fetal personhood under the Fourteenth Amendment, an option Republican Senate Minority Leader Mitch McConnell had termed "possible" (*Vanity Fair*, May 8, 2022).

Medical experts charged that the draft simply ignored the physical implications of pregnancy for women, pointing to the high rate of maternal mortality in the United States and citing recent government statistics showing that 861 women died from pregnancy-related conditions in 2020, almost 100 more than in 2018. They warned that overturning *Roe* would lead to increased deaths, especially among Black women, who were about three times as likely to die from pregnancy-related causes as white women (US Department of Health and Human Services, Centers for Disease Control and Prevention 2020b). Other scholars expressed serious concerns that overturning *Roe* would have an adverse impact on women and their children, depressing their economic, educational, and health status and increasing child poverty. The poorest and most vulnerable among them would suffer the most, they stressed, citing a research project known as the Turnaway Study, a multiyear survey comparing the financial outcomes of women who succeeded in obtaining abortions with those who sought them but did not get them. Among other things, the study found long-term effects, with the latter disadvantaged by their inability to finish their education and establish themselves in the workforce (Talbot 2020; NBC News, May 5, 2022). Reacting to the leaked opinion, Biden released a statement reaffirming his support for abortion rights and declaring, "I believe that a woman's right to choose is fundamental" and challenging the "nation's elected officials at all levels of government to protect" it if the Court overturns *Roe* (Biden 2022).

On June 24, 2022, the Supreme Court announced *Dobbs v. Jackson Women's Health Organization* (2022), voting 6–3 to uphold the Mississippi law and 5–3 to overturn *Roe*. Essentially mirroring the draft opinion, Alito dramatically proclaimed on behalf of the five justices: "We hold that *Roe* and *Casey* must be overruled" (*Dobbs v. Jackson Women's Health Organization* 2022, 2242). He ended by reiterating, "The Constitution does not prohibit the citizens of each State from regulating or prohibiting abortion." In overruling *Roe* and *Casey*, he added, we "return that authority to the people and their elected representatives" (*Dobbs v. Jackson Women's Health Organization* 2022, 2284).

With the thrust of the ruling previewed by the leaked draft, most eyes were on the concurring and dissenting opinions. Thomas's concurring opinion garnered the most attention, for he raised the possibility that *Dobbs* was merely a prelude to further limitations on constitutional rights related to the right to privacy. Despite Alito's effort to limit the ruling to abortion rights, Thomas wrote separately to indicate his oft-stated view that certain rights guaranteed by the due process clause were not entitled to constitutional protection. He saw no reason to limit the analysis to abortion, more broadly objecting to a panoply of rights the Court had singled out for protection under the umbrella of due process guarantees. In his view, the clause only requires the government to follow correct procedures when infringing on the right to life, liberty, or property. The primary focus of his attack was the doctrine of substantive due process, emanating from the due process clause, which has been interpreted to preclude the government from placing "unreasonable, arbitrary, or unnecessary restraints on the substance of liberty or property" (Lewis 2001, 21; Williams 2010).

Thomas specified a need to revisit the four leading examples of substantive due process rights, encompassed under the rubric of the right to privacy: the right to abortion, the right to contraception, the right to same-sex consensual relations, and the right to same-sex marriage. Because he believed all substantive due process decisionmaking was "demonstrably erroneous" and "dangerous," he urged the Court to "reconsider all substantive due process precedents," and recommended righting the constitutional wrongs reflected in them by overturning those rulings (*Dobbs v. Jackson Women's Health Organization* 2022, 2301–2302).

To reassure the nation that the Court was not about to heed Thomas's advice on the demise of substantive due process, Kavanaugh's concurring opinion began by attempting to present a nuanced approach to abortion rights. Echoing his stance during the oral arguments, he depicted the Constitution as neutral on abortion and therefore, he said, the "Court also must be scrupulously neutral" and allow access to abortion to be resolved through the democratic process (2305). He criticized *Roe* for removing the decision from the people and their representatives by declaring a national right to abortion. Consistent with his effort to appear neutral, Kavanaugh rejected the call for a nationwide abortion ban. He hastened to add that he respects people with those views as well as those who supported abortion rights. The beliefs of both sides are irrelevant, he insisted, as are those of the nine justices, because the Constitution's silence on abortion demands the Court remain neutral, allowing both sides to attempt to persuade their representatives to adopt their perspective.

Kavanaugh also endeavored to distance himself from Alito's assertion that abortion rights are outside the Constitution because they did not exist at the nation's founding or the adoption of the Fourteenth Amendment. But, he said, while new rights are not universally proscribed, the justices do not have the authority "to rewrite the Constitution to create new rights and liberties based on our own moral or policy views" (2306).

Kavanaugh quickly disposed of the question whether adhering to stare decisis was a command, requiring a recommitment to *Roe*. To demonstrate the Court's need for flexibility to overturn erroneously decided cases, he cited the notorious *Plessy v. Ferguson* (1896)—establishing the separate but equal doctrine—that the Court had overturned fifty years later in *Brown v. Board of Education* (1954). Like *Plessy*, he said, *Roe* was "egregiously wrong" and the decision to overrule it is correct. Emphasizing his "deep and unyielding respect" for the *Casey* plurality, Kavanaugh dismissed it for failing to "resolve the abortion debate," as its authors had intended (*Dobbs v. Jackson Women's Health Organization* 2022, 2307–2308). Finally, Kavanaugh, having established to his satisfaction that the Court would no longer be the deciding factor in abortion care policies, sought to reassure abortion rights supporters on the limits of the decision. To reinforce Alito's disclaimer and respond to Thomas, he stressed that the Court is not seeking to limit other privacy rights emanating from the substantive due process clause. Second, he said, in his view, the constitutional right to interstate travel bars states from prohibiting their residents from seeking abortions in other states.

As appeared likely from Roberts's questioning at the oral arguments, the chief justice did not join the majority in voting to overturn *Roe* but concurred in the judgment, providing the sixth vote to eliminate the viability standard and uphold the Mississippi law. Echoing the view he expressed during the oral arguments, Roberts declared that fifteen weeks afforded most women a "reasonable opportunity" to choose to terminate a pregnancy, which, in his view, was the key to *Roe* (*Dobbs v. Jackson Women's Health Organization* 2022, 2310).

In contrast to the other five justices in the majority who sought to justify their retreat from the doctrine of stare decisis, Roberts instead called attention to it, expressing concern at its jarring effect on the legal system. He believed it inappropriate to depart from the principle of "judicial restraint," which posits that cases should be decided as narrowly as possible, without unnecessarily reaching a broader question. Adhering to judicial restraint is especially important, he insisted, "where the broader path the Court chooses entails repudiating a constitutional right we have not only previously recognized, but also expressly reaffirmed applying the doctrine of stare decisis." Praising the majority opinion for being "thoughtful and thorough," he reiterated that the "dramatic and consequential ruling is unnecessary to decide the case before us" (2311).

Roberts reminded his colleagues that the state had initially argued the Court could refrain from overruling *Roe* to reach a decision on the merits of the Mississippi law. But, he noted, the state shifted its approach and argued that *Roe* is inconsistent with the law. He criticized the majority for "reward[ing] that gambit" and accepting the state's current drastic formulation that the Court must either allow *Roe* and *Casey* to stand or reduce them to rubble. The case can and should be resolved on narrower grounds, Roberts graphically stated, "without overruling *Roe* all the way down to the studs: recognize that the viability line must be discarded, as the majority rightly does, and leave it for another day whether to reject any right to an abortion at all" (*Dobbs v. Jackson Women's Health Organization* 2022, 2313).

Unlike the majority opinion, Kagan's dissent (for herself, Breyer, and Sotomayor) stressed the realistic outcomes of the ruling (as opposed to the idyllic picture Alito painted), forcefully explaining its impact on women's equality and bodily autonomy. She accused the Court of declaring "that from the very moment of fertilization, a woman has no rights to speak of" (2317). With states now only required to show a law is rational, and the Court holding that protecting fetal life is rational, there will be no limits on state abortion restrictions, including bans at fertilization. So far, she asserted, many states have outlawed medication abortions and permit abortions only under narrow exceptions for immediate life-threatening conditions in which mere threats to women's health do not override the law, nor do severe fetal abnormalities. In sum, she declared, "across a vast array of circumstances, a State will be able to impose its moral choice on a woman and coerce her to give birth to a child" (2318).

Kagan charged that the ruling "erases the woman's interest and recognizes only the State's (or the Federal Government's)" (2323). She warned that states will be free to enforce their laws by criminalizing women as well as providers and allowing private citizens to spy on each other following the Texas model. Moreover, she rebutted the majority's attempt to reassure the nation that abortion will be decided on a statewide basis, pointing to existing state restrictions on interstate travel and bans on mail-order abortion pills from outside the state. Last, she cautioned that Congress remained free to impose a national ban on abortion, with any specifications it chooses, subject only to rational basis Supreme Court review.

Rejecting Alito's and Kavanaugh's assurances, Kagan also delved into the potential impact of Thomas's concurring opinion. Although she acknowledged the majority's attempt to carve out abortion, she noted that other rights (same-sex marriage, contraception, and interracial marriage) derived from the right to privacy are also not explicitly protected in the Fourteenth Amendment, nor are they "deeply rooted" in the nation's history. Such rights, she cautioned, can also be excised from the Constitution by the Court and left to state decisionmakers, especially with the majority's apparent disdain for stare decisis. She ended by charging that no legal changes justify the Court's reversal on abortion, a right on which women have relied for fifty years and one that was reaffirmed numerous times since then. The only change has been in the replacement of Court personnel. In a harsh attack on the majority, she reproached it for "overrul[ing] *Roe* and *Casey* for one and only one reason: because it has always despised them, and now it has the votes to discard them." In doing so, she caustically added, "the majority thereby substitutes a rule by judges for the rule of law" (*Dobbs v. Jackson Women's Health Organization* 2022, 2335).

Post-*Dobbs* Policies

Ironically, Alito had depicted *Roe* as divisive and "spark[ing] a national controversy" (2241). But states soon began to implement myriad laws to ban or severely restrict abortion care, with most only allowing exceptions for the life of the woman. California Democrat Anna Eshoo charged that the high court's "devastating" ruling "created a patchwork of states with differing laws and restrictions causing societal chaos and confusion" (*New York Times*, July 15, 2022; Winter 2022). Most states with trigger laws or pre-*Roe* bans announced the laws would take effect; others turned to measures to limit access to abortion care, including calling for special legislative sessions, amending state constitutions, and holding statewide referendums on abortion regulations. In states with Democratic governors, such as Michigan, Wisconsin, California, Washington state, and New York, government officials announced measures to protect women within their borders as well as those outside the state. State attorneys general and prosecutors vowed not to enforce laws banning abortion in their states, and abortion rights supporters launched numerous legal challenges in state courts (*New York Times*, June 27, 2022; NBC News, June 27, 2022; *New York Times*, July 2, 2022).

Public opinion showed a nation deeply at odds with the decision. One of the first surveys taken after the ruling revealed that 59 percent of the respondents disapproved of overturning *Roe*, with 52 percent calling it "a step backwards"; among women, 56 percent believed it will "make [women's] lives worse" (CBS News, June 26, 2022). Soon after, another survey reported comparable results, with 56 percent of the respondents opposing the ruling; most women, men, whites, and nonwhites disagreed with the Court (NPR/PBS/Marist poll 2022). A month later a CNN poll demonstrated even more opposition to the decision. The survey found that 63 percent of the respondents disapproved of *Dobbs*, with 58 percent believing it would have a "negative effect" on women in their state and 68 percent saying it would have a "negative effect" on the entire nation (CNN, July 28, 2022).

The media speculated on the potential consequences of the ruling. The discussion ranged from health officials reporting suspected illegal abortions to law enforcement; punishing women for abortions; forbidding interstate travel for abortions; scrutinizing women's out-of-state travel; monitoring women's text messages and internet search histories; blocking internet access to abortion information; defining personhood at conception or fertilization; investigating stillborn births and miscarriages; banning medication abortions; imposing narrow rape and incest exceptions; regulating telehealth appointments; federal and state court involvement in abortion litigation; the constraints of the Hyde Amendment; access to certain kinds of contraception and in vitro fertilization; permanent storage of frozen embryos; prenatal testing for anatomical anomalies; and abortions for women with ectopic pregnancies, preeclampsia, sepsis, or other life-threatening conditions (*Washington Post*, June 27, 2022; *New York Times*, June 27, 2022; NBC News, June 27, 2022).

Dobbs highlighted the limits of state enforcement mechanisms that conflicted with the constitutional right to travel and the FDA's authority to regulate public health. Even before the Court announced the decision, states had curtailed access to medication abortions, outlawed telemedicine appointments, and made it illegal to prescribe, sell, and mail pills. After *Dobbs*, state officials asserted they were constitutionally empowered to block women from seeking abortion care outside their borders.

The Federal Government and Abortion Rights

While states were embroiled in abortion policymaking in the summer of 2022, the federal government also entered the fray. Although House Democrats had succeeded in approving legislation to bypass the courts to establish a statutory right to abortion during 2021 and 2022—most recently in July 2022—the measures failed to secure the sixty votes needed to overcome the Republican filibuster in the Senate. All eyes turned to the Biden administration, which was forced to weigh the federal government's ability to prevail in conflicts with states over their autonomy, cognizant that its actions would be challenged in court and almost certainly lead to Supreme Court review. The day the opinion was announced, Biden warned that "the health and life of women of this nation are now at risk," calling the opinion "a tragic error by the Supreme Court" and the day "a sad one for this country." Underscoring the constraints on federal authority, restricted among other things, by the Hyde Amendment's ban on federal spending for abortion care with limited exceptions, he reminded the nation that Congress represented the most viable approach to restoring reproductive rights in the nation (*Politico,* June 24, 2022).

It was clear from the outset that the battle lines would be most sharply drawn over the state's authority to prevent its residents from seeking abortion care out of state and deny them access to medication abortions. In a news release, Garland addressed these issues, reaffirming that "under bedrock constitutional principles, women who reside in states that have banned access to comprehensive reproductive care must remain free to seek that care in states where it is legal." He also confirmed the FDA's authority to regulate medication abortions, warning states that they cannot override federal policy and may not "ban Mifepristone based on disagreement with the FDA's expert judgment about its safety and efficacy" (US Department of Justice, Office of Public Affairs 2022a).

Shortly thereafter, DOJ announced the formation of a reproductive rights task force. Chaired by Associate Attorney General Vanita Gupta, the task force committed itself to assessing state and local regulations that threaten the reproductive rights women are entitled to under federal law. The press release specified such restrictive policies as banning mifepristone, blocking information on abortion care, and denying women the right to access abortion care in other states. It pledged that the federal government would respond appropriately in such situations. Echoing Biden's words, it ended with a reminder that "the best way to protect reproductive freedom is through congressional action" (US Department of Justice, Office of Public Affairs 2022b).

Acknowledging the limits of federal authority over abortion policy-making, on July 8, 2022, Biden announced he was signing Executive Order 14076 to direct federal officials to help expand rights to abortion care, especially for women living in states that banned or greatly restricted access to abortion. His primary focus was on keeping medication abortions available for women living with state bans, calling on HHS to report on additional options to guarantee access. Biden forcefully stated that "eliminating the right recognized in *Roe* has already had and will continue to have devastating implications for women's health and public health more broadly." He reiterated the importance of voting to restore abortion rights (American Presidency Project 2022). Understandably, there was a range of reactions to Biden's speech; some called it extreme, some criticized him for not taking more immediate concrete steps, and others said it was "a good start" (*Washington Post*, July 8, 2022; *New York Times*, July 8, 2022).

In the continuing effort to establish the preeminence of federal authority over the states, HHS Secretary Xavier Becerra released a clarifying guidance for health care providers, informing them that the Emergency Medical Treatment and Labor Act (EMTALA) requires doctors to perform abortions on women in emergency rooms—even in states where the procedure is banned—if they consider it "the stabilizing treatment necessary" to deal with an emergent medical situation. The letter specified that the federal law preempts state laws that would deny abortions to women on the basis of state prohibitions or narrow definitions of emergencies (US Department of Health and Human Services, Centers for Medicare and Medicaid Services 2022). On August 2, 2022, DOJ filed a federal lawsuit against Idaho, claiming the state's "near-absolute ban on abortion," which provides an exception for saving the woman's life but not her health, violates EMTALA by withholding necessary emergency care (*New York Times*, August 2, 2022). A subsequent guidance warned pharmacies that refusing to fill prescriptions for abortion pills could place them in jeopardy of violating federal civil rights law against discrimination on the basis of sex or disability. It emphasized that pharmacies cannot deny women access to medication based on suspicions they will be used to induce abortions, noting that such pills are also used to treat miscarriages, hormonal imbalances, cancer, rheumatoid arthritis, stomach ulcers, and ectopic pregnancies (US Department of Health and Human Services 2022).

The Voters Respond

In 2022, while the nation was still reacting to the Supreme Court ruling overturning *Roe*, voters across the country cast their ballots on abortion rights in six states; in each, proponents of abortion rights won, many handily. In August, shortly after the Court announced *Dobbs*, Kansas, once known for its anti-abortion activism, rejected a measure to amend the state constitution to restrict abortion rights. Titled the "Kansas No State Constitutional Right to Abortion and Legislative Power to Regulate Abortion Amendment," it would have allowed the legislature to further limit access to abortion—and even ban it—in the state. When the votes were counted, almost 60 percent of voters had rejected the measure (*Politico,* August 3, 2022; *Washington Post,* August 3, 2022). In the November 2022 midterm elections, exit polls showed that a large number of voters said the issue of abortion was important to them and influenced their vote choice. A majority (61 percent) said they were "angry" or "dissatisfied" about the Court's decision to overturn *Roe*; of these, almost three-quarters voted for the Democrat, the candidate supporting abortion rights (NBC News, November 9, 2022).

The 2022 elections gave voters in five states an opportunity to directly express their views on abortion. Three states (Vermont, Michigan, and California) enshrined the right to abortion in their state constitutions, while voters in two other states (Kentucky and Montana) rejected efforts to further limit access to abortion care in their states. Vermont's Proposal 5 amended the state constitution to guarantee an individual's right to "personal reproductive autonomy"; it was approved by 76 percent of the voters. Michigan's Proposal 3 established a state constitutional right to "reproductive freedom"; 57 percent of the voters favored it. Its passage nullified an existing 1931 state law prohibiting abortion with no exceptions for rape or incest. In California, 66 percent of voters supported Proposition 1 to amend the state constitution to prohibit the state from "deny[ing] or interfer[ing] with an individual's reproductive freedom in their most intimate decisions." Like the amendment proposed in Kansas, Kentucky's Constitutional Amendment 2 would have explicitly affirmed that "nothing in the state constitution creates a right to abortion"; 52 percent of the voters rejected it. In a measure indirectly related to abortion, Montana's L-R 131 would have enacted a law punishing providers who failed to "take necessary actions to preserve the life of a born-alive infant"; it lost when only 47 percent of the voters supported it *(Ballotpedia,* November 8, 2022 [updated November 12, 2022]; *New York Times,* November 8, 2022 [updated November 11, 2022]; *New York Times,* November 10, 2022; NBC News, November 9, 2022; *Washington Post,* November 9, 2022). The 2022 elections show that, far from settling the controversy, the high court overturning *Roe* all but guaranteed that the politics of abortion would engulf the nation in the foreseeable future.

Conclusion

This chapter presented the story of access to abortion care in the United States, beginning with *Roe v. Wade* (1973), the case that constitutionalized abortion rights. In it, the Supreme Court formulated the trimester framework, barring the state from regulating abortion during the first trimester, allowing it to restrict it on certain grounds during the second trimester, and permitting it to ban abortion entirely during the third trimester unless it is necessary to preserve the woman's life and health. In the first decade following *Roe*, a majority of the Court remained committed to preserving abortion rights. Soon after though, justices became increasingly willing to uphold restrictions on abortion. In *Planned Parenthood of Southeastern Pennsylvania v. Casey* (1992), the Court reaffirmed *Roe* but abandoned the trimester framework by merging the first and second trimesters into a previability stage and allowing the state to regulate abortion care unless it imposed an undue burden on a woman. In the postviability stage, the state was empowered to prohibit abortion entirely but required to allow exceptions for the woman's life or health.

With *Casey* opening the floodgates, regulations abounded as anti-abortion groups exerted increasing influence over abortion policymaking. For decades, the Court remained unwilling to accede to their requests to overturn *Roe* and *Casey*, but by 2020, the stage was set for a new round of abortion policymaking ushered in by a battle over a Texas law with a novel enforcement mechanism. In refusing to rule on the constitutionality of the Texas six-week limit on abortion, the Court signaled that it would not interfere with the state's effort to shield an unconstitutional law from federal court review. In *Dobbs v. Jackson Women's Health Organization* (2022), the Court voted to uphold Mississippi's fifteen-week abortion ban and overturn *Roe* and *Casey*. The majority held that the Constitution does not protect a right to abortion and granted the citizens and their elected representatives the power to formulate abortion policy—including a total ban on abortion. *Dobbs* led to uncertainty, with a patchwork of state and local laws and policies dividing the nation, as the debate on the issue continues to rage. Following *Dobbs*, the controversy over abortion has become even more politicized, with abortion rights proponents and opponents likely to continue battling each other on ballot measures, as well as in the legislatures and courts.

7

Chasing Equality: Where Are We Now?

AUGUST 26, 2020, MARKED THE 100-YEAR ANNIVERSARY OF THE ratification of the Nineteenth Amendment, expanding women's roles as US citizens by guaranteeing their right to vote. Women have since made significant gains toward achieving equal status in social, political, and economic arenas, but there are disturbing signs that they remain second-class citizens. Women are more likely than men to attend college, but they also have a much greater chance of being sexually assaulted while at school. Even though women make up about half of the US workforce, a gender pay gap endures. Women employees are often harassed on the job and passed over for promotions regardless of their qualifications. At home, they continue to bear most of the burden of housework and caregiving responsibilities, regardless of their employment status. Although many women have gained greater access to contraception and abortion care, they continue to face relentless challenges to their reproductive autonomy, a clear indication that the fight for women's rights is far from over. As we demonstrate throughout the book, women's rights advocates must be mindful of the larger political context for, as we have shown, the interactions among the branches and levels of government play an important role in determining the parameters of women's rights.

By the 1980s, most public institutions of higher learning had opened their doors to men and women. When some remained segregated by sex, the courts intervened. In 1982, the Supreme Court ruled that the single-sex admissions policy of the School of Nursing at Mississippi University for Women was unconstitutional because it violated the equal protection clause of the Fourteenth Amendment. In 1996, the Court stepped in again to strike the long-standing male-only admission policy of the Virginia Military Institute, one of the last military academies in the United States to exclude women.

Congress expanded gender-based equality by passing Title IX of the Education Amendments of 1972. The statute broadly prohibited sex-based discrimination in educational institutions receiving federal funds. With the law in place, its interpretation was primarily left to the judicial and executive branches. Initially, the courts took a narrow view of Title IX, ruling that only programs directly receiving federal funding, such as college financial aid programs, were covered by the statute. In 1988, Congress again turned its attention to equality in education by enacting a law making it clear that all programs and activities in the institution were subject to the antidiscrimination guarantees of Title IX.

One of the thorniest debates over the interpretation of Title IX was the extent to which it governed secondary and postsecondary school athletic programs as shifts in the executive branch affected the interpretation of the law's ban on sex discrimination. The statute's influence on equality in sports is reflected in women's successes in the Olympics and other international and national competitions, but the glaring differences in women's and men's treatment in recent collegiate tournaments in basketball, softball, and baseball show that more must be done to carry out the objectives of Title IX's congressional sponsors.

Despite state and local governments' power to regulate education, the executive branch plays a key role in interpreting Title IX's ban on sex discrimination, with the courts largely deferring to its regulatory authority over the statute. Within the executive branch, the Department of Education has played an outsized role in addressing gender equality issues in education, with its Office for Civil Rights (OCR) responsible for enforcing Title IX and its regulations. OCR is empowered to investigate student complaints of Title IX violations, and though it can withdraw federal funding from noncomplying institutions, it is more likely to enter into settlement agreements with schools it finds have failed to adhere to the statute.

Reflecting the priorities of the occupant of the White House, the Obama, Trump, and Biden administrations have adopted different policies to alleviate sexual harassment and assault on campuses. The Obama administration took a proactive approach, requiring schools to deal expeditiously and forcefully with student complaints of sexual misconduct; the Trump administration reversed most of these policies, focusing on protecting the rights of the accused. Since Biden took office, his administration has committed itself to reinstating the Obama-era interpretations of Title IX, swinging the pendulum back to emphasizing the needs of the victims.

During the two world wars, the federal government made a concerted effort to recruit women to fill the jobs vacated by the men fighting overseas. In World War II, the government even heavily subsidized childcare so mothers with young children could join the workforce. When the war ended, society expected women to return to the home and the government concluded its employment initiatives for women. In the 1960s, the issue of women's employment gained renewed attention when Congress passed Title VII of the 1964 Civil Rights Act, which, among other things, bans sex discrimination in the workplace. As a result of the new law, the Equal Employment Opportunity Commission (EEOC) was charged with enforcing Title VII.

Sex discrimination in the workplace has been prohibited for over fifty years, yet women remain overrepresented in low-paying and low-prestige jobs. In addition, a sizable proportion of them have experienced sexual harassment at work. The courts were initially reticent to rule that sexual harassment was a form of sex discrimination, in part because judges believed it could affect both women and men. But by 1980, the EEOC formally recognized that sexual harassment constitutes sex discrimination, and within a few years, the courts followed suit. However, these changes in the law did not mean that the sexual misconduct—in and out of the workplace—ceased, as demonstrated by the explosion of the #MeToo movement in which millions of women joined in the social media call to declare that they had been victims of sexual assault or harassment.

Lawmakers have attempted to halt the staggering rates of sexual harassment and assault of women in the military by proposing legislation to remove the decision to prosecute such crimes from the chain of command. Advocates of this move believe it will lead to a greater number of assailants facing charges. At the state level, some legislatures have begun to close loopholes that permit women's continued harassment at work by barring nondisclosure agreements that prevent workers from making public the sexual misconduct they experienced.

Beyond bringing attention to the widespread problem of sexual harassment and assault in the workplace, the #MeToo movement also instigated a conversation about the broader inequalities women face at work, such as the persistent gender wage gap. In 1963, full-time women workers earned fifty-nine cents for every dollar men working full-time earned; that year, Congress passed the Equal Pay Act (EPA).

Twenty years later, the gap had only narrowed by five cents. Although there has been progress, neither the EPA nor Title VII has been able to eradicate gender inequality in the labor market and close the wage gap. To reverse the Supreme Court's narrow interpretation of Title VII to combat sex discrimination in pay, Congress passed the 2009 Lilly Ledbetter Fair Pay Act to allow employees to challenge gender pay discrimination in the courts. But by 2022, women working in full-time, year-round jobs were still earning only eighty-three cents for every dollar earned by their male counterparts.

For most of the nation's history, individual employees were left to determine how to balance their work and family lives on their own. In the wake of the passage of Title VII, the federal government began to take a more active role, with all three branches addressing pregnancy in the workplace. Initially, the courts ruled that treating pregnant employees differently from nonpregnant employees did not violate Title VII. Even after the EEOC released guidelines in 1972 equating pregnancy discrimination with sex discrimination, numerous courts challenged the agency's interpretation of the law. Throughout the 1970s, the courts ruled that discrimination against pregnant women did not constitute sex discrimination because any disparity in treatment was based on pregnancy, not sex. In 1978, in response to substantial public outrage, Congress passed the Pregnancy Discrimination Act (PDA), explicitly stating that pregnancy discrimination is sex discrimination. In spite of the passage of the PDA, the courts have issued inconsistent rulings on the role of pregnant women in the workplace.

Congress was initially the most significant actor in formulating the nation's family leave policy by enacting the 1993 Family and Medical Leave Act, affording eligible employees the opportunity to take unpaid leave for up to twelve weeks. Since then, Congress has played a minor role in family leave policymaking, consigning it to state and local governments and private industry to compensate for the gaps in the legislation, particularly the fact that the leaves—except for federal workers as of 2019—are unpaid. As of 2022, eleven states and Washington, DC, as well as over 100 cities and counties, have enacted paid family leave policies. In addition, 23 percent of employees receive paid leave from their employers. With subnational governments and private industry leading the way in implementing paid leave policies, eligibility and benefits vary greatly, and public pressure continues to mount for Congress to pass a nationwide paid family leave program. Even though there is growing support among lawmakers for the idea of paid leave, there is also a significant partisan divide regarding funding sources. In the current era of extreme party polarization, it is doubtful that Congress will establish a national paid family leave policy in the near future.

Childcare has long been considered a private responsibility in the United States. When the government has gotten involved, it has primarily been to assist low-income families. The only childcare assistance most middle- and upper-income families have received is in the form of federal income tax credits—which are inadequate to cover the cost of care. Biden and progressive Democrats in Congress attempted to incorporate paid leave and childcare into the Build Back Better plan, but they faced substantial opposition from Republicans and more conservative members of their own party, and these programs were excluded from the Inflation Reduction Act of 2022.

The battle for women's reproductive freedom initially centered on the need to overcome government restrictions on access to effective means of contraception. In 1965, the Supreme Court established a constitutional right to privacy in the due process clause of the Fourteenth Amendment, guaranteeing the right of married couples to use birth control. In subsequent years, the Court expanded its interpretation of the right to privacy to include contraception for single people and to remove age limits on access to contraception.

In 1970, Congress enacted the Title X Family Planning Program to provide funding for family planning services, primarily for low-income women and their families. For the most part, state legislatures have not played an active role in regulating women's access to contraception; similarly, the courts have also been less engaged in family planning policy-making and are divided over states' authority to take away funding for family planning services within their borders. As part of their efforts to impose limits on access to abortion care, several states as well as the federal government attempted to restrict the services of Planned Parenthood for contraceptive care and other medical services, a process described as "defunding" Planned Parenthood.

As a result of such policies, family planning services became increasingly politicized because they were intertwined with abortion regulations and, as with most women's rights policies, they reflect the views of state and federal lawmakers. Shortly before his second term ended in 2017, President Barack Obama sought to prohibit states from blocking family planning clinics that provide or refer abortion services from receiving Title X funding. When President Donald Trump took office, he immediately annulled this policy, forcing Title X recipients to choose between receiving federal funding and ceasing to provide abortion care. Once in office, President Joe Biden's administration revoked the Trump-era rule and removed the limits on abortion referrals by Title X recipients.

There was also a significant debate over contraception coverage in the passage of the 2010 Affordable Care Act (ACA), better known as Obamacare. The law included a requirement (the contraceptive mandate) that private insurance plans cover a variety of female contraceptive methods with no co-payments. After enacting the ACA, Congress left its interpretation to the judicial and executive branches. Most of the disagreement revolved around the extent to which the mandate violates the rights of employers who claim that it interferes with their religious beliefs. When religious institutions challenged the mandate in federal court, they argued it violates their constitutional right to free exercise in the First Amendment. The Supreme Court agreed and expanded religious liberty at the expense of access to contraceptive care.

Abortion policymaking is largely reserved for the states by virtue of their authority to enact laws to promote the health and welfare of their citizens. Because Congress and the executive branch only intermittently involved themselves in abortion politics, state legislatures play the largest role in determining the parameters of women's abortion rights. The state's authority to regulate access to abortion is limited by judicial interpretation by the state and federal courts. In the landmark case of *Roe v. Wade* in 1973, the Supreme Court ruled that criminalizing abortion violated a woman's constitutional right to privacy derived from the due process clause of the Fourteenth Amendment. It established the trimester framework for determining the proper balance between the right to an abortion and the state's interest in protecting maternal and fetal health.

Throughout the 1970s and 1980s, the Supreme Court upheld abortion rights with exceptions to allow restrictions on minors through parental consent or notification laws. Likewise, the Court acquiesced when states denied abortion funding to women receiving Medicaid; it also upheld the 1976 Hyde Amendment, approved by Congress to bar the use of federal funds for abortions under most circumstances. In the 1992 ruling in *Planned Parenthood of Southeastern Pennsylvania v. Casey*, the Supreme Court both reaffirmed *Roe* and allowed states greater latitude to regulate abortions. Subsequently, abortion restrictions began to proliferate, especially after the 2010 election led to Republican dominance in most state legislatures. In 2020, with three Trump justices on the Court, it seemed apparent that a new regime of abortion policymaking was in place.

The 2022 ruling in *Dobbs v. Jackson Women's Health Organization* upheld a Mississippi law banning abortion after fifteen weeks of pregnancy. More importantly, the ruling overturned *Roe* and *Casey*, with a majority declaring that *Roe* had been wrongly decided. Overruling the fifty-year-old precedent, the Court returned abortion policymaking to the states, granting them virtually unlimited power over women's ability to exercise control over their reproductive decisionmaking. The setback for women's rights was incomparable, with states hastening to impose restrictions on access to abortion care, which fall most heavily on low-income women and women of color. Many were modeled on the Texas pre-*Roe* statute that only permitted abortions to save a woman's life, placing abortion providers in the untenable position of choosing between their patients' needs and conforming to state law.

Where Are We Now?

This book has documented the challenges women face while attempting to secure equal rights in US society. Since the nation's founding, women struggled to nullify laws and policies that treated them as second-class citizens, denying them the right to vote, own property, participate in the economy, receive an equal education, and control their reproductive autonomy. From the perspective of 2023, women have made considerable advances in securing rights, as measured in the legal and cultural shifts at home, in the workplace, and in schools. Despite these gains, we show their work is far from over and they must continue to fight to achieve a truly egalitarian society in which they are compensated according to their worth, assisted in balancing their work and family responsibilities, guaranteed equal opportunities at work and school, and able to assert control over their reproductive decisionmaking.

This book signifies our belief that women must engage in continuous efforts to attain these goals while simultaneously fighting to preserve the gains they have already made. In presenting the historical foundations of gender inequality in the United States, *Chasing Equality* underscores the fragility of equal rights guarantees. Throughout the book, as we examine women's rights policymaking by discussing interactions among elected and appointed public officials at the national and subnational levels, we highlight the linkages among legislatures, courts, and executive agencies as they form the contours of women's rights policies. We demonstrate that changes in public officeholders at all levels can significantly advance or abruptly halt—

and even reverse—women's progress, as government institutions some-times promote equal rights and at other times undermine them. Changes in political leadership can lead to policy shifts that deprive women of their gains and force them to redouble their efforts in the fight for equal rights. In particular, our book underscores the revolving door of rights guarantees that follows transfers of power between political parties and their leaders. Because voting has consequences and elections matter, women's rights advocates must devote significant energies to ensuring the outcomes that will advance their equal status in society. Therefore, we urge women's rights supporters to recognize that to advocate effec-tively for policies that promote equality, they must understand the role that government institutions play in their lives.

References

AARP and National Alliance for Caregiving. 2020. *Caregiving in the United States*. Available at https://www.aarp.org/content/dam/aarp/ppi/2020/05/full-report-caregiving-in-the-united-states.doi.10.26419-2Fppi.00103.001.pdf.

A Better Balance. 2010. "Fact Sheet: The Business Case for Workplace Flexibility." Available at https://www.abetterbalance.org/resources/business-case-workplace-flexibility-factsheet/.

Acker, Joan. 1992. "From Sex Roles to Gendered Institutions." *Contemporary Sociology* 21: 565–569.

Acosta, Joie D., Matthew Chinman, and Amy L. Shearer. 2021. "Countering Sexual Assault and Sexual Harassment in the U.S. Military: Lessons from RAND Research." RAND Corporation. Available at https://www.rand.org/pubs/research_reports/RRA1318-1.html.

AG Shapiro. 2020. "New Title IX Rule Unlawful, Limits Protections for Sexual Harassment Victims." June 4. Available at https://www.attorneygeneral.gov/taking-action/ag-shapiro-new-title-ix-rule-unlawful-limits-protections-for-sexual-harassment-victims/.

Ambrosius, Brenda L. 2012. "Title IX: Creating Unequal Equality Through Application of the Proportionality Standard in Collegiate Athletics." *Valparaiso University Law Review* 46: 557–606.

American Association of University Women. 2020. "Title IX Rollbacks: Has the #MeToo Backlash Begun?" February 27. Available at https://www.aauw.org/resources/news/media/insights/title-ix-rollbacks-this-is-what-metoo-backlash-looks-like/.

American Civil Liberties Union. 2017. "Re: Religious Exemptions and Accommodations for Coverage of Certain Preventive Services Under the Affordable Care Act [CMS-9940-IFC]." December 5. Available at https://www.aclu.org/sites/default/files/field_document/17_12_5_aclu_comments_re_birth_control_religious_ifr.pdf.

————. 2020a. "ACLU Sues Betsy DeVos for Allowing Schools to Ignore Sexual Harassment and Assault." May 14. Available at https://www.aclu.org/press-releases/aclu-sues-betsy-devos-allowing-schools-ignore-sexual-harassment-and-assault.

———. 2020b. "ACOG Led Coalition of Medical Experts and Reproductive Justice Advocates as Plaintiffs in the Lawsuit." July 13. Available at https://www.aclu .org/press-releases/federal-court-blocks-fda-restriction-unnecessarily-imposes -covid-19-risks-patients.

———. 2021a. "Challenges to The Federal Contraceptive Coverage Rule." Available at https://www.aclu.org/challenges-federal-contraceptive-coverage-rule.

———. 2021b. "Federal Appeals Court Allows Texas Abortion Ban to Remain in Effect." October 14. Available at https://www.aclu.org/press-releases/federal -appeals-court-allows-texas-abortion-ban-remain-effect.

———. 2021c. "Texas Abortion Ban Blocked for Now." October 6. Available at https://www.aclu.org/press-releases/texas-abortion-ban-blocked-now.

———. 2021d. "Texas Abortion Ban Goes to Supreme Court for the Third Time." October 28. Available at https://www.aclu.org/press-releases/texas-abortion -ban-goes-supreme-court-third-time.

———. 2021e. "The ACLU Urges Supreme Court to End Discriminatory Sex-Based Registration for the Draft." January 8. Available at https://www.aclu .org/press-releases/aclu-urges-supreme-court-end-discriminatory-sex-based -registration-draft.

American College of Obstetricians and Gynecologists. 2017. "Periviable Birth." October. Available at https://www.acog.org/clinical/clinical-guidance/obstetric -care-consensus/articles/2017/10/periviable-birth.

American Presidency Project. 2022. "Executive Order 14076—Protecting Access to Reproductive Healthcare Services." July 8. Available at https://www .presidency.ucsb.edu/documents/executive-order-14076-protecting-access -reproductive-healthcare-services.

Amnesty International. 2021. "Key Facts on Abortion." Available at https://www .amnesty.org/en/what-we-do/sexual-and-reproductive-rights/abortion-facts/.

Anderson, Greta. 2019. "More Title IX Lawsuits by Accusers and Accused." *Inside Higher Ed*, October 3. Available at https://www.insidehighered.com/news /2019/10/03/students-look-federal-courts-challenge-title-ix-proceedings.

Anderson, Paul M. 2012. "Title IX at Forty: An Introduction and Historical Review of Forty Legal Developments That Shaped Gender Equity Law." *Marquette Sports Law Review* 22: 325–393.

Anthony, Deborah J. 2008. "The Hidden Harms of the Family and Medical Leave Act: Gender-Neutral Versus Gender-Equal." *Journal of Gender, Social Policy & the Law* 16: 459–501.

Appelbaum, Eileen, and Ruth Milkman. 2011. "Leaves that Pay: Employer and Worker Experiences with Paid Family Leave in California." Center for Economic and Policy Research. Available at http://www.cepr.net/documents/publications /paid-family-leave-1-2011.pdf.

———. 2013. *Unfinished Business: Paid Family Leave in California and the Future of U.S. Work-Family Policy*. Ithaca, NY: Cornell University Press.

Armenia, Amy, and Naomi Gerstel. 2006. "Family Leave, the FMLA and Gender Neutrality: The Intersection of Race and Gender." *Social Science Research* 35: 871–891.

Asher, Lauren J., and Donna R. Lenhoff. 2001. "Family and Medical Leave: Making Time for Family Is Everyone's Business." *Caring for Infants and Toddlers* 11: 115–121.

Atkins, Chloe. 2021. "What U.S. Abortion Access Looks Like, in Graphics." NBC News, July 25. Available at https://www.nbcnews.com/news/us-news/what-u-s -abortion-access-looks-graphics-n1274859.

Bailey, Martha J. 2012. "Reexamining the Impact of Family Planning Programs on US Fertility: Evidence from the War on Poverty and the Early Years of Title X." *American Economic Journal: Applied Economics* 4: 62–97.

———. 2013. "Fifty Years of Family Planning: New Evidence on the Long-Run Effects of Increasing Access to Contraception." *Brookings Papers on Economic Activity* (Spring): 341–395. Available at https://www.brookings.edu/wp-content /uploads/2016/07/2013a_bailey.pdf.

Baker, Paula. 1984. "The Domestication of Politics: Women and American Political Society, 1780–1920." *American Historical Review* 89: 620–647.

Bakst, Dina, Elizabeth Gedmark, and Sarah Brafman. 2019. *Long Overdue: It Is Time for the Federal Pregnant Workers Fairness Act*. A Better Balance. Available at https://www.abetterbalance.org/wp-content/uploads/2019/05/Long -Overdue.pdf.

Banaszak, Lee Ann. 1996. *Why Movements Succeed or Fail: Opportunity, Culture, and the Struggle for Woman Suffrage*. Princeton, NJ: Princeton University Press.

Barnard, Thomas H., and Adrienne L. Rapp. 2009. "Pregnant Employees, Working Mothers, and the Workplace: Legislation, Social Change, and Where We Are Today." *Cleveland State Journal of Law and Health* 32: 197–239.

Baum, Charles L., and Christopher J. Ruhm. 2016. "The Effects of Paid Family Leave in California on Labor Market Outcomes." *Journal of Policy Analysis and Management* 35: 333–356.

Bazelon, Emily. 2015. "What Are the Limits of 'Religious Liberty'?" *New York Times Magazine*, July 7. Available at https://www.nytimes.com/2015/07/12 /magazine/what-are-the-limits-of-religious-liberty.html.

Becker, Nora V., and Daniel Polsky. 2015. "Women Saw Large Decreases in Out-of-Pocket Spending for Contraceptives After ACA Mandate Removed Cost-Sharing." *Health Affairs* 7: 1204–1211.

Bednarek, Lucy B. 1998. "The Gender Wage Gap: Searching for Equality in a Global Economy." *Indiana Journal of Global Legal Studies* 6: 213–236.

Behti, Anjalee. 2019. "Trump's Ruthless Expansion of the Mexico City Policy Threatens Reproductive Health Abroad." *University of San Francisco Law Review* 53: 117–142.

Belkoff, Corinne. 2020. "The Impact of Title IX on Women in Intercollegiate Sports Administration and Coaching." *Entertainment and Sports Law* 36: 45–58.

Bellafaire, Judith A. 2005. "The Women's Army Corps: A Commemoration of World War II Service." Available at https://history.army.mil/brochures/wac /wac.htm.

Bennett, Jessica. 2017. "The 'Click' Moment: How the Weinstein Scandal Unleashed a Tsunami." *New York Times*, November 5. Available at https://www.nytimes.com /2017/11/05/us/sexual-harrasment-weinstein-trump.html.

Berger, Lawrence M., Jennifer Hill, and Jane Waldfogel. 2005. "Maternity Leave, Early Maternal Employment and Child Health and Development in the U.S." *Economic Journal* 115: F29–F47.

Bernstein, Anya. 2001. *The Moderation Dilemma: Legislative Coalitions and the Politics of Family and Medical Leave*. Pittsburgh, PA: University of Pittsburgh Press.

Bernstein, Janessa L. 2008. "The Underground Railroad to Reproductive Freedom: Restrictive Abortion Laws and the Resulting Backlash." *Brooklyn Law Review* 73: 1463–1508.

Berry, Mary Frances. 1986. *Why ERA Failed: Politics, Women's Rights, and the Amending Process of the Constitution*. Bloomington: Indiana University Press.

Bertrand, Marianne, Claudia Goldin, and Lawrence F. Katz. 2010. "Dynamics of the Gender Gap for Young Professionals in the Financial and Corporate Sectors." *American Economic Journal: Applied Economics* 2: 228–255.

Biden, Joseph. 2020. "Statement by Vice President Joe Biden on Birth Control Case Before the U.S. Supreme Court." May 7. Available at https://medium.com /@JoeBiden/statement-by-vice-president-joe-biden-on-birth-control-case -before-the-u-s-supreme-court-fe16addb28d4.

———. 2021. "Memorandum on Protecting Women's Health at Home and Abroad." January 28. Available at https://www.whitehouse.gov/briefing-room/presidential -actions/2021/01/28/memorandum-on-protecting-womens-health-at-home-and -abroad/.

———. 2022. "Statement by President Joe Biden." The White House. May 3. Available at https://www.whitehouse.gov/briefing-room/statements-releases/2022/05/03 /statement-by-president-joe-biden-4/.

Blair, Karen J. 1980. *The Clubwoman as Feminist: True Womanhood Redefined, 1868–1914.* New York: Holmes and Meier.

Blau, Francine D., and Lawrence M. Kahn. 2017. "The Gender Wage Gap: Extent, Trends, and Explanations." *Journal of Economic Literature* 55: 789–865.

Bleiweis, Robin. 2020. "Quick Facts About the Gender Wage Gap." Center for American Progress. Available at https://www.americanprogress.org/issues/women /reports/2020/03/24/482141/quick-facts-gender-wage-gap/.

Blumrosen, Ruth G. 1979. "Wage Discrimination, Job Segregation, and Title VII of the Civil Rights Act of 1964." *University of Michigan Journal of Law Reform* 12: 397–502.

Boisseau, Tracey Jean, and Tracy A. Thomas. 2018. "After Suffrage Comes Equal Rights? ERA as the Next Logical Step." In *100 Years of the Nineteenth Amendment: An Appraisal of Women's Political Activism*, edited by Holly J. McCammon and Lee Ann Banaszak, 227–253. New York: Oxford University Press.

Bolan, A. J. 2018. "Deliberate Indifference: Why Universities Must Do More to Protect Students from Sexual Assault." *George Washington Law Review* 86: 804–839.

Bonn, Kyle. 2022. "USA Qualified for World Cup 2022: USMNT History, Stars, Coach, and Everything You Need to Know." *Sporting News*, March 31. Available at https://www.sportingnews.com/us/soccer/news/usa-qualified-world-cup -2022-usmnt-history-stars-coach/pbkksh0llseonlvoks5pthlx.

Boonstra, Heather D. 2007. "The Heart of the Matter: Public Funding of Abortion for Poor Women in the United States." Guttmacher Institute, March 5. Available at https://www.guttmacher.org/gpr/2007/03/heart-matter-public-funding-abortion -poor-women-united-states.

Bordin, Ruth. 1981. *Woman and Temperance: The Quest for Power and Liberty, 1873–1900.* Philadelphia: Temple University Press.

Boushey, Heather, and Sarah Jane Glynn. 2012. "There Are Significant Business Costs to Replacing Employees." Center for American Progress. Available at https:// www.americanprogress.org/issues/economy/reports/2012/11/16/44464/there -are-significant-business-costs-to-replacing-employees/.

Bowles, Hannah Riley, Linda Babcock, and Lei Lai. 2007. "Social Incentives for Gender Differences in the Propensity to Initiate Negotiations: Sometimes It Does Hurt to Ask." *Organizational Behavior and Human Decision Processes* 103: 84–103.

Brenan, Megan. 2022. "Americans Say Birth Control, Divorce Most 'Morally Acceptable.'" Gallup, June 9. Available at https://news.gallup.com/poll/393515 /americans-say-birth-control-divorce-morally-acceptable.

Brenner, Guy, Laura Fant, and Raymond Arroyo. 2022. "Paid Family Leave Is Coming to Maryland." Available at https://www.lawandtheworkplace.com/2022/04/paid-family-and-medical-leave-is-coming-to-maryland/.

Bridge, Diane L. 1997. "The Glass Ceiling and Sexual Stereotyping: Historical and Legal Perspectives of Women in the Workplace." *Virginia Journal of Social Policy and the Law* 4: 581–644.

Brown, Alec. 2021. "Trigger Laws: What They Are and Which States Have Them." Human Defense Initiative, April 2. Available at https://humandefense.com/trigger-laws-what-are-they-and-which-states-have-them/.

Brown, Olivia, Melanie Collins, Hange (Hera) Liao, Lydia Tsao, and Tracey Zhang. 2019. "Twentieth Annual Review of Gender and the Law." *Georgetown Journal of Gender and the Law* 20: 397–420.

Brown, Scott, Jane Herr, Radha Roy, and Jacob Alex Klerman. 2020. *Employee and Worksite Perspectives of the Family and Medical Leave Act: Results from the 2018 Surveys*. Rockville, MD: Abt Associates. Available at https://www.dol.gov/sites/dolgov/files/OASP/evaluation/pdf/WHD_FMLA2018SurveyResults_FinalReport_Aug2020.pdf.

Budig, Michelle J. 2014. "The Fatherhood Bonus and the Motherhood Penalty: Parenthood and the Gender Gap in Pay." Third Way, September 2. Available at https://www.thirdway.org/report/the-fatherhood-bonus-and-the-motherhood-penalty-parenthood-and-the-gender-gap-in-pay.

Burt, Jonathan. 2018. "Equal Protection and Scrutinizing Scrutiny: The Supreme Court's Decision in *Sessions v. Morales-Santana*." *Utah Law Review*: 787–809.

Buzuvis, Erin E. 2017. "Title IX and Procedural Fairness: Why Disciplined-Student Litigation Does Not Undermine the Role of Title IX in Campus Sexual Assault." *Montana Law Review* 78: 71–108.

California Employment Development Department. n.d. "Paid Family Leave." Available at https://edd.ca.gov/disability/paid-family-leave/ (accessed July 31, 2022).

Canales, Bilma. 2018. "Closing the Federal Gender Pay Gap Through Wage Transparency." *Houston Law Review* 55: 969–997.

Cantalupo, Nancy Chi. 2019. "Dog Whistles and Beachheads: The Trump Administration, Sexual Violence, and Student Discipline in Education." *Wake Forest Law Review* 54: 303–361.

Carpenter, Daniel, and Colin D. Moore. 2014. "When Canvassers Became Activists: Antislavery Petitioning and the Political Mobilization of American Women." *American Political Science Review* 108: 479–498.

Chamberlain, Elaine, Hannah Cornett, and Adam Yohanan. 2018. "Athletics & Title II of the 1972 Education Amendments." *Georgetown Journal of Gender and the Law* 19: 231–263.

Chatterji, Pinka, and Sara Markowitz. 2012. "Family Leave After Childbirth and the Mental Health of New Mothers." *Journal of Mental Health Policy and Economics* 15: 61–76.

Chen, Melissa J., and Mitchell Creinin. 2015. "Mifepristone with Buccal Misoprostol for Medical Abortion: A Systematic Review." *Obstetrics & Gynecology* 16: 12–21.

Chi, Keon S. 1986. "Comparable Worth in State Government: Trends and Issues." *Policy Studies Review* 5: 800–814.

Chiwaya, Nigel. 2018. "New Data on #MeToo's First Year Shows 'Undeniable' Impact." NBC News, October 11. Available at https://www.nbcnews.com/news/us-news/new-data-metoo-s-first-year-shows-undeniable-impact-n918821.

Churches, Kimberly. 2020. "Title IX Rollbacks: Has the #MeToo Backlash Begun?" AAUW, February 27. Available at https://www.aauw.org/resources/news/media/insights/title-ix-rollbacks-this-is-what-metoo-backlash-looks-like/.

Cohen, Cathren. 2018. "'Beyond Rational Belief': Evaluating Health-Justified Abortion Restrictions After *Whole Woman's Health.*" *New York University Review of Law & Social Change* 42: 173–220.

Cohen, Robert H. 1995. "Pay Equity: A Child of the 80s Grows Up." *Fordham Law Review* 63: 1461–1493.

Cohn, D'Vera, Gretchen Livingston, and Wendy Wang. 2014. "After Decades of Decline, a Rise in Stay-at-Home Mothers." Pew Research Center, April 8. Available at https://www.pewresearch.org/social-trends/2014/04/08/after-decades-of-decline-a-rise-in-stay-at-home-mothers/.

Coleman, Doriane Lambelet, Michael J. Joyner, and Donna Lopiano. 2020. "Re-Affirming the Value of the Sports Exception to Title IX's General Non-Discrimination Rule." *Duke Journal of Gender Law and Policy* 27: 69–134.

Collins, Gail. 2009. *When Everything Changed: The Amazing Journey of American Women from 1960 to the Present.* New York: Little, Brown.

Collins, Lauren. 2022. "The Complicated Life of the Abortion Pill." *New Yorker,* July 5. Available at https://www.newyorker.com/science/annals-of-medicine/emile-baulieu-the-complicated-life-of-the-abortion-pill.

Colorado Department of Labor and Employment. n.d. "Family and Medical Leave Insurance Program (FAMLI)." Available at https://famli.colorado.gov/ (accessed July 31, 2022).

Committee on Education and Labor Republicans. 2020. "Foxx Statement on Education Department's Title IX Rule." Available at https://republicans-edlabor.house.gov/news/documentsingle.aspx?DocumentID=406948.

Congress of the United States. 2021. "Letter to the Honorable Miguel Cardona." September 13. Available at https://s3.documentcloud.org/documents/21061559/2021-09-13-nprm-title-ix-letter-to-sec-cardona.pdf.

"Connecticut Paid Leave." n.d. Available at https://ctpaidleave.org/s/?language=en_US (accessed July 31, 2022).

Conover, Pamela Johnston, and Virginia Gray. 1983. *Feminism and the New Right: Conflict over the American Family.* New York: Praeger.

Conway, M. Margaret, David W. Ahern, and Gertrude A. Steuernagel. 2005. *Women and Public Policy: A Revolution in Progress,* 3rd ed. Washington, DC: CQ Press.

Corbin, Caroline Mala. 2016. "Punting on Substantial Religious Burden, the Supreme Court Provides No Guidance for Future RFRA Challenges to Anti-discrimination Laws." *SCOTUSblog,* May 17. Available at https://www.scotusblog.com/2016/05/symposium-punting-on-substantial-religious-burden-the-supreme-court-provides-no-guidance-for-future-rfra-challenges-to-anti-discrimination-laws-2/.

Cott, Nancy F. 1990a. "Across the Great Divide: Women in Politics Before and After 1920." In *Women, Politics, and Change,* edited by Louise Tilly and Patricia Gurin, 153–176. New York: Russell Sage Foundation.

———. 1990b. "The Equal Rights Amendment Conflict in the 1920s." In *Conflicts in Feminism,* edited by Marianne Hirsch and Evelyn Fox Keller, 44–59. New York: Routledge.

Dabrowski, Julie. 2014. "The Exception That Doesn't Prove the Rule: Why Congress Should Narrow ENDA's Religious Exemption to Protect the Rights of LGBT Employees." *American University Law Review* 63: 1957–1984.

Daku, Mark, Amy Raub, and Jody Heymann. 2012. "Maternal Leave Policies and Vaccination Coverage: A Global Analysis." *Social Science & Medicine* 74: 120–124.

Daniels, Kimberly, and Joyce C. Abma. 2020. "Current Contraceptive Status Among Women Aged 15–49." National Center for Health Statistics, Data Brief no. 388, October. Available at https://www.cdc.gov/nchs/products/databriefs/db388.htm.

Danielsson, Krissi. 2022 "What Is Fetal Viability?" *Verywell Family*, Updated September 17. Available at https://www.verywellfamily.com/premature-birth-and-viability-2371529#age-of-viability.

Darrah, Denise. 2012. "Frederick Douglass, Supporter of Equal Rights for All People." *Counterpoints* 406: 151–162.

Das, Andrew. 2022a. "U.S. Soccer and Women's Players Agree to Settle Equal Pay Lawsuit." *New York Times*, February 22. Available at https://www.nytimes.com/2022/02/22/sports/soccer/us-womens-soccer-equal-pay.html.

———. 2022b. "U.S. Soccer and Top Players Agree to Guarantee Equal Pay." *New York Times*, May 18. Available at https://www.nytimes.com/2022/05/18/sports/soccer/us-soccer-equal-pay-deal.html.

Davidson, Jennifer. 2019. "Lessons from *Trinity Lutheran*: An Entity-Based Approach to Unconstitutional Conditions and Abortion Defunding Laws." *New York University Review of Law & Social Change* 43: 581–610.

Davis, Elizabeth Lindsay. 1933. *Lifting as They Climb*. Washington, DC: National Association of Colored Women.

Daw, K., Austin Donohue, Courtney Hinkle, Hyun Seo Lee, Maureen Milmoe, Katherine Shea, and Myunghee Tuttle. 2020. "Twenty-First Annual Review of Gender and the Law: Sexual Harassment in Education." *Georgetown Journal of Gender and Law* 21: 439–478.

Delchin, Steven A. 1997. "*United States v. Virginia* and Our Evolving 'Constitution': Playing Peek-a-Boo with the Standard of Scrutiny for Sex-Based Classifications." *Case Western Reserve Law Review* 47: 1121–1155.

Dellinger, Walter, and Gene B. Sperling. 1989. "Abortion and the Supreme Court: The Retreat from *Roe v. Wade*." *University of Pennsylvania Law Review* 138: 83–118.

Denniston, Lyle. 2015. "The ACA Birth-Control Controversy, Made Simple." *SCOTUSblog*, July 15. Available at https://www.scotusblog.com/2015/07/the-aca-birth-control-controversy-made-simple/.

———. 2016. "Opinion Analysis: A Compromise, with Real Impact, on Birth Control." *SCOTUSblog*, May. Available at https://www.scotusblog.com/2016/05/opinion-analysis-a-compromise-with-real-impact-on-birth-control/.

Densmore, Kristyn. 2018–2019. "The Struggle of a Woman's Body in a Man's World." *Appalachian Law Review* 18: 25–44.

DeWitt, Ethan. 2021. "Sununu Gets His Paid Family Leave Plan, but Some See Pitfalls in the Program." *New Hampshire Bulletin*, July 7. Available at https://newhampshirebulletin.com/2021/07/07/sununu-gets-his-paid-family-leave-plan-but-some-see-pitfalls-in-the-program/.

DiCaro, Julie. 2021. *Sidelined: Sports, Culture, and Being a Woman in America*. New York: Dutton.

Dingell, Debbie. 2021. "Dingell, Hayes Unveil Legislation to Hold Educational Institutions Accountable for Sexual Assault." September 28. Available at https://debbiedingell.house.gov/news/documentsingle.aspx?DocumentID=3229.

Dinner, Deborah. 2010. "The Universal Childcare Debate: Rights Mobilization, Social Policy, and the Dynamics of Feminist Activism, 1966–1974." *Law and History Review* 28: 577–628.

District of Columbia Department of Employment Services. n.d. "D.C. Paid Family Leave." Available at https://does.dc.gov/page/dc-paid-family-leave (accessed July 31, 2022).

Djavaherian, Jennifer, Devlin Healey, M. Annie Houghton-Larsen, Alison Tanner, and Greyson Wallis. 2017. "Eighteenth Annual Review of Gender and the Law: Abortion." *Georgetown Journal of Gender and Law* 18: 395–437.

Donaldson, Chelsea M. 2018. "Breaking the TRAP: How *Whole Woman's Health* Protects Abortion Access, and the Substantive Due Process Clause's Rebuke of Anti-Abortion Regulations." *New England Law Review* 40: 257–298.

Donley, Greer. 2019. "Contraceptive Equity: Curing the Sex Discrimination in the ACA's Mandate." *Alabama Law Review* 71: 499–559.

Donovan, Megan K. 2017. "D&E Abortion Bans: The Implications of Banning the Most Common Second-Trimester Procedure." Guttmacher Policy Review, February 21. Available at https://www.guttmacher.org/gpr/2017/02/de-abortion-bans-implications-banning-most-common-second-trimester-procedure.

Donovan, Patricia. 1980. "Informed Consent to Abortion: Ensuring a Knowledgeable Choice or Interfering with a Woman's Constitutional Right?" *Family Planning Population Reporter* 9: 10–13.

Dow, Nicole. 2021. "How High Are Child Care Costs? 40% of Parents Have Gone into Debt over It." *Penny Hoarder*, October 18. Available at https://www.thepennyhoarder.com/save-money/child-care-costs/.

Dunham, Rachel. 2020. "Title IX Beyond School Lines: The Proposed Regulations That Will Limit Colleges and Universities' Jurisdictional Scope of Responsibility." *Roger Williams University Law Review* 25: 265–306.

Duong, Viet-An, Phu Pham, Ritwik Bose, and Jiebo Luo. 2020. "#MeToo on Campus: Studying College Sexual Assault at Scale Using Data Reported on Social Media." Cornell University. Available at https://arxiv.org/abs/2001.05970.

Eckes, Suzanne. 2003. "The Thirtieth Anniversary of Title IX: Women Have Not Reached the Finish Line." *Southern California Review of Law and Women's Studies* 13: 3–34.

Economic Policy Institute. n.d. "Child Care Costs in the United States." Available at https://www.epi.org/child-care-costs-in-the-united-states/#/FL (accessed November 7, 2021).

Edgar, Caroline. 2020. "A Preponderance of the Evidence: The Appropriate Standard in Title IX Sexual Harassment Proceedings." *Administrative Law Review Accord* 6: 85–112.

Edwards, Sarah. 2015. "The Case in Favor of OCR's Tougher Title IX Policies: Pushing Back Against the Pushback." *Duke Journal of Gender Law and Policy* 23: 121–144.

Eisenberg, Deborah Thompson. 2010. "Shattering the Equal Pay Act's Glass Ceiling." *Southern Methodist University Law Review* 63: 17–72.

Elesser, Kim. 2019. "The Latest Consequence of #MeToo: Not Hiring Women." *Forbes*, September 5. Available at https://www.forbes.com/sites/kimelsesser/2019/09/05/the-latest-consequence-of-metoo-not-hiring-women/?sh=c615c72280b0.

Elison, Sonja Klueck. 1997. "Policy Innovation in a Cold Climate: The Family and Medical Leave Act of 1993." *Journal of Family Issues* 18: 30–54.

Elving, Ronald D. 1995. *Conflict and Compromise: How Congress Makes the Law.* New York: Simon & Schuster.

"Equal Rights Amendment." 2021. Available at https://www.equalrightsamendment.org/.

Evans, Sara M. 1989. *Born for Liberty: A History of Women in America.* New York: Free Press.

Eversman, Caroline. 2019. "Using Medicaid Funds for Planned Parenthood: Is the Medicaid Act's Choice of Free Provider Really a Free Choice?" *Ohio State Law Journal* 80: 133–158.

Ewing-Nelson, Claire, and Jasmine Tucker. 2021. "A Year into the Pandemic, Women Are Still Short Nearly 5.1 Million Jobs." National Women's Law Center. Available at https://nwlc.org/wp-content/uploads/2021/03/Feb-Jobs-Day-v2.pdf.

Executive Order 13798. 2017. "Promoting Free Speech and Religious Liberty." May 4.
Executive Order 14020. 2021. "Executive Order on Establishment of the White House Gender Policy Council." March 11.
Executive Order 14021. 2021. "Executive Order on Guaranteeing an Educational Environment Free from Discrimination on the Basis of Sex, Including Sexual Orientation or Gender Identity." March 11.
Federal Register. 1972. "Employment Policies Relating to Pregnancy and Childbirth." 37 F.R. 6837. April 5.
———. 1988. "Statutory Prohibition on Use of Appropriated Funds in Programs Where Abortion Is a Method of Family Planning; Standard of Compliance for Family Planning Services Projects." 53 F.R. 2922. February 2.
———. 2000. "Standards of Compliance for Abortion-Related Services in Family Planning Services Projects." 65 F.R. 41269. July 3.
———. 2013. "Coverage of Certain Preventive Services Under the Affordable Care Act." 78 F.R. 39870. July 2.
———. 2016. "Compliance with Title X Requirements by Project Recipients in Selecting Subrecipients." 81 F.R. 91852. December 19.
———. 2017a. "Moral Exemptions and Accommodations for Coverage of Certain Preventive Services Under the Affordable Care Act." 82 F.R. 47838. October 13.
———. 2017b. "Religious Exemptions and Accommodations for Coverage of Certain Preventive Services Under the Affordable Care Act." 82 F.R. 47792. October 13.
———. 2018. "Moral Exemptions and Accommodations for Coverage of Certain Preventive Services Under the Affordable Care Act." 83 F.R. 57592. November 15.
———. 2019. "Compliance with Statutory Program Integrity Requirements." 84 F.R. 7714. March 4.
———. 2020. "Nondiscrimination on the Basis of Sex in Education Programs or Activities Receiving Federal Financial Assistance." 85 F.R. 30026. May 19.
———. 2021a. "Ensuring Access to Equitable, Affordable, Client-Centered, Quality Family Planning Services." 86 F.R. 19812. April 15.
———. 2021b. "Ensuring Access to Equitable, Affordable, Client-Centered, Quality Family Planning Services." 86 F.R. 56144. October 7.
Federal Reserve Board. 2020. "Update on the Economic Well-Being of U.S. Households: July 2020 Results." Available at https://www.federalreserve.gov /publications/files/2019-report-economic-well-being-us-households-update -202009.pdf.
Feldblum, Chai R., and Victoria A. Lipnic. 2016. "Select Task Force on the Study of Harassment in the Workplace." Equal Employment Opportunity Commission. Available at https://www.eeoc.gov/select-task-force-study-harassment-workplace.
Filler-Corn, Eileen, Charniele Herring, Vivian Watts, Jeion Ward, Delores McQuinn, Kaye Kory, Jennifer Carroll Foy, and Hala Ayala. 2020. "Virginia Just Passed the ERA. Here's Why We Still Need It." *Washington Post,* January 27. Available at https://www.washingtonpost.com/opinions/2020/01/27/virginia-just-passed-era -heres-why-we-still-need-it/.
FINDLAW. 2016. "Federal Religious Freedom Restoration Act Overview." June 20. Available at https://civilrights.findlaw.com/discrimination/federal-religious -freedom-restoration-act-overview.html.
Finer, Lawrence B., and Stanley K. Henshaw. 2003. "Abortion Incidence and Services in the United States in 2000." *Perspectives on Sexual and Reproductive Health* 35: 6–16.
Finley, Lucinda M. 1986. "Transcending Equality Theory: A Way Out of the Maternity and the Workplace Debate." *Columbia Law Review* 86: 1118–1182.

Fins, Amanda. 2020. "Women and the Lifetime Wage Gap: How Many Woman Years Does It Take to Equal 40 Man Years?" National Women's Law Center. Available at https://nwlc.org/wp-content/uploads/2017/03/Women-and-the-Lifetime-Wage -Gap-2017-1.pdf.

First Five Years Fund. 2021. "Voters Agree: Child Care and Early Learning Is Smart Policy and Smart Politics." Available at https://www.ffyf.org/2021-policy-poll -fact-sheet/.

Fiss, Owen. 1976. "Groups and the Equal Protection Clause." *Philosophy and Public Affairs* 5: 107–177.

Fitzgerald, Wendy A. 1988. "Toward Dignity in the Workplace: *Miller-Wohl* and Beyond." *Montana Law Review* 49: 147–179.

Flaherty, Colleen. 2020. "Teaching Me Too." *Inside Higher Ed*, January 14. Available at https://www.insidehighered.com/news/2020/01/14/me-too-was-major -theme-years-modern-language-association-meeting.

Flexner, Eleanor, and Ellen F. Fitzpatrick. 1996. *Century of Struggle: The Women's Rights Movement in the United States*. Cambridge, MA: Belknap Press of Harvard University Press.

Ford, Linda G. 1991. *Iron-Jawed Angels: The Suffrage Militancy of the National Woman's Party, 1912–1920*. Lanham, MD: University Press of America.

Freeman, Jo. 1991. "How 'Sex' Got into Title VII: Persistent Opportunism as a Maker of Public Policy." *Law and Inequality* 9: 163–184.

———. 1996. "What's in a Name? Does It Matter How the Equal Rights Amendment Is Worded?" Available at https://www.jofreeman.com/lawandpolicy /eraname.htm.

Friedan, Betty. 1963. *The Feminine Mystique*. New York: W. W. Norton.

Friedman, Dana E. 1990. "Corporate Responses to Family Needs." *Marriage and Family Review* 15: 77–98.

Frost, Jennifer J., Lori F. Frohwirth, Nakisha Blades, Mia R. Zolna, Ayana Douglas-Hall, and Jonathan Bearak. 2017. "Publicly Funded Contraceptive Services at U.S. Clinics, 2015." Guttmacher Institute, April. Available at https://www .guttmacher.org/report/publicly-funded-contraceptive-services-us-clinics-2015.

Fry, Richard. 2019. "U.S. Women Near Milestone in the College-Educated Labor Force." Pew Research Center, June 20. Available at https://www.pewresearch .org/fact-tank/2019/06/20/u-s-women-near-milestone-in-the-college-educated -labor-force/.

Frye, Jocelyn. 2017. "Not Just the Rich and Famous: The Pervasiveness of Sexual Harassment Across Industries Affects All Women." Center for American Progress, November 20. Available at https://www.americanprogress.org/article /not-just-rich-famous/.

Fuentes, Liza, and Jenna Jerman. 2019. "Distance Traveled to Obtain Clinical Abortion Care in the United States and Reasons for Clinic Choice." *Journal of Women's Health* 28: 1623–1631.

Fullerton, Howard N., Jr. 1999. "Labor Force Participation: 75 Years of Change, 1950–98 and 1998–2025." *Monthly Labor Review* 122: 3–12.

Gallardo, Samantha. 2018. "How Strong Is Your American Blood?" *Suffolk Journal of Trial and Appellate Advocacy* 23: 265–283.

Gallup. 2021. "Abortion." Available at https://news.gallup.com/poll/1576/Abortion .aspx.

Garcia, Sandra E. 2017. "The Woman Who Created #MeToo Long Before Hashtags." *New York Times*, October 20. Available at https://www.nytimes.com/2017 /10/20/us/me-too-movement-tarana-burke.html.

Geiger, A. W., Gretchen Livingston, and Kristen Bialik. 2019. "6 Facts About U.S. Moms." Pew Research Center, May 8. Available at https://www.pewresearch.org /fact-tank/2019/05/08/facts-about-u-s-mothers/.

Gelb, Joyce, and Marian Lief Palley. 1987. *Women and Public Policies*. Princeton, NJ: Princeton University Press.

George, B. Glenn. 2010. "Forfeit: Opportunity, Choice, and Discrimination Theory Under Title IX." *Yale Journal of Law and Feminism* 22: 1–52.

Giele, Janet Zollinger. 1995. *Two Paths to Women's Equality: Temperance, Suffrage, and the Origins of Modern Feminism*. New York: Twayne.

Gillette-Pierce, Kiersten, and Jamila K. Taylor. 2017. "The Threat to Title X Family Planning: Why It Matters and What's at Stake for Women." Center for American Progress, February 9. Available at https://www.americanprogress.org /article/the-threat-to-title-x-family-planning/.

Gilley, Allison. 2019. "Protecting Planned Parenthood: Is Planned Parenthood Funding a Justiciable Right Under the Medicaid Freedom-of-Choice Provision?" *Wisconsin Journal of Law, Gender and Society* 34: 69–82.

Glass, Jennifer L., and Sarah Beth Estes. 1997. "The Family Responsive Workplace." *Annual Review of Sociology* 23: 289–313.

Glynn, Sarah Jane. 2018. "An Unequal Division of Labor: How Equitable Workplace Policies Would Benefit Working Mothers." Center for American Progress. Available at https://www.americanprogress.org/issues/women/reports/2018/05/18 /450972/unequal-division-labor/.

———. 2020. "The Rising Cost of Inaction on Work-Family Policies." Center for American Progress. Available at https://www.americanprogress.org/issues/women /news/2020/01/21/479555/rising-cost-inaction-work-family-policies/.

Glynn, Sarah Jane, and Jane Farrell. 2012. "Latinos Least Likely to Have Paid Leave or Workplace Flexibility." Center for American Progress. Available at https://www.americanprogress.org/issues/economy/reports/2012/11/20/45394 /latinos-least-likely-to-have-paid-leave-or-workplace-flexibility/.

Gold, Rachel Benson. 2003. "Lessons from Before Roe: Will Past Be Prologue?" Guttmacher Institute. Available at https://www.guttmacher.org/gpr/2003/03/lessons -roe-will-past-be-prologue.

Gold, Rachel Benson, and Megan K. Donovan. 2017. "Lessons from Before Abortion Was Legal." *Scientific American*, September 1. Available at https://www .scientificamerican.com/article/lessons-from-before-abortion-was-legal/.

Gold, Rachel Benson, and Elizabeth Nash. 2013. "TRAP Laws Gain Political Traction While Abortion Clinics—And the Women They Serve—Pay the Price." *Guttmacher Policy Review* 16: 7–12.

Goldin, Claudia. 2014. "A Grand Gender Convergence: Its Last Chapter." *American Economic Review* 104: 1091–1119.

Goldvaser, Amalia. 2008. "Inflating Goodyear's Bottom Line: Paying Women Less and Getting Away with It." *Cardozo Journal of Law and Gender* 15: 99–116.

Good, Hannah. 2021. "It's the 100th Anniversary of the First Conference on Birth Control. Here's a Look at Contraception's Lesser-known Legacy." *The Lily*, November 6. Available at https://www.thelily.com/its-the-100th-anniversary-of -the-first-conference-on-birth-control-heres-a-look-at-contraceptions-lesser -known-legacy/.

Gornick, Janet C., and Marcia K. Meyers. 2003. *Families That Work: Policies for Reconciling Parenthood and Employment*. New York: Russell Sage Foundation.

GovTrack. 2021a. "H.R. 804: FAMILY Act." Available at https://www.govtrack .us/congress/bills/117/hr804.

————. 2021b. "H.R. 4445: Ending Forced Arbitration of Sexual Assault and Sexual Harassment Act of 2021." Available at https://www.govtrack.us/congress/bills/117/hr4445.

————. 2021c. "S. 248: FAMILY Act." Available at https://www.govtrack.us/congress/bills/117/s248.

————. 2021d. "S. 1520: Military Justice Improvement and Increasing Prevention Act of 2021." Available at https://www.govtrack.us/congress/bills/117/s1520.

————. 2021e. "S. 2342: Ending Forced Arbitration of Sexual Assault and Sexual Harassment Act of 2021." Available at https://www.govtrack.us/congress/bills/117/s2342.

Gravely, Alexis. 2021. "Proposed Title IX Rule Changes Expected May 2022." *Inside Higher Ed*, June 24. Available at https://www.insidehighered.com/quicktakes/2021/06/24/proposed-title-ix-rule-changes-expected-may-2022.

Green, Emma. 2015. "Even Nuns Aren't Exempt from Obamacare's Birth-Control Mandate." *The Atlantic*, July 14. Available at https://www.theatlantic.com/politics/archive/2015/07/obama-beats-the-nuns-on-contraception/398519/.

Green, Tristin K. 2008. "Insular Individualism: Employment Discrimination Law After *Ledbetter v. Goodyear*." *Harvard Civil Rights–Civil Liberties Law Review* 43: 353–383.

Greenhouse, Linda. 2020. "How Chief Justice Roberts Solved His Abortion Dilemma." *New York Times*, July 2. Available at https://www.nytimes.com/2020/07/02/opinion/supreme-court-abortion-roberts.html.

————. 2022. "Justice Alito's Invisible Women." *New York Times*, May 5. Available at https://www.nytimes.com/2022/05/05/opinion/abortion-alito-discrimination.html.

Greenhouse, Linda, and Reva B. Siegel. 2016. "*Casey* and the Clinic Closings: When 'Protecting Health' Obstructs Choice." *Yale Law Journal* 125: 1428–1480.

Griffin, Leslie. 2016. "Workers Remain at Risk Post–*Zubik v. Burwell*." *SCOTUSblog*, May 17. Available at https://www.scotusblog.com/2016/05/symposium-workers-remain-at-risk-post-zubik-v-burwell/.

Guendelman, Sylvia, Julia Goodman, Martin Kharrazi, and Maureen Lahiff. 2014. "Work-Family Balance After Childbirth: The Association Between Employer-Offered Leave Characteristics and Maternity Leave Duration." *Maternal and Child Health Journal* 18: 200–208.

Gunther, Gerald. 1972. "Foreword: In Search of Evolving Doctrine on a Changing Court: A Model for a Newer Equal Protection." *Harvard Law Review* 86: 1–48.

Gupta, Alisha Haridasani. 2020. "Why Some Women Call This Recession a 'Shecession.'" *New York Times*, May 9. Available at https://www.nytimes.com/2020/05/09/us/unemployment-coronavirus-women.html.

Gupta, Alisha Haridasani, and Alexandra E. Petri. 2021. "There's a New Pregnancy Discrimination Bill in the House. This Time It Might Pass." *New York Times*, March 4. Available at https://www.nytimes.com/2021/03/04/us/pregnancy-discrimination-congress-women.html.

Gupta, Pronita, Tanya Goldman, Eduardo Hernandez, and Michelle Rose. 2018. "Paid Family and Medical Leave Is Critical for Low-Wage Workers and Their Families." Center for Law and Social Policy. Available at https://www.clasp.org/publications/fact-sheet/paid-family-and-medical-leave-critical-low-wage-workers-and-their-families.

Guskin, Emily. 2018. "Republicans' Changing Views Fuel Sharp Rise in Concerns About Harassment, *Post*-ABC Poll Finds." *Washington Post*, January 24. Available at https://www.washingtonpost.com/news/the-fix/wp/2018/01/24/republicans-fuel-sharp-rise-in-concerns-about-sexual-harassment-post-abc-poll-finds/.

Guttmacher Institute. 2000. "Title X 'Gag Rule' Is Formally Repealed." Guttmacher Policy Review, August 1. Available at https://www.guttmacher.org/gpr/2000/08/title-x-gag-rule-formally-repealed#.

———. 2019. "Induced Abortion in the United States." September. Available at https://www.guttmacher.org/fact-sheet/induced-abortion-united-states#2000.

———. 2020. "The Broad Benefits of Contraceptive Use in the United States." April. Available at https://www.guttmacher.org/sites/default/files/factsheet/broad-benefits-contraceptive-use-united-states.pdf.

———. 2021a. "Contraceptive Use in the United States by Demographics." May. Available at https://www.guttmacher.org/fact-sheet/contraceptive-use-united-states.

———. 2021b. "Contraceptive Use in the United States by Method." May. Available at https://www.guttmacher.org/fact-sheet/contraceptive-method-use-united-states.

———. 2022a. "About." Available at https://www.guttmacher.org/about.

———. 2022b. "An Overview of Abortion Laws." June 1. Available at https://www.guttmacher.org/state-policy/explore/overview-abortion-laws.

———. 2022c. "Bans on Specific Abortion Methods Used After the First Trimester." June 1. Available at https://www.guttmacher.org/state-policy/explore/bans-specific-abortion-methods-used-after-first-trimester.

———. 2022d. "Parental Involvement in Minors' Abortions." June 1. Available at https://www.guttmacher.org/state-policy/explore/parental-involvement-minors-abortions.

———. 2022e. "State Funding of Abortion Under Medicaid." June 1. Available at https://www.guttmacher.org/state-policy/explore/state-funding-abortion-under-medicaid#.

———. 2022f. "Targeted Regulation of Abortion Providers." June 1. Available at https://www.guttmacher.org/print/state-policy/explore/targeted-regulation-abortion-providers.

Haksgaard, Hannah. 2017. "Rural Women and Developments in the Undue Burden Analysis: The Effect of *Whole Woman's Health v. Hellerstedt*." *Drake Law Review* 65: 663–717.

Halpin, John, Karl Agne, and Nisha Jain. 2020. "What Do Voters Want on Child Care Ahead of the 2020 Elections? Results from a National Survey of Registered Voters." Center for American Progress. Available at https://www.americanprogress.org/issues/early-childhood/reports/2020/09/25/490772/voters-want-child-care-ahead-2020-elections/.

Han, Lori Cox, and Caroline Heldman. 2018. *Women, Power, and Politics: The Fight for Gender Equality in the United States*. New York: Oxford University Press.

Harnik, Michelle J. 2018. "University Title IX Compliance: A Work in Progress in the Wake of Reform." *Nevada Law Journal* 19: 647–687.

Harrington, Brad, Fred Van Deusen, Jennifer Sabatini Fraone, Samantha Eddy, and Linda Hass. 2014. "The New Dad: Take Your Leave. Perspectives on Paternity Leave from Fathers, Leading Organizations, and Global Policies." Boston College Center for Work & Family. Available at https://www.fatherhood.gov/sites/default/files/resource_files/e000003974.pdf.

Harrison, Cynthia Ellen. 1988. *On Account of Sex: The Politics of Women's Issues, 1945–1968*. Berkeley: University of California Press.

Hartmann, Heidi I., and Stephanie Aaronson. 1994. "Pay Equity and Women's Wage Increases: Success in the States, a Model for the Nation." *Duke Journal of Gender Law and Policy* 1: 69–88.

Harvard Law Review. 2016. "Religious Liberty—Religious Freedom Restoration Act—Seventh Circuit Denies Preliminary Injunction to Wheaton College—

Wheaton College v. Burwell, 791 F.3d 792 (7th Cir. 2015)." *Harvard Law Review* 129: 851–858.

Hasday, Jill Elaine. 2022. "Opinion on *Roe*, Alito Cites a Judge Who Treated Women as Witches and Property." *Washington Post*, May 5. Available at https://www.washingtonpost.com/opinions/2022/05/09/alito-roe-sir-matthew-hale-misogynist/.

Hefferan, James J., Jr. 2016. "A Sporting Chance: *Biediger v. Quinnipiac University* and What Constitutes a Sport for Purposes of Title IX." *Marquette Sports Law Review* 26: 583–633.

Hendricks, Wanda A. 1994. "'Vote for the Advantage of Ourselves and Our Race': The Election of the First Black Alderman in Chicago." *Illinois Historical Journal* 87: 171–184.

Herbst, Chris M. 2017. "Universal Child Care, Maternal Employment, and Children's Long-Run Outcomes: Evidence from the US Lanham Act of 1940." *Journal of Labor Economics* 35: 519–564.

Herr, Jane, Radha Roy, and Jacob Alex Klerman. 2020. *Gender Differences in Needing and Taking Leave*. Rockville, MD: Abt Associates. Available at https://www.dol.gov/sites/dolgov/files/OASP/evaluation/pdf/WHD_FMLAGenderShortPaper_January2021.pdf.

Hersh, Adam. 2018. "Daniel in the Lion's Den: A Structural Reconsideration of Religious Exemptions from Nondiscrimination Laws Since *Obergefell*." *Stanford Law Review* 70: 265–317.

Hess, Cynthia, Tanima Ahmed, and Jeff Hayes. 2020. "Providing Unpaid Household and Care Work in the United States: Uncovering Inequality." Institute for Women's Policy Research. Available at https://www.nationalpartnership.org/our-work/resources/economic-justice/fmla/updating-the-fmla.pdf.

Hewlett, Sylvia Ann, Carolyn Buck Luce, Lisa J. Servon, Laura Sherbin, Peggy Shiller, Eytan Sosnovich, and Karen Sumberg. 2008. "The Athena Factor: Reversing the Brain Drain in Science, Engineering, and Technology." *Harvard Business Review*, June. Available at https://www.google.com/url?sa=t&rct=j&q=&esrc=s&source=web&cd=&ved=2ahUKEwjLq7jZ7ob7AhXVrokEHdPaCSMQFnoECAwQAQ&url=https%3A%2F%2Flawcat.berkeley.edu%2Frecord%2F1127365%2Ffiles%2F0-Athena_Factor___Brain_Drain_in_Scienc.pdf&usg=AOvVaw1FPXiQ6zjKIurdH5z7RlPQ.

Hillstrom, Laurie Collier. 2019. *The #MeToo Movement*. Santa Barbara, CA: ABC-CLIO.

Holley, Peter, and Dan Solomon. 2021. "Your Questions About Texas's New Abortion Law, Answered." *Texas Monthly*, October 7. Available at https://www.texasmonthly.com/news-politics/texas-abortion-law-explained/.

Houser, Linda, and Thomas P. Vartanian. 2012. *Pay Matters: The Positive Economic Impact of Paid Family Leave for Families, Businesses and the Public*. New Brunswick, NJ: Center for Women and Work at Rutgers, State University of New Jersey. Available at https://www.nationalpartnership.org/our-work/resources/economic-justice/other/pay-matters.pdf.

Howe, Amy. 2021a. "Court Dismisses Abortion 'Gag Rule' Cases, Adds Arbitration and Habeas Cases to Docket." *SCOTUSblog*, May 17. Available at https://www.scotusblog.com/2021/05/court-dismisses-abortion-gag-rule-cases-adds-arbitration-and-habeas-cases-to-docket/.

———. 2021b. "Court to Weigh In on Mississippi Abortion Ban Intended to Challenge *Roe v. Wade*." *SCOTUSblog*, May 17. Available at https://www.scotusblog

.com/2021/05/court-to-weigh-in-on-mississippi-abortion-ban-intended-to
-challenge-roe-v-wade/.

―――. 2021c. "Court Won't Block Texas Abortion Ban but Fast-Tracks Cases for
Argument on Nov. 1." *SCOTUSblog*, October 22. Available at https://www
.scotusblog.com/2021/10/court-wont-block-texas-abortion-ban-but-fast-tracks
-cases-forargument-on-nov-1/.

―――. 2021d. "Texas Tells Justices to Leave Abortion Plan in Place, but Suggests
Overruling *Roe* and *Casey*." *SCOTUSblog*, October 21. Available at https://
www.scotusblog.com/2021/10/texas-tells-justices-to-leave-abortion-plan-in
-place-but-suggests-overruling-roe-and-casey/.

Huckle, Patricia. 1981. "The Womb Factor: Pregnancy Policies and Employment of
Women." *Western Political Quarterly* 34: 114–126.

Human Rights Watch. 2016. "Booted: Lack of Recourse for Wrongfully Discharged U.S. Military Rape Survivors." Available at https://www.hrw.org
/report/2016/05/19/booted/lack-recourse-wrongfully-discharged-us-military
-rape-survivors#.

Institute for Women's Policy Research. 2020. "The Gender Wage Gap by Occupation and by Race and Ethnicity 2019." Available at https://iwpr.org/wp-content
/uploads/2020/07/2020-Occupational-wage-gap-FINAL.pdf.

Institute of Medicine. 2011. "Clinical Preventive Services for Women: Closing the
Gaps." Washington, DC: National Academies Press. Available at https://www
.nap.edu/catalog/13181/clinical-preventive-services-for-women-closing-the
-gaps.

Jagoda, Naomi. 2020. "Trump Urges Congress to Pass Bill Allowing New Parents
to Advance Tax Credits." *The Hill*, February 4. Available at https://thehill.com
/policy/finance/481543-trump-urges-congress-to-pass-bill-that-would-allow
-new-parents-to-advance-tax.

James, Letitia, Attorney General. 2020. "Attorney General James Acts to Protect
Students from Sexual Harassment." June 5. Available at https://ag.ny.gov/press
-release/2020/attorney-general-james-acts-protect-students-sexual-harassment.

Jansson, Bruce S. 2019. *The Reluctant Welfare State: Engaging History to Advance
Social Work Practice in Contemporary Society*, 9th ed. Boston, MA: Cengage.

Jee, Eunjung, Joya Misra, and Marta Murray-Close. 2019. "Motherhood Penalties in
the U.S., 1986–2014." *Journal of Marriage and Family* 81: 434–449.

Jenkins, Sally. 2021. "The NCAA's Shameful Neglect of Women's Basketball Has
Been Exposed, and It Starts at the Top." *Washington Post*, August 5. Available
at https://www.washingtonpost.com/sports/2021/08/05/ncaas-shameful-neglect
-womens-basketball-has-been-exposed-it-starts-top/.

Jerman, Jenna, Rachel K. Jones, and Tsuyoshi Onda. 2016. "Characteristics of U.S.
Abortion Patients in 2014 and Changes Since 2008." Guttmacher Institute, May.
Available at https://www.guttmacher.org/report/characteristics-us-abortion-patients
-2014#8.

Johannson, Elly-Ann. 2010. "The Effect of Own and Spousal Parental Leave on
Earnings." Working Paper 2010:4, Institute for Evaluation of Labour Market
and Education Policy. Available at https://onlabor.org/wp-content/uploads/2016
/05/623752174.pdf.

Johnson, Stefanie K., Ksenia Keplinger, and Jessica F. Kirk. 2019. "Has Sexual
Harassment at Work Decreased Since #MeToo?" *Harvard Business Review*, July
18. Available at https://hbr.org/2019/07/has-sexual-harassment-at-work-decreased
-since-metoo.

Jones, Martha S. 2020. *Vanguard: How Black Women Broke Barriers, Won the Vote, and Insisted on Equality for All.* New York: Basic Books.

Jones, Rachel K., and Heather D. Boonstra. 2016. "The Public Health Implications of the FDA Update to the Medication Abortion Label." Guttmacher Institute, June 30. Available at https://www.guttmacher.org/article/2016/06/public-health-implications-fda-update-medication-abortion-label.

Jones, Rachel K., and Jenna Jerman. 2017. "Population Group Abortion Rates and Lifetime Incidence of Abortion: United States, 2008–2014." *American Journal of Public Health* 107: 1904–1909.

Jordan, Karen A. 2015. "The Emerging Use of a Balancing Approach in *Casey*'s Undue Burden Analysis." *University of Pennsylvania Journal of Constitutional Law* 18: 657–723.

Jorgensen, Helene, and Eileen Appelbaum. 2014. *Expanding Federal Family and Medical Leave Coverage: Who Benefits from Changes in Eligibility Requirements?* Washington, DC: Center for Economic and Policy Research. Available at https://cepr.net/documents/fmla-eligibility-2014-01.pdf.

Jou, Judy, Katy B. Kozhimannil, Jean M. Abraham, Lynn A. Blewett, and Patricia M. McGovern. 2018. "Paid Maternity Leave in the United States: Associations with Maternal and Infant Health." *Maternal and Child Health Journal* 22: 216–225.

Jurewitz, Ross A. 2000. "Playing at Even Strength: Reforming Title IX Enforcement in Intercollegiate Athletics." *American University Journal of Gender, Social Policy and the Law* 8: 283–351.

Kaiser Family Foundation. 2019. "Abortions Later in Pregnancy." December 5. Available at https://www.kff.org/womens-health-policy/fact-sheet/abortions-later-in-pregnancy/.

———. 2020. "The Mexico City Policy: An Explainer." November 4. Available at https://www.kff.org/global-health-policy/fact-sheet/mexico-city-policy-explainer/.

———. 2022. "The Availability and Use of Medication Abortion." April 6. Available at https://www.kff.org/womens-health-policy/fact-sheet/the-availability-and-use-of-medication-abortion/#:~:text=Medication%20abortion%20is%20a%20safe,than%200.001%20percent%20(0.00064%25).

Kaitin, Katharine Karr. 1994. "Congressional Responses to Families in the Workplace: The Family and Medical Leave Act of 1987–1988." In *More than Kissing Babies? Current Child and Family Policy in the United States*, edited by Francine H. Jacobs and Margery W. Davies, 91–120. Westport, CT: Auburn House.

Kalyanaraman, Srividya. 2018. "Is the #MeToo Movement Helping Women Get Better Jobs?" BostInno, November 29. Available at https://www.bizjournals.com/boston/inno/stories/news/2018/11/29/is-the-metoo-movement-helping-women-get-better.html.

Kantor, Jodi. 2018. "#MeToo Called for an Overhaul. Are Workplaces Really Changing?" *New York Times*, March 23. Available at https://www.nytimes.com/2018/03/23/us/sexual-harassment-workplace-response.html.

Kapp, Marshall B. 1982. "Abortion and Informed Consent Requirements." *American Journal of Obstetrics and Gynecology* 144: 1–4.

Kay, Julie F., and Kathryn Kolbert. 2020. "The Supreme Court's Abortion Decision Could Reshape American Jurisprudence." *Slate*, March 3. Available at https://slate.com/news-and-politics/2020/03/scotus-june-medical-services-abortion-legal-principles.html.

Keller, Leah H., Adam Sonfield, Megan K. Donovan, Ruth Dawson, and Zara Ahmed. 2020. "Reviving Sexual and Reproductive Health and Rights in the

Biden-Harris Era." Guttmacher Institute, November 10. Available at https://www.guttmacher.org/article/2020/11/reviving-sexual-and-reproductive-health-and-rights-biden-harris-era.

Kelly, Erin, and Frank Dobbin. 1999. "Civil Rights Law at Work: Sex Discrimination and the Rise of Maternity Leave Policies." *American Journal of Sociology* 105: 455–492.

Kendis, Becca. 2019. "Faute De Mieux: Recognizing and Accepting *Whole Woman's Health* for Its Strengths and Weaknesses." *Case Western Reserve Law Review* 69: 1007–1055.

Kimball, Nina Joan. 1984. "Not Just Any Factor Other Than Sex: An Analysis of the Fourth Affirmative Defense of the Equal Pay Act." *George Washington Law Review* 52: 318–336.

Kimof, Sarah. 2019. "To Exempt or Not Exempt: Religion, Nonreligion, and the Contraceptive Mandate." *San Diego Law Review* 56: 779–828.

Kirzinger, Ashley, Lunna Lopes, Alina Salganicoff, Brittni Frederiksen, Cailey Muñana, Usha Ranji, and Mollyann Brodie. 2019. "Public Opinion and Knowledge on Reproductive Health Policy." Kaiser Family Foundation, May 3. Available at https://www.kff.org/womens-health-policy/poll-finding/kff-poll-public-opinion-and-knowledge-on-reproductive-health-policy/.

Kitchener, Caroline. 2021a. "In One Month, Abortion Could Be Essentially Illegal in Texas." *The Lily*, August 4. Available at https://www.thelily.com/in-one-month-abortion-could-be-essentially-illegal-in-texas/.

———. 2021b. "There Has Never Been an Antiabortion Law Like the One Just Passed in Texas." *The Lily*, May 25. Available at https://www.thelily.com/there-has-never-been-an-antiabortion-law-like-the-one-just-passed-in-texas/.

Klatch, Rebecca E. 1987. *Women of the New Right*. Philadelphia: Temple University Press.

Klein, Abbie Gordon. 1992. *The Debate over Child Care, 1969–1990*. Albany: State University of New York Press.

Klerman, Jacob Alex, Kelly Daley, and Alyssa Pozniak. 2012. *Family and Medical Leave in 2012: Technical Report*, revised April 18, 2014. Cambridge, MA: Abt Associates.

Kleven, Henrik, Camille Landais, and Jakob Egholt Søgaard. 2019. "Children and Gender Inequality: Evidence from Denmark." *American Economic Journal: Applied Economics* 11: 181–209.

Knott, Katherine. 2022. "A Step Forward or Backward? Title IX Public Comments Show Deep Divisions." *Inside Higher Ed*, September 14. Available at https://www.insidehighered.com/news/2022/09/14/thousands-weigh-new-title-ix-rules.

Kraditor, Aileen S. 1981. *The Ideas of the Woman Suffrage Movement, 1890–1920*. New York: W. W. Norton.

Kramer, Sarah. 2018. "Not Your Mouthpiece: Abortion, Ideology, and Compelled Speech in Physician-Patient Relationships." *University of Pennsylvania Journal of Law and Social Change* 21: 1–26.

Kubak, Katherine, Shelby Martin, Natasha Mighell, Madison Winey, and Rachel Wofford, eds. 2019. "Twentieth Annual Review of Gender and the Law: Abortion." *Georgetown Journal of Gender and Law* 20: 265–311.

Lamb, Michael E. 2010. *The Role of the Father in Child Development*, 5th ed. Hoboken, NJ: Wiley.

Landivar, Liana Christin, Leah Ruppanner, Lloyd Rouse, William J. Scarborough, and Caitlyn Collins. 2022. "Research Note: School Reopenings During the

COVID-19 Pandemic and Implications for Gender and Racial Equity." *Demography* 59: 1–12.

Law, Sylvia A. 1998. "Sex Discrimination and Insurance for Contraception." *Washington Law Review* 73: 363–402.

Laycock, Douglas, and Oliver S. Thomas. 1994. "Interpreting the Religious Freedom Restoration Act." *Texas Law Review* 73: 209–245.

LegiScan. 2018. "Bill Text: MS HB1510 | 2018 | Regular Session | Enrolled." Available at https://legiscan.com/MS/text/HB1510/2018.

———. 2021. "Bill Text: TX SB8 | 2021-2022 | 87th Legislature | Enrolled." Available at https://legiscan.com/TX/text/SB8/id/2395961.

Lenhart, Amanda, Haley Swenson, and Brigid Schulte. 2019. "Navigating Work and Care: Women Want Better Work Conditions. More Time to Care." New America's Better Life Lab. Available at https://www.newamerica.org/better-life-lab/reports/navigating-work-and-care/.

Lenhoff, Donna R., and Lissa Bell. n.d. "Government Support for Working Families and for Communities: Family and Medical Leave as a Case Study." Available at https://www.nationalpartnership.org/our-work/resources/economic-justice/fmla/fmla-case-study-lenhoff-bell.pdf (accessed April 8, 2021).

Leo, John. 1986. "Sexes: Are Women Male Clones?" *Time*, August 18. Available at http://content.time.com/time/subscriber/article/0,33009,962052-1,00.html.

Lerner, Sharon. 2015. "The Real War on Families: Why the U.S. Needs Paid Leave Now." *In These Times*, August 18. Available at https://inthesetimes.com/article/the-real-war-on-families.

Levanon, Asaf, Paula England, and Paul Allison. 2009. "Occupational Feminization and Pay: Assessing Causal Dynamics Using 1950–2000 U.S. Census Data." *Social Forces* 88: 865–891.

Lewis, Helen. 2021. "Why I'll Keep Saying 'Pregnant Women.'" *The Atlantic*, October 26. Available at https://www.theatlantic.com/ideas/archive/2021/10/pregnant-women-people-feminism-language/620468/.

Lewis, Thomas Tandy. 2001. "The Ironic History of Substantive Due Process: Three Constitutional Revolutions." *International Social Science Review* 76: 21–35.

Liner, Emily. 2016. "A Dollar Short: What's Holding Women Back from Equal Pay?" Third Way, March 18. Available at https://www.thirdway.org/report/a-dollar-short-whats-holding-women-back-from-equal-pay.

Lithwick, Dahlia. 2020. "Roberts Isn't a Liberal. He's a Perfectionist Who Wants to Win." *Slate*, June 29. Available at https://slate.com/news-and-politics/2020/06/roberts-june-medical-strategy.html.

Lithwick, Dahlia, and Mark Jacob Stern. 2021. "The Supreme Court Has Just Two Days to Decide the Fate of *Roe v. Wade*." *Slate*, August 30. Available at https://slate.com/news-and-politics/2021/08/texas-abortion-supreme-court-roe-wade.html.

Lohr, Patricia A. 2008. "Surgical Abortion in the Second Trimester." *Reproductive Health Matters* 16: 151–161.

Luhby, Tami, and Katie Lobosco. 2022. "What's in the Manchin-Schumer Deal on Climate, Health Care and Taxes." CNN, July 28. Available at https://www.cnn.com/2022/07/15/politics/biden-build-back-better-manchin/index.html.

Lupu, Ira C. 2015. "Hobby Lobby and the Dubious Enterprise of Religious Exemptions." *Harvard Journal of Law and Gender* 38: 35–101.

Lynch, Michael Leone, and Roy P. Salins. 2022. "Delaware Becomes the Latest State to Enact a Paid Family and Medical Leave Law." Available at https://www

.dwt.com/blogs/employment-labor-and-benefits/2022/05/delaware-paid-family
-medical-leave.

MacKinnon, Catharine A. 1979. *Sexual Harassment of Working Women*. New Haven, CT: Yale University Press.

———. 2016. "In Their Hands: Restoring Institutional Liability for Sexual Harassment in Education." *Yale Law Journal* 125: 2038–2105.

Malik, Rasheed. 2019. "Working Families Are Spending Big Money on Child Care." Center for American Progress. Available at https://www.americanprogress.org/issues/early-childhood/reports/2019/06/20/471141/working-families-spending-big-money-child-care/.

Mann, Naomi M. 2018. "Taming Title IX Tensions." *University of Pennsylvania Journal of Constitutional Law* 20: 631–675.

Mansbridge, Jane J. 1986. *Why We Lost the ERA*. Chicago: University of Chicago Press.

Marshall, Susan E. 1991. "Who Speaks for American Women? The Future of Antifeminism." *The Annals of the American Academy of Political and Social Science* 515: 50–62.

Masters, Hannah L. E. 2020. "Red Card on Wage Discrimination: U.S. Soccer Pay Disparity Highlights Inadequacy of the Equal Pay Act." *Vanderbilt Journal of Entertainment and Technology* 22: 895–922.

Mayeri, Serena. 2004. "Constitutional Choices: Legal Feminism and the Historical Dynamics of Change." *California Law Review* 92: 755–839.

McCammon, Sarah. 2019. "Planned Parenthood Withdraws from Title X Program over Trump Abortion Rule." NPR, August 19. Available at https://www.npr.org/2019/08/19/752438119/planned-parenthood-out-of-title-x-over-trump-rule.

McConnaughy, Corrine M. 2013. *The Woman Suffrage Movement in America: A Reassessment*. New York: Cambridge University Press.

McDonagh, Eileen L., and H. Douglas Price. 1985. "Woman Suffrage in the Progressive Era: Patterns of Opposition and Support in Referenda Voting, 1910–1918." *American Political Science Review* 79: 415–435.

McGovern, Patricia, Bryan Dowd, Dwenda Gjerdingen, Ira Moscovice, Laura Kockevar, and Sarah Murphy. 2000. "The Determinants of Time Off Work After Childbirth." *Journal of Health Politics, Policy and Law* 25: 527–564.

McMullan, Courtney Joy. 2019. "Flip It and Reverse It: Examining Reverse Gender Discrimination Claims Brought Under Title IX." *Washington and Lee Law Review* 76: 1825–1874.

McNulty, Patrick J., and Joseph F. Moser. 2019. "Absolution for Opting Out of the Contraception Mandate: Substantial Burden Gone Awry." *Drake Law Review* 67: 89–136.

McShane, Julianne. 2021. "You Can Get the Abortion Pill by Mail for Now, the FDA Ruled. But It's Still an Ongoing Legal Battle." *The Lily*, April 26. Available at https://www.thelily.com/you-can-get-the-abortion-pill-by-mail-for-now-the-fda-ruled-but-its-still-an-ongoing-legal-battle/.

Mezey, Susan Gluck. 2011. *Elusive Equality: Women's Rights, Public Policy, and the Law*, 2nd ed. Boulder, CO: Lynne Rienner.

Michel, Sonya. 1999. *Children's Interests/Mother's Rights: The Shaping of America's Child Care Policy*. New Haven, CT: Yale University Press.

Miller, Claire Cain. 2014. "Pay Gap Is Because of Gender, Not Jobs." *New York Times*, April 23. Available at https://www.nytimes.com/2014/04/24/upshot/the-pay-gap-is-because-of-gender-not-jobs.html.

————. 2021. "How Other Nations Pay for Child Care. The U.S. Is an Outlier." *New York Times*, October 6. Available at https://www.nytimes.com/2021/10/06 /upshot/child-care-biden.html.

Miller, Stephen. 2019. "GOP Rolls Out 'New Parents Act' to Provide Paid Family Leave." Society for Human Resource Management, March 28. Available at https://www.shrm.org/resourcesandtools/hr-topics/benefits/pages/gop-rolls-out -new-parents-act-for-paid-family-leave.aspx.

Mirakian, Christopher. 2008. "*Gonzales v. Carhart*: A New Paradigm for Abortion Legislation." *University of Missouri Kansas City Law Review* 77: 197–225.

Mizrahi, Ramit, and John L. Schwab. 2019. "Timing Is Everything: AB 9, Statutes of Limitations and the Exhaustion of Administrative Remedies." Available at https://mizrahilaw.com/statutes-of-limitations/.

Mohr, James C. 1978. *Abortion in America: The Origins and Evolution of National Policy*. Oxford: Oxford University Press.

Monmouth University Polling Institute. 2021. "Public Pans Texas Abortion Law." September 20. Available at https://www.monmouth.edu/pollinginstitute/reports /monmouthpoll_us_092021/.

Montes, Andrea. 2018. "Reinstatement of the Global Gag Rule in 2017: Playing Politics with Women's Lives Around the World." *Nova Law Review* 42: 285– 315.

Moorman, Anita M., and Barbara Osborne. 2016. "Are Institutions of Higher Education Failing to Protect Students? An Analysis of Title IX's Sexual Violence Protections and College Athletics." *Marquette Sports Law Review* 26: 545–582.

Moss-Racusin, Corinne A., John F. Dovidio, Victoria L. Brescoll, Mark J. Graham, and Jo Handelsman. 2012. "Faculty's Subtle Gender Biases Favor Male Students." *Proceedings of the National Academy of Sciences* 109: 16474–16479.

Moyer, Melinda Wenner. 2021. "'A Poison in the System': The Epidemic of Military Sexual Assault." *New York Times*, August 3. Available at https://www .nytimes.com/2021/08/03/magazine/military-sexual-assault.html.

Napili, Angela. 2017. "Title X (Public Health Service Act) Family Planning Program." Congressional Research Services, August 31. Available at https://sgp.fas .org/crs/misc/RL33644.pdf.

Nash, Elizabeth. 2019. "State Abortion Policy Landscape: From Hostile to Supportive." Guttmacher Institute, August. Available at https://www.guttmacher.org /article/2019/08/state-abortion-policy-landscape-hostile-supportive#.

Nash, Elizabeth, and Lauren Cross. 2021. "26 States Are Certain or Likely to Ban Abortion Without *Roe*: Here's Which Ones and Why." Guttmacher Institute. October 21. Available at https://www.guttmacher.org/article/2021/10/26-states -are-certain-or-likely-ban-abortion-without-roe-heres-which-ones-and-why.

Nash, Elizabeth, Rachel Benson Gold, Lizamarie Mohammed, Zohra Ansari-Thomas, and Olivia Cappello. 2018. "Policy Trends in Brief." Guttmacher Institute, January. Available at https://www.guttmacher.org/article/2018/01/policy -trends-states-2017#.

Nash, Elizabeth, Lizamarie Mohammed, Zohra Ansari-Thomas, Olivia Cappello, and Sophia Naide. 2019. "State Policy Trends 2019: A Wave of Abortion Bans, but Some States Are Fighting Back." Guttmacher Institute, December 10. Available at https://www.guttmacher.org/article/2019/12/state-policy-trends -2019-wave-abortion-bans-some-states-are-fighting-back.

Nash, Elizabeth, and Sophia Naide. 2021. "State Policy Trends at Midyear 2021: Already the Worst Legislative Year Ever for U.S. Abortion Rights." Guttmacher

Institute, July 1. Available at https://www.guttmacher.org/article/2021/07/state
-policy-trends-midyear-2021-already-worst-legislative-year-ever-us-abortion#.

National Coalition for Women and Girls in Education. 2012. "Title IX at 40: Working to Ensure Gender Equity in Education." Available at https://www.ncwge
.org/PDF/TitleIXat40.pdf.

National Organization for Women. 2011. "Founding." Available at https://now.org
/about/history/founding-2/.

National Partnership for Women and Families. 2016. "Expecting Better: A State-by-
State Analysis of Laws that Help Expecting and New Parents, fourth ed." Available at https://www.nationalpartnership.org/our-work/resources/economic-justice
/expecting-better-2016.pdf.

———. 2018. "Voters' Views on Paid Family + Medical Leave: Findings from a
National Survey." Available at https://www.nationalpartnership.org/our-work
/resources/economic-justice/paid-leave/voters-views-on-paid-family-medical
-leave-survey-findings-august-2018.pdf.

———. 2020a. "Legislative Proposals for Updating the Family and Medical Leave
Act." Available at https://www.nationalpartnership.org/our-work/resources
/economic-justice/fmla/updating-the-fmla.pdf.

———. 2020b. "New Polling Confirms Strong, Broad Support for Paid Family and
Medical Leave." Available at https://www.nationalpartnership.org/our-work
/resources/economic-justice/paid-leave/new-polling-paid-family-and-medical
-leave.pdf.

———. 2021a. "The Family and Medical Insurance Leave (FAMILY) Act." Available at https://www.nationalpartnership.org/our-work/resources/economic-justice
/paid-leave/family-act-fact-sheet.pdf.

———. 2021b. "The Paycheck Fairness Act." Available at www.nationalpartnership
.org/our-work/resources/economic-justice/fair-pay/the-paycheck-fairness-act
.pdf.

———. 2022a. "America's Women and the Wage Gap." Available at https://www
.nationalpartnership.org/our-work/resources/economic-justice/fair-pay/americas
-women-and-the-wage-gap.pdf.

———. 2022b. "Asian American, Native Hawaiian and Pacific Islander Women and
the Wage Gap." Available at www.nationalpartnership.org/our-work/resources
/economic-justice/fair-pay/asian-women-and-the-wage-gap.pdf.

National Women's Law Center. 2020a. "Limiting Nondisclosure and Nondisparage-
ment Agreements that Silence Workers: Policy Recommendations." Available at
https://nwlc.org/wp-content/uploads/2020/04/NDA-Factsheet-4.27.pdf.

———. 2020b. "NWLC Files Lawsuit Against Betsy DeVos, Trump Administration's Sexual Harassment Rules." June 10. Available at https://nwlc.org/press
-releases/nwlc-files-lawsuit-against-betsy-devos-trump-administrations-sexual
-harassment-rules/.

National Women's Law Center and Center on Poverty & Social Policy at Columbia
University. 2021. "A Lifetime's Worth of Benefits: The Effects of Affordable,
High-Quality Child Care on Family Income, the Gender Earnings Gap, and
Women's Retirement Security." Available at https://nwlc.org/resource/a-lifetimes
-worth-of-benefits-the-effects-of-affordable-high-quality-child-care-on-family
-income-the-gender-earnings-gap-and-womens-retirement-security/.

NCAA. 2021. "March Madness Brand Will Be Used for DI Women's Basketball
Championship." September 29. Available at https://www.ncaa.com/news
/basketball-women/article/2021-09-29/march-madness-brand-will-be-used
-di-womens-basketball-championship.

Nepomnyaschy, Lenna, and Jane Waldfogel. 2007. "Paternity Leave and Fathers' Involvement with Their Young Children." *Community, Work and Family* 10: 427–453.

Neuwirth, Jessica. 2015. *Equal Means Equal: Why the Time for an Equal Rights Amendment Is Now.* New York: New Press.

Neverdon-Morton, Cynthia. 1989. *Afro-American Women of the South and the Advancement of the Race, 1895–1925.* Knoxville: University of Tennessee Press.

New America. 2020. "Universal Pre-K." Available at https://www.newamerica.org /education-policy/reports/2020-education-tracker/universal-pre-k/.

New Jersey Department of Labor and Workforce Development. n.d. "Family Leave Insurance." Available at https://www.myleavebenefits.nj.gov/worker/fli/?_ga=2 .114919296.660330013.1621461645-1151666889.1621461645 (accessed July 31, 2022).

New York State. n.d. "New York State Paid Family Leave." Available at https:// paidfamilyleave.ny.gov/ (accessed July 31, 2022).

Nicelli, Natalie. 2017. "Repealing Essential Health Benefits Hurts and Harms Women." *New York University Review of Law and Social Change Harbinger* 41: 39–56.

Nixon, Richard. 1969. "Special Message to the Congress on Problems of Population Growth." Center for Research on Population and Security, July 18. Available at http://www.population-security.org/09-CH1.html.

North, Anna. 2020. "Biden Can Do 3 Things on Day One to Unwind Trump's War on Reproductive Health." Vox, November 16. Available at https://www.vox.com /2020/11/16/21561232/biden-birth-control-contraception-health-trump-congress.

O'Connor, Sandra Day. 1996. "The History of the Women's Suffrage Movement." *Vanderbilt Law Review* 49: 657–676.

OECD Family Database. n.d. "Parental Leave Systems." Available at https://www .oecd.org/els/soc/PF2_1_Parental_leave_systems.pdf (accessed July 18, 2022).

Ohlheiser, Abby. 2017. "The Woman Behind 'Me Too' Knew the Power of the Phrase When She Created It—10 Years Ago." *Washington Post,* October 19. Available at https://www.washingtonpost.com/news/the-intersect/wp/2017/10 /19/the-woman-behind-me-too-knew-the-power-of-the-phrase-when-she-created -it-10-years-ago/.

Oppermann, Brenda. 2019. "Women and Gender in the U.S. Military: A Slow Process of Integration." In *Women and Gender Perspectives in the Military: An International Comparison,* edited by Robert Egnell and Mayesha Alam, 113–140. Washington, DC: Georgetown University Press.

Oregon Employment Department. n.d. "Paid Family and Medical Leave Insurance." Available at https://www.oregon.gov/employ/PFMLI/Pages/default.aspx (accessed July 31, 2022).

Ortiz-Ospina, Esteban, Sandra Tzvetkova, and Max Roser. 2018. "Women's Employment." Available at https://ourworldindata.org/female-labor-supply#citation.

Osterman, Rachel. 2009. "Origins of a Myth: Why Courts, Scholars, and the Public Think Title VII's Ban on Sex Discrimination Was an Accident." *Yale Journal of Law and Feminism* 20: 409–440.

Padavic, Irene, and Barbara F. Reskin. 2002. *Women and Men at Work,* 2nd ed. Thousand Oaks, CA: Pine Forge Press.

"Paid Family and Medical Leave Massachusetts." n.d. Available at https://www .mass.gov/get-to-know-pfml (accessed July 31, 2022).

Palley, Elizabeth. 2010. "Who Cares for Children? Why Are We Where We Are with American Child Care Policy?" *Children and Youth Services Review* 32: 155–163.

Palley, Elizabeth, and Corey S. Shdaimah. 2014. *In Our Hands: The Struggle for U.S. Child Care Policy*. New York: New York University Press.

Panorama and American Sustainable Business Council. 2019. "The Business Impacts of Paid Leave: Insights from a Financial Analysis of Companies Offering Paid Family and Medical Leave." Available at https://www.asbcouncil.org/sites/main/files/file-attachments/panorama_report_-_business_impacts_of_pid_leave.pdf.

Parker, Kim. 2018. "Women in Majority-male Workplaces Report Higher Rates of Gender Discrimination." Pew Research Center, March 7. Available at https://www.pewresearch.org/fact-tank/2018/03/07/women-in-majority-male-workplaces-report-higher-rates-of-gender-discrimination/.

Patton, Alisha. 2018. *"Harris* and *Whole Woman's Health* Collide: No Funding Provisions Unduly Burden Reproductive Freedom." *Hastings Law Journal* 70: 297–329.

Patton, Dana, Julia F. Costich, and Niklas Lidströmer. 2017. "Paid Parental Leave Policies and Infant Mortality Rates in OECD Countries: Policy Implications for the United States." *World Medical and Health Policy* 9: 6–23.

Paul, Ellen Frankel. 1989. *Equity and Gender: The Comparable Worth Debate*. New Brunswick, NJ: Transaction Publishers.

Persson, Petra, and Maya Rossin-Slater. 2019. "When Dad Can Stay Home: Fathers' Workplace Flexibility and Maternal Health." National Bureau of Economic Research Working Paper No. 25902. Available at https://www.nber.org/system/files/working_papers/w25902/w25902.pdf.

Peterson, Anne Helen. 2020. "Other Countries Have Social Safety Nets. The U.S. Has Women." Available at https://annehelen.substack.com/p/other-countries-have-social-safety.

Petts, Richard J., and Chris Knoester. 2018. "Paternity Leave-Taking and Father Engagement." *Journal of Marriage and Family* 80: 1144–1162.

Pew Research Center. 2016. "Most Say Birth Control Should Be Covered by Employers, Regardless of Religious Objections." September 28. Available at https://www.pewresearch.org/religion/2016/09/28/1-most-say-birth-control-should-be-covered-by-employers-regardless-of-religious-objections/.

———. 2019. "Mothers, More than Fathers, Experience Career Interruptions." March 21. Available at https://www.pewresearch.org/ft_19-03-22_genderpaygap_mothersmorethanfathers/.

———. 2021. "Key Facts About the Abortion Debate in America." June 17. Available at https://www.pewresearch.org/fact-tank/2021/06/17/key-facts-about-the-abortion-debate-in-america/.

Phillips-Fein, Kim. 2009. *Invisible Hands: The Making of the Conservative Movement from the New Deal to Reagan*. New York: W. W. Norton.

Piccirillo, Mary. 1988. "The Legal Background of a Parental Leave Policy and Its Implications." In *The Parental Leave Crisis: Toward a National Policy*, edited by Edward F. Zigler and Meryl Frank, 293–314. New Haven, CT: Yale University Press.

Planned Parenthood. 2016–2017. "Annual Report." Available at https://www.plannedparenthood.org/uploads/filer_public/71/53/7153464c-8f5d-4a26-bead-2a0dfe2b32ec/20171229_ar16-17_p01_lowres.pdf.

———. 2020 "Affordable Care Act (ACA)." Available at https://www.plannedparenthoodaction.org/issues/health-care-equity/affordable-care-act-aca.

———. 2021. "Global Gag Rule." Available at https://www.plannedparenthoodaction.org/tracking-trump/policy/global-gag-rule?_ga=2.266239375.1814061895.1613439267-1940969207.1613439247.

PL + US (Paid Leave for the United States). n.d. "Businesses Call on Congress to Act on Paid Leave in Biden-Harris Recovery Package." Available at https://paidleave .us/biz-for-paid-leave (accessed May 19, 2021).

PL + US (Paid Leave for the United States), Promundo, and Parental Leave Corporate Task Force. 2021. "Paid Leave and the Pandemic: Effective Workplace Policies and Practices for a Time of Crisis and Beyond." Available at https://paidleave .us/paidleaveandthepandemic.

Polachek, Solomon W. 2014. "Equal Pay Legislation and the Gender Wage Gap." *IZA World of Labor*, May. Available at https://wol.iza.org/articles/equal-pay -legislation-and-the-gender-wage-gap/long.

Poggi, Stephanie. 2005. "Abortion Funding for Poor Women: The Myth of the Rape Exception." Center for American Progress, April 28. Available at https://www .americanprogress.org/issues/women/news/2005/04/28/1427/abortion-funding -for-poor-women-the-myth-of-the-rape-exception/.

Powell, Farran, Emma Kerr, and Sarah Wood. 2021. "See the Average College Tuition in 2021–2022." *U.S. News and World Report*, September 13. Available at https://www.usnews.com/education/best-colleges/paying-for-college/articles /paying-for-college-infographic.

Primrose, Sarah. 2012. "The Attack on Planned Parenthood: A Historical Analysis." *UCLA Women's Law Journal* 19: 165–211.

Radford, Mary F. 1988. "*Wimberly* and Beyond: Analyzing the Refusal to Award Unemployment Compensation to Women Who Terminate Prior Employment Due to Pregnancy." *New York University Law Review* 63: 532–610.

Radigan, Anne L. 1988. *Concept & Compromise: The Evolution of Family Leave Legislation in the U.S. Congress*. Washington, DC: Women's Research and Education Institute. Available at https://files.eric.ed.gov/fulltext/ED320652.pdf.

Re, Richard M., and Christopher M. Re. 2012. "Voting and Vice: Criminal Disenfranchisement and the Reconstruction Amendments." *Yale Law Journal* 121: 1584–1670.

Reagan, Leslie R. 1998. *When Abortion Was a Crime: Women, Medicine, and the Law in the United States, 1867–1973*. Berkeley: University of California Press.

Rehel, Erin M. 2014. "When Dad Stays Home Too: Paternity Leave, Gender, and Parenting." *Gender and Society* 28: 110–132.

Rehel, Erin, and Emily Baxter. 2015. "Men, Fathers, and Work-Family Balance." Center for American Progress. Available at https://www.americanprogress .org/issues/women/reports/2015/02/04/105983/men-fathers-and-work-family -balance/.

Relias Media. 2020a. "Title X Final Rule Is Troubling for Providers." May 1. Available at https://www.reliasmedia.com/articles/146025-title-x-final-rule-is-troubling -for-providers.

———. 2020b. "Title X Problems Worsen with Recent Court Decisions." March 27. Available at https://www.reliasmedia.com/articles/146024-title-x-problems-worsen -with-recent-court-decision.

Rhode Island Department of Labor and Training. n.d. "Temporary Disability/ Caregiver Insurance." Available at https://dlt.ri.gov/tdi/ (accessed July 31, 2022).

Rock, Stephanie. 2018. "One Step Forward and Two Steps Back: The Victory and Setback Issued by the Supreme Court of the United States in *Morales-Santana*." *Wisconsin Journal of Law, Gender and Society* 33: 177–197.

Rosario, Isabella. 2021. "Iowa State University Could Rename Catt Hall. Here's Why the Name Is Controversial." *Ames Tribune*, August 22. https://www.amestrib .com/story/news/2021/08/22/carrie-chapman-catt-legacy-controversial-iowa -state-university-isu-womens-suffrag-racism-voting/8197034002/.

Rose, Elizabeth R. 1999. *A Mother's Job: The History of Day Care, 1890–1960*. New York: Oxford University Press.

Rossin-Slater, Maya, Christopher J. Ruhm, and Jane Waldfogel. 2013. "The Effects of California's Paid Family Leave Program on Mothers' Leave-Taking and Subsequent Labor Market Outcomes." *Journal of Policy Analysis and Management* 32: 224–245.

Rothwell, Jonathan, and Lydia Saad. 2021. "How Have U.S. Working Women Fared During the Pandemic?" Gallup, March 8. Available at https://news.gallup.com /poll/330533/working-women-fared-during-pandemic.aspx.

Rutenberg, Jim, Rachel Abrams, and Melena Ryzik. 2017. "Harvey Weinstein's Fall Opens the Floodgates in Hollywood." *New York Times*, October 16. Available at https://www.nytimes.com/2017/10/16/business/media/harvey-weinsteins-fall -opens-the-floodgates-in-hollywood.html.

Salganicoff, Alina, Laurie Sobel, and Amrutha Ramaswamy. 2021. "The Hyde Amendment and Coverage for Abortion Services." Kaiser Family Foundation, March 5. Available at https://www.kff.org/womens-health-policy/issue-brief /the-hyde-amendment-and-coverage-for-abortion-services/.

Samar, Vincent. 2015. "Interpreting Hobby Lobby to Not Harm LGBT Civil Rights." *South Dakota Law Review* 60: 457–473.

Sanger, Carol. 2008. "Seeing and Believing: Mandatory Ultrasound and the Path to a Protected Choice." *UCLA Law Review* 56: 351–408.

Sanger, Margaret. 1921. "The Morality of Birth Control." *American Rhetoric*, November 18. Available at https://www.americanrhetoric.com/speeches/margaretsanger moralityofbirthcontrol.htm.

Satinoff, Debra L. 1998. "Sex-Based Discrimination in U.S. Immigration Law: The High Court's Lost Opportunity to Bridge the Gap Between What We Say and What We Do." *American University Law Review* 47: 1353–1392.

Schieder, Jessica, and Elise Gould. 2016. "'Women's Work' and the Gender Pay Gap: How Discrimination, Societal Norms, and Other Forces Affect Women's Occupational Choices—and Their Pay." Economic Policy Institute, July 20. Available at https://www.epi.org/publication/womens-work-and-the-gender-pay -gap-how-discrimination-societal-norms-and-other-forces-affect-womens -occupational-choices-and-their-pay/.

Schwartzman, Micah, Richard Schragger, and Nelson Tebbe. 2016. "Zubik and the Demands of Justice." *SCOTUSblog*, May 16. Available at https://www.scotusblog .com/2016/05/symposium-zubik-and-the-demands-of-justice/.

Scott, Anne Firor, and Andrew M. Scott. 1982. *One Half the People: The Fight for Woman Suffrage*. Urbana: University of Illinois Press.

Sepinwall, Amy J. 2015. "Conscience and Complicity: Assessing Pleas for Religious Exemptions in *Hobby Lobby*'s Wake." *University of Chicago Law Review* 82: 1897–1979.

Shaw, Elyse, Ariane Hegewisch, and Cynthia Hess. 2018. "Sexual Harassment and Assault at Work: Understanding the Costs." Institute for Women's Policy Research, October. Available at https://iwpr.org/wp-content/uploads/2020/09 /IWPR-sexual-harassment-brief_FINAL.pdf.

Shinkman, Paul D. 2018. "#MeTooMilitary Protests Defense Department Sexual Assault at the Pentagon." *U.S. News and World Report*, January 8. Available at https://www.usnews.com/news/national-news/articles/2018-01-08/metoomilitary -protests-defense-department-sexual-assault-at-the-pentagon.

Sholar, Megan A. 2016a. *Getting Paid While Taking Time: The Women's Movement and the Development of Paid Family Leave Policies in the United States*. Philadelphia: Temple University Press.

————. 2016b. "Donald Trump and Hillary Clinton Both Support Paid Family Leave. That's a Breakthrough." *Washington Post (The Monkey Cage)*, September 22. Available at https://www.washingtonpost.com/news/monkey-cage/wp/2016/09/22/donald-trump-and-hillary-clinton-both-support-paid-family-leave-thats-a-breakthrough/.

Shook, Susan. 1996. "The Title IX Tug-of-War and Intercollegiate Athletics in the 1990s: Nonrevenue Men's Teams Join Women Athletes in the Scramble for Survival." *Indiana Law Journal* 71: 773–814.

Sindt, Jordyn. 2020. "Title IX's Feeble Efforts Against Sexual Harassment: The Need for Heightened Requirements Within Title IX to Provide Comparable University and PreK–12 Policies." *Journal of Gender, Race and Justice* 23: 495–527.

Skemp, Sheila L. 2016. "Women and Politics in the Era of the American Revolution." *Oxford Research Encyclopedia of American History*. Available at https://oxfordre.com/view/10.1093/acrefore/9780199329175.001.0001/acrefore-9780199329175-e-216.

Sobel, Laurie, Adara Beamesderfer, and Alina Salganicoff. 2016. "Private Insurance Coverage of Contraception." Kaiser Family Foundation. Available at https://www.kff.org/womens-health-policy/issue-brief/private-insurance-coverage-of-contraception/.

Sobel, Laurie, Alina Salganicoff, and Brittni Frederiksen. 2019. "New Title X Regulations: Implications for Women and Family Planning Providers." Kaiser Family Foundation, March 8. Available at https://www.kff.org/womens-health-policy/issue-brief/new-title-x-regulations-implications-for-women-and-family-planning-providers/.

Sobel, Laurie, Alana Salganicoff, and Ivette Gomez. 2018. "State and Federal Contraceptive Coverage Requirements: Implications for Women and Employers." Kaiser Family Foundation, March 29. Available at https://www.kff.org/womens-health-policy/issue-brief/state-and-federal-contraceptive-coverage-requirements-implications-for-women-and-employers/.

Sobel, Laurie, Alina Salganicoff, and Caroline Rosenzweig. 2018. "New Regulations Broadening Employer Exemptions to Contraceptive Coverage: Impact on Women." Kaiser Family Foundation, November 19. Available at https://www.kff.org/health-reform/issue-brief/new-regulations-broadening-employer-exemtions-to-contraceptive-coverage-impact-on-women/.

Sonfield, Adam. 2012. "The Religious Exemption to Mandated Insurance Coverage of Contraception." *AMA Journal of Ethics* 14: 37–145.

————. 2013. "Implementing the Federal Contraceptive Coverage Guarantee: Progress and Prospects." *Guttmacher Policy Review* 16: 8–12.

Sonfield, Adam, Kinsey Hasstedt, Megan L. Kavanaugh, and Ragnar Anderson. 2013. "The Social and Economic Benefits of Women's Ability to Determine Whether and When to Have Children." Guttmacher Institute, March 13. Available at https://www.guttmacher.org/report/social-and-economic-benefits-womens-ability-determine-whether-and-when-have-children.

Sonfield, Adam, Athena Tapales, Rachel K. Jones, and Lawrence B. Finer. 2015. "Impact of the Federal Contraceptive Coverage Guarantee on Out-of-Pocket Payments for Contraceptives: 2014 Update." *Contraception* 91: 44–48.

Staff, Jeremy, and Jeylan T. Mortimer. 2012. "Explaining the Motherhood Wage Penalty During the Early Occupational Career." *Demography* 49: 1–21.

Stearns, Jenna. 2015. "The Effects of Paid Maternity Leave: Evidence from Temporary Disability Insurance." *Journal of Health Economics* 43: 85–102.

Steidinger, Joan. 2020. *Stand Up and Shout Out: Women's Fight for Equal Pay, Equal Rights, and Equal Opportunities in Sports*. Lanham, MD: Rowman & Littlefield.

Steiner, Gilbert Y. 1985. *Constitutional Inequality: The Political Fortunes of the Equal Rights Amendment*. Washington, DC: Brookings Institution.

Stewart, Emily. 2018. "The Equal Rights Amendment's Surprise Comeback, Explained." Vox, May 31. Available at https://www.vox.com/policy-and-politics /2018/5/31/17414630/equal-rights-amendment-metoo-illinois.

Stiehm, Judith Hicks. 1989. *Arms and the Enlisted Woman*. Philadelphia: Temple University Press.

Stop Street Harassment. 2018. "The Facts Behind the #MeToo Movement: A National Study on Sexual Harassment and Assault." Available at https:// stopstreetharassment.org/wp-content/uploads/2018/01/Full-Report-2018 -National-Study-on-Sexual-Harassment-and-Assault.pdf.

Strasser, Mark P. 2017. *"Rust* in the First Amendment Scaffolding." *University of Pennsylvania Journal of Constitutional Law* 19: 861–877.

Stroman, Trish, Wendy Woods, Gabrielle Fitzgerald, Shalini Unnikrishnan, and Liz Bird. 2017. "Why Paid Family Leave Is Good Business." Boston Consulting Group. Available at http://media-publications.bcg.com/BCG-Why-Paid-Family -Leave-Is-Good-Business-Feb-2017.pdf.

Suk, Julie C. 2020. "The Trump Administration Says the ERA Is Dead on Arrival. It Isn't." *Washington Post*, January 21. Available at https://www.washingtonpost .com/outlook/2020/01/21/trump-administration-says-era-is-dead-arrival-it-isnt/.

Sullivan, Patricia. 2020. "U.S. House Removes ERA Ratification Deadline, One Obstacle to Enactment." *Washington Post*, February 13. Available at https:// www.washingtonpost.com/local/legal-issues/us-house-removes-era-ratification -deadline-one-obstacle-to-enactment/2020/02/13/e82aa802-4de5-11ea-b721 -9f4cdc90bc1c_story.html.

Swenson, Kyle. 2017. "Who Came Up with the Term 'Sexual Harassment'?" *Washington Post*, November 22. Available at https://www.washingtonpost.com/news /morning-mix/wp/2017/11/22/who-came-up-with-the-term-sexual-harassment/.

Swers, Michele L. 2002. *The Difference Women Make: The Policy Impact of Women in Congress*. Chicago: University of Chicago Press.

Symes, Beth. 1987. "Equality Theories and Maternity Benefits." In *Equality and Judicial Neutrality*, edited by Sheilah L. Martin and Kathleen E. Mahoney, 207– 217. Toronto: Carswell.

Szayna, Thomas S., Eric V. Larson, Angela O'Mahony, Sean Robson, Agnes Gereben Schaefer, Miriam Matthews, J. Michael Polich, Lynsay Ayer, Derek Eaton, William Marcellino, Lisa Miyashiro, Marek Posard, James Syme, Zev Winkelman, Cameron Wright, Megan Zander-Cotugno, and William Welser IV. 2016. "Considerations for Integrating Women into Closed Occupations in U.S. Special Operations Forces." RAND Corporation. Available at https://www .rand.org/pubs/research_reports/RR1058.html.

Szitanyi, Stephanie. 2020. *Gender Trouble in the U.S. Military: Challenges to Regimes of Male Privilege*. Cham, Switzerland: Palgrave Macmillan.

Talbot, Margaret. 2020. "The Study That Debunks Most Anti-Abortion Arguments." *New Yorker*, July 7. Available at https://www.newyorker.com/books/under-review /the-study-that-debunks-most-anti-abortion-arguments.

Tanaka, Sakiko. 2005. "Parental Leave and Child Health Across OECD Countries." *Economic Journal* 115: F7–F28.

Tani, Karen M. 2017. "An Administrative Right to Be Free from Sexual Violence? Title IX Enforcement in Historical and Institutional Perspective." *Duke Law Journal* 6: 1847–1903.

Taub, Nadine. 1985. "From Parental Leaves to Nurturing Leaves." *New York University Review of Law and Social Change* 13: 381–405.

Teghtsoonian, Katherine. 1993. "Neo-Conservative Ideology and Opposition to Federal Regulation of Child Care Services in the United States and Canada." *Canadian Journal of Political Science* 26: 97–121.

Terborg-Penn, Rosalyn. 1978. "Discrimination Against Afro-American Women in the Woman's Movement, 1830–1920." In *The Afro-American Woman: Struggles and Images*, edited by Sharon Harley and Rosalyn Terborg-Penn, 17–27. Port Washington, NY: Kennikat Press.

———. 1998. *African American Women in the Struggle for the Vote, 1850–1920*. Bloomington: Indiana University Press.

Tetrault, Lisa. 2014. *The Myth of Seneca Falls: Memory and the Women's Suffrage Movement, 1848–1898*. Chapel Hill: University of North Carolina Press.

Thomas, Sue. 1994. *How Women Legislate*. New York: Oxford University Press.

"Transcript: Betsy DeVos' Remarks on Campus Sexual Assault." 2017. *Washington Post*, September 7. Available at https://www.washingtonpost.com/news/grade-point/wp/2017/09/07/transcript-betsy-devoss-remarks-on-campus-sexual-assault/.

"Transcript of Supreme Court Oral Arguments in *Dobbs v. Jackson Women's Health*." 2021. CNN, December 1. Available at https://www.cnn.com/2021/12/01/politics/read-transcript-dobbs-jackson-womens-health/index.html.

Tucker, Jasmine. 2021. "Native American Women Need Action That Closes the Wage Gap." National Women's Law Center. Available at https://bit.ly/3de1gvv.

———. 2022. "The Wage Gap Robs Women of Economic Security as the Harsh Impact of COVID-19 Continues." National Women's Law Center. Available at https://nwlc.org/wp-content/uploads/2022/03/Equal-Pay-Day-Factsheet-2022.pdf.

Tussman, Joseph, and Jacobus ten Broek. 1949. "The Equal Protection of the Laws." *California Law Review* 37: 341–381.

Underwood, Montre. 1999. "*Gebser v. Lago Vista Independent School District*: The Supreme Court Adopts Actual Knowledge Standard as Basis for School District's Liability Under Title IX." *Tulane Law Review* 73: 2181–2193.

UN Women. 2020. "From Insights to Action: Gender Equality in the Wake of Covid-19." Available at https://www.unwomen.org/en/digital-library/publications/2020/09/gender-equality-in-the-wake-of-covid-19.

Upadhyay, Ushma D., Sheila Desai, Vera Zlidar, Tracy Weitz, Daniel Grossman, Patricia Anderson, and Diana Taylor. 2015. "Incidence of Emergency Department Visits and Complications After Abortion." *Obstetrics & Gynecology* 125: 175–183.

US Council of Economic Advisers. 2015. "Gender Pay Gap: Recent Trends and Explanations." Available at https://obamawhitehouse.archives.gov/sites/default/files/docs/equal_pay_issue_brief_final.pdf.

US Department of Defense. 2020. "Appendix B: Statistical Data on Sexual Assault." Available at https://www.sapr.mil/sites/default/files/Appendix_B_Statistical_Data_On_Sexual_Assault_FY2020.pdf.

US Department of Defense, Sexual Assault Prevention and Response Office. 2019. "SAPRO Report Metrics Overview." Available at https://www.sapr.mil/sites/default/files/public/docs/reports/SAPRO_Report_Metrics_Overview_ReferenceCopy.pdf.

US Department of Education. 2017a. "Department of Education Issues New Interim Guidance on Campus Sexual Misconduct." September 22. Available at https://content.govdelivery.com/accounts/USED/bulletins/1b8b87c.

———. 2017b. "Q&A on Campus Sexual Misconduct." September. Available at https://www2.ed.gov/about/offices/list/ocr/docs/qa-title-ix-201709.pdf.

————. 2018. "Nondiscrimination on the Basis of Sex in Education Programs or Activities Receiving Federal Financial Assistance." November 29. Available at https://www.federalregister.gov/documents/2018/11/29/2018-25314/nondiscrimination-on-the-basis-of-sex-in-education-programs-or-activities-receiving-federal.

————. 2021. "Department of Education's Office for Civil Rights Announces Virtual Public Hearing to Gather Information for the Purpose of Improving Enforcement of Title IX." May 17. Available at https://www.ed.gov/news/press-releases/department-educations-office-civil-rights-announces-virtual-public-hearing-gather-information-purpose-improving-enforcement-title-ix.

————. 2022a. "Fact Sheet: U.S. Department of Education's 2022 Proposed Amendments to Its Title IX Regulations." June. Available at https://www2.ed.gov/about/offices/list/ocr/docs/t9nprm-factsheet.pdf.

————. 2022b. "Nondiscrimination on the Basis of Sex in Education Programs or Activities Receiving Federal Financial Assistance." Available at https://www2.ed.gov/about/offices/list/ocr/docs/t9nprm.pdf.

————. 2022c. "The U.S. Department of Education Releases Proposed Changes to Title IX Regulations, Invites Public Comment." Available at https://www.ed.gov/news/press-releases/us-department-education-releases-proposed-changes-title-ix-regulations-invites-public-comment.

US Department of Education, Office for Civil Rights. 1996. "Clarification of Intercollegiate Athletics Policy Guidance: The Three-Part Test." January 16. Available at https://www2.ed.gov/about/offices/list/ocr/docs/clarific.html.

————. 1997. "Sexual Harassment Guidance 1997: Harassment of Students by School Employees, Other Students, or Third Parties." March 13. Available at https://www2.ed.gov/about/offices/list/ocr/docs/sexhar01.html.

————. 2001. "Revised Sexual Harassment Guidance: Harassment of Students by School Employees, Other Students, or Third Parties." January. Available at https://www2.ed.gov/about/offices/list/ocr/docs/shguide.pdf.

————. 2003. "Further Clarification of Intercollegiate Athletics Policy Guidance Regarding Title IX Compliance." July 11. Available at https://www2.ed.gov/about/offices/list/ocr/title9guidanceFinal.html.

————. 2005. "Additional Clarification of Intercollegiate Athletics Policy: Three-Part Test—Part Three." March 17. Available at https://www2.ed.gov/about/offices/list/ocr/letters/200503017-additional-clarification-three-part-test.pdf.

————. 2010. "Intercollegiate Athletics Policy: Three-Part Test—Part Three." April 20. Available at https://www2.ed.gov/print/about/offices/list/ocr/docs/title9-qa-20100420.html.

————. 2011. "Dear Colleague Letter." April 4. Available at https://www2.ed.gov/about/offices/list/ocr/letters/colleague-201104.html.

————. 2014. "Questions and Answers on Title IX and Sexual Violence." April 29. Available at https://www2.ed.gov/about/offices/list/ocr/docs/qa-201404-title-ix.pdf.

US Department of Health and Human Services. 2017. "Trump Administration Issues Rules Protecting the Conscience Rights of All Americans." October 6. Available at https://www.hhs.gov/about/news/2017/10/06/trump-administration-issues-rules-protecting-the-conscience-rights-of-all-americans.html.

————. 2018. "Fact Sheet: Final Rules on Religious and Moral Exemptions and Accommodation for Coverage of Certain Preventive Services Under the Affordable Care Act." November 7. Available at https://www.hhs.gov/about/news/2018/11/07/fact-sheet-final-rules-on-religious-and-moral-exemptions-and

-accommodation-for-coverage-of-certain-preventive-services-under-affordable-care-act.html.

———. 2021. "HHS Issues Final Regulation Aimed at Ensuring Access to Equitable, Affordable, Client-Centered, Quality Family Planning Services." October 4. Available at https://www.hhs.gov/about/news/2021/10/04/hhs-issues-final-regulation-aimed-at-ensuring-access-to-equitable-affordable-client-centered-quality-family-planning-services.html.

———. 2022. "HHS Issues Guidance to the Nation's Retail Pharmacies Clarifying Their Obligations to Ensure Access to Comprehensive Reproductive Health Care." July 13. Available at https://www.hhs.gov/about/news/2022/07/13/hhs-issues-guidance-nations-retail-pharmacies-clarifying-their-obligations-ensure-access-comprehensive-reproductive-health-care-services.html.

US Department of Health and Human Services, Assistant Secretary for Planning and Evaluation. 2015. "The Affordable Care Act Is Improving Access to Preventive Services for Millions of Americans Today." May 13. Available at https://aspe.hhs.gov/reports/affordable-care-act-improving-access-preventive-services-millions-americans.

US Department of Health and Human Services, Centers for Disease Control and Prevention. "Abortion Surveillance—United States, 2018." 2020a. November 27. Available at https://www.cdc.gov/mmwr/volumes/69/ss/ss6907a1.htm.

———. 2020b. "Maternal Mortality Rates in the United States, 2020." Available at https://www.cdc.gov/nchs/data/hestat/maternal-mortality/2020/maternal-mortality-rates-2020.htm.

US Department of Health and Human Services, Centers for Medicare and Medicaid Services. 2022. "Following President Biden's Executive Order to Protect Access to Reproductive Health Care, HHS Announces Guidance to Clarify that Emergency Medical Care Includes Abortion Services." July 11. Available at https://www.hhs.gov/about/news/2022/07/11/following-president-bidens-executive-order-protect-access-reproductive-health-care-hhs-announces-guidance-clarify-that-emergency-medical-care-includes-abortion-services.html.

US Department of Health and Human Services, Office of Population Affairs. 2019. "Title X Program Funding History." Available at https://opa.hhs.gov/grant-programs/archive/title-x-program-archive/title-x-program-funding-history.

US Department of Health, Education and Welfare. 1979. "Title IX 1979 Policy Interpretation on Intercollegiate Athletics." December 11. Available at https://www2.ed.gov/about/offices/list/ocr/docs/t9interp.html.

US Department of Justice. 2021. "Attorney General Merrick B. Garland Delivers Remarks Announcing Lawsuit Against the State of Texas to Stop Unconstitutional Senate Bill 8." September 9. Available at https://www.justice.gov/opa/speech/attorney-general-merrick-b-garland-delivers-remarks-announcing-lawsuit-against-state-0.

US Department of Justice, Civil Rights Division and U.S. Department of Education, Office for Civil Rights. 2016. "Dear Colleague Letter on Transgender Students." May 13. Available at https://www.justice.gov/opa/file/850986/download.

US Department of Justice, Office of Public Affairs. 2022a. "Attorney General Merrick B. Garland Statement on Supreme Court Ruling in *Dobbs v. Jackson Women's Health Organization*." June 24. Available at https://www.justice.gov/opa/pr/attorney-general-merrick-b-garland-statement-supreme-court-ruling-dobbs-v-jackson-women-s.

———. 2022b. "Justice Department Announces Reproductive Rights Task Force." July 12. Available at https://www.justice.gov/opa/pr/justice-department-announces-reproductive-rights-task-force.

US Department of Labor. 2010. "Administrator's Interpretation No. 2010-3." Available at http://www.dol.gov/WHD/opinion/adminIntrprtn/FMLA/2010/FMLAAI2010_3.pdf.

———. 2015a. "Fact Sheet: Final Rule to Amend the Definition of Spouse in the Family and Medical Leave Act Regulations." Available at http://www.dol.gov/whd/fmla/spouse/factsheet.htm.

———. 2015b. "The Cost of Doing Nothing: The Price We All Pay Without Paid Leave Policies to Support America's 21st Century Working Families." Available at https://ecommons.cornell.edu/bitstream/handle/1813/78447/The_Cost_of_Doing_Nothing.pdf?sequence=1&isAllowed=y.

US Department of Labor, Bureau of Labor Statistics. n.d. "Labor Force Statistics from the Current Population Survey." Available at https://data.bls.gov/PDQWeb/ln (accessed July 9, 2022).

———. 2000. "Changes in Women's Labor Force Participation in the 20th Century." Available at https://www.bls.gov/opub/ted/2000/feb/wk3/art03.htm.

———. 2021a. "Employment Characteristics of Families—2020." April 21. Available at https://www.bls.gov/news.release/pdf/famee.pdf.

———. 2021b. "Labor Force Participation Rate—Women." September 3. Available at https://fred.stlouisfed.org/series/LNS11300002.

———. 2021c. "National Compensation Survey: Employee Benefits in the United States, March 2021." Available at https://www.bls.gov/ncs/ebs/benefits/2021/home.htm.

———. 2021d. "Women in the Labor Force: A Databook." Available at https://www.bls.gov/opub/reports/womens-databook/2020/home.htm.

———. 2022. "A Look at Paid Family Leave by Wage Category in 2021." Available at https://www.bls.gov/opub/ted/2022/a-look-at-paid-family-leave-by-wage-category-in-2021.htm.

US Department of Labor, Women's Bureau. 1993. "State Maternity/Family Leave." Available at https://archive.org/details/statematernityfa00unit.

———. 2020. "Labor Force Participation Rate by Sex, Race and Hispanic Ethnicity." Available at https://www.dol.gov/agencies/wb/data/latest-annual-data/labor-force-participation-rates.

US Department of the Treasury, Internal Revenue Service. 2021a. "Child and Dependent Care Credit FAQs." Available at https://www.irs.gov/newsroom/child-and-dependent-care-credit-faqs.

———. 2021b. "Topic No. 602 Child and Dependent Care Credit." Available at https://www.irs.gov/taxtopics/tc602.

US Departments of Labor, Health and Human Services, and Internal Revenue Service. 2021. "FAQs About Affordable Care Act Implementation Part 48." August 16. Available at https://www.hhs.gov/guidance/document/faqs-about-affordable-care-act-implementation-part-48.

US Equal Employment Opportunity Commission. n.d. "Sex-Based Discrimination." Available at https://www.eeoc.gov/sex-based-discrimination (accessed November 19, 2021).

———. 2000a. "Commission Decision on Coverage of Contraception." December 14. Available at http://www.eeoc.gov/commission-decision-coverage-contraception.

———. 2000b. "The Story of the United States Equal Employment Opportunity Commission: Ensuring the Promise of Opportunity for 35 Years, 1965–2000." Washington, DC: U.S. Equal Employment Opportunity Commission.

———. 2010. "Enforcement Guidance: Vicarious Employer Liability for Unlawful Harassment by Supervisors." Available at https://www.eeoc.gov/sites/default/files/migrated_files/policy/docs/harassment.pdf.

————. 2015. "Women in the American Workforce." Available at https://www.eeoc
.gov/special-report/women-american-workforce.

US Government Accountability Office. 2020. "Gender Pay Difference: The Pay Gap
for Federal Workers Has Continued to Narrow, but Better Quality Data on Promotions Are Needed." Available at https://www.gao.gov/products/gao-21-67.

US Senate Committee on Health, Education, Labor and Pensions. 2020. "Senator
Murray Slams Secretary DeVos' Title IX Rule, Calls on the Department to
Focus on COVID-19 Response." May 6. Available at https://www.help.senate
.gov/ranking/newsroom/press/senator-murray-slams-secretary-devos-title-ix
-rule-calls-on-the-department-to-focus-on-covid-19-response.

Vail, Katie. 2019. "The Failings of Title IX for Survivors of Sexual Violence: Uti-
lizing Restorative Justice on College Campuses." *Washington Law Review* 94:
2085–2118.

Valenza, Charles A. 1985. "Was Margaret Sanger a Racist?" *Family Planning Perspectives* 17: 44–46.

Vogel, Lise. 1990. "Debating Difference: Feminism, Pregnancy, and the Workplace." *Feminist Studies* 16: 9–32.

————. 1995. "Considering Difference: The Case of the U.S. Family and Medical
Leave Act of 1993." *Social Politics: International Studies in Gender, State and
Society* 2: 111–120.

Voss, Gretchen. 2015. "Mother F*cker." *Women's Health* 12: 162–167.

Ward, Cynthia V. 2018. "Restoring Fairness to Campus Sex Tribunals." *Tennessee
Law Review* 85: 1073–1138.

"Washington Paid Family & Medical Leave." n.d. Available at https://paidleave.wa
.gov/ (accessed July 31, 2022).

Weissman, Sara. 2021. "NCAA Inequitably Reliant on Men's Basketball." *Inside
Higher Ed*, August 4. Available at https://www.insidehighered.com/quicktakes
/2021/08/04/report-ncaa-inequitably-reliant-men%E2%80%99s-basketball.

Weldon, S. Laurel. 2006. "Inclusion, Solidarity, and Social Movements: The Global
Movement Against Gender Violence." *Perspectives on Politics* 4: 55–74.

Wells, Mildred White. 1953. *Unity in Diversity: The History of the General Federation of Women's Clubs*. Washington, DC: General Federation of Women's
Clubs.

Whalen, Charles W., and Barbara Whalen. 1985. *The Longest Debate: A Legislative
History of the 1964 Civil Rights Act*. Cabin John, MD: Seven Locks Press.

Wheeler, Marjorie Spruill. 1993. *New Women of the New South: The Leaders of the
Woman Suffrage Movement in the Southern States*. New York: Oxford University Press.

White, Karl, Gracia Sierra, Laura Dixon, Elizabeth Sepper, and Ghazaleh Moayedi.
2021. "Texas Senate Bill 8: Medical and Legal Implications." Texas Policy
Evaluation Project, July. Available at http://sites.utexas.edu/txpep/files/2021
/07/TxPEP-research-brief-senate-bill-8.pdf.

White, Linda A. 2009. "Explaining Differences in Child Care Policy Development
in France and the USA: Norms, Frames, Programmatic Ideas." *International
Political Science Review* 30: 385–405.

The White House. n.d. "The Child Tax Credit." Available at https://www.whitehouse
.gov/child-tax-credit/ (accessed August 1, 2022).

Wiessner, Daniel. 2021. "Senate Panel Approves Increased Protections for Pregnant Workers." Reuters, August 3. Available at https://www.reuters.com/legal
/transactional/senate-panel-approves-increased-protections-pregnant-workers
-2021-08-03/.

Williams, Ryan C. 2010. "The One and Only Substantive Due Process Clause." *Yale Law Journal* 120: 408–512.

Williams, Wendy. 1984–1985. "Equality's Riddle: Pregnancy and the Equal Treatment/Special Treatment Debate." *New York University Review of Law & Social Change* 13: 325–380.

Wines, Michael. 1992. "Bush Vetoes Bill Making Employers Give Family Leave." *New York Times*, September 23. Available at https://www.nytimes.com/1992/09/23/us/bush-vetoes-bill-making-employers-give-family-leave.html.

Wingfield, Nick, and Jessica Silver-Greenberg. 2017. "Microsoft Moved to End Secrecy in Sexual Harassment Claims." *New York Times*, December 19. Available at https://www.nytimes.com/2017/12/19/technology/microsoft-sexual-harassment-arbitration.html.

Winkler, Bridget. 2020. "Deviation from the Principles of Stare Decisis in Abortion Jurisprudence, and an Analysis of *June Medical Services L.L.C. v. Russo* Oral Arguments." *UCLA Law Review Discourse* 68: 14–38.

Winter, Jessica. 2022. "The *Dobbs* Decision Has Unleashed Legal Chaos for Doctors and Patients." *New Yorker*, July 2. Available at https://www.newyorker.com/news/news-desk/the-dobbs-decision-has-unleashed-legal-chaos-for-doctors-and-patients.

Wisensale, Steven K. 2001. *Family Leave Policy: The Political Economy of Work and Family in America*. Armonk, NY: M. E. Sharpe.

———. 2003. "Two Steps Forward, One Step Back: The Family and Medical Leave Act as Retrenchment Policy." *Review of Policy Research* 20: 135–152.

Wood, Susan F. 2017. "A Women's Health Legacy of the Obama Administration." *American Journal of Public Health* 107: 27–28.

Wright, Susan. 1992. "*Franklin v. Gwinnett County Public Schools*: The Supreme Court Implies a Damage Remedy for Title IX Sex Discrimination." *Vanderbilt Law Review* 45: 1367–1386.

Yackee, Susan Webb. 2021. "Guidance on Regulatory Guidance: What the Government Needs to Know and Do to Engage the Public." IBM Center for the Business of Government. Available at https://www.businessofgovernment.org/sites/default/files/Guidance%20on%20Regulatory%20Guidance.pdf.

Yahoo News/YouGov. 2021. "COVID-19 Vaccination Survey." Available at https://docs.cdn.yougov.com/y4mb321uuq/20210406_yahoo_vaccine_tabs.pdf.

Zhou, Li. 2022. "How Democrats Plan to Overhaul Taxes, Climate Spending, and Health Care Before the Midterm." Vox, July 28. Available at https://www.vox.com/23281547/build-back-better-joe-manchin-inflation-reduction-act.

Ziegler, Mary. 2018. "Rethinking an Undue Burden: *Whole Woman's Health*'s New Approach to Fundamental Rights." *Tennessee Law Review* 85: 461–515.

Zigler, Edward, Katherine W. Marsland, and Heather Lord. 2009. *The Tragedy of Child Care in America*. New Haven, CT: Yale University Press.

Zigler, Edward, and Susan Muenchow. 1992. *Head Start: The Inside Story of America's Most Successful Educational Experiment*. New York: Basic Books.

Index of Cases

Index

About the Book

Despite women's many gains in the political, economic, and social spheres, equality remains elusive—and in some areas, ground is being lost. Why? Why does the pay gap between women and men persist? Why is sexual harassment and assault so prevalent in schools and universities? Why are efforts to diminish women's individual autonomy, restricting their access to reproductive health care, succeeding?

Susan Mezey and Megan Sholar address these disturbing questions, tracing the struggle for women's equal rights and opportunities in the United States across more than a century.

Susan Gluck Mezey is professor emeritus in the Department of Political Science, Loyola University Chicago. **Megan A. Sholar** is advanced lecturer in the Interdisciplinary Honors Program at Loyola University Chicago.